RECONSIDERING LAW AND POLICY DEBATES

This book offers fresh approaches to a variety of social and political issues that have become highly polarized and resistant to compromise by examining them through a population-based, public health perspective. The topics included are some of the most contentious: abortion and reproductive rights; end-of-life issues, including the right to die and the treatment of pain; the connection between racism and poor health outcomes for African Americans; the right of same-sex couples to marry; the toll of gun violence and how to reduce it; domestic violence and how the criminal justice model fails to deal with it effectively; and how tort compensation and punitive damages can further public health goals. People at every point along the political spectrum will find the book enlightening and informative.

Written by ten authors, all of whom have cross-disciplinary expertise, this book shifts the focus away from the point of view of rights, politics, or morality and examines the effect of laws and policies from the perspective of public health and welfare.

John G. Culhane is a Professor of Law and Director of the Health Law Institute at Widener University, School of Law. He is a lecturer at Yale University School of Public Health and a Senior Fellow with the Jefferson School of Population Health at Thomas Jefferson University. He is the author of more than two dozen law review articles that have appeared in journals at Yale Law School, North Carolina School of Law, University of Wisconsin School of Law, Fordham University School of Law, and William and Mary School of Law. Culhane is regularly featured in national and local broadcast and print media for his scholarship on a wide range of topics including public health issues, government responsibility, and compensation for victims of mass disasters. He appears in the feature-length documentary *America Betrayed.* He blogs at wordinedgewise.org and writes a weekly column for 365gay.com.

Reconsidering Law and Policy Debates

A PUBLIC HEALTH PERSPECTIVE

Edited by

John G. Culhane

Health Law Institute, Widener University, School of Law

CAMBRIDGE
UNIVERSITY PRESS

CAMBRIDGE UNIVERSITY PRESS
Cambridge, New York, Melbourne, Madrid, Cape Town, Singapore,
São Paulo, Delhi, Dubai, Tokyo, Mexico City

Cambridge University Press
32 Avenue of the Americas, New York, NY 10013-2473, USA

www.cambridge.org
Information on this title: www.cambridge.org/9780521195058

First published 2011

Printed in the United States of America

A catalog record for this publication is available from the British Library.

Library of Congress Cataloging in Publication data
Reconsidering law and policy debates: a public health perspective / [edited by]
John G. Culhane.
p. cm.
Includes bibliographical references.
ISBN 978-0-521-19505-8
1. Public health laws – United States. 2. Public health – Government policy – United States. 3. United States – Social policy. 4. Civil rights – United States. I. Culhane, John G. II. Title.
KF3775.R388 2010
344.7304–dc22 2010031689

ISBN 978-0-521-19505-8 Hardback

CONTENTS

Contributors . . . . *page* vii

Introduction 1
John G. Culhane

Part I: Birth and Death

1. Beyond Privacy: A Population Approach to Reproductive Rights 15
Wendy E. Parmet

2. Stretching the Boundaries of Public Health: Should We Consider End-of-Life Care a Public Health Issue? 40
Diane E. Hoffmann

Part II: The Limits of Civil Rights

3. Dying While Black in America: Maslow's Hierarchy of Need and Racial Policy Making 69
Vernellia R. Randall

4. Public Health and Marriage (Equality). 89
John G. Culhane

Part III: Dimensions of Violence

5. Using Public Health to Reform the Legal and Justice Response to Domestic Violence 125
Evan Stark

6. Law and Policy Approaches to Keeping Guns from High-Risk People 153
Jon S. Vernick, Daniel W. Webster and Katherine A. Vittes

Part IV: Beyond Compensation: Public Features of Private Litigation

7. Tort Litigation for the Public's Health 187
Elizabeth Weeks Leonard

8. Punitive Damages and the Public Health Agenda 221
Jean Macchiaroli Eggen

Index 255

CONTRIBUTORS

John G. Culhane
Professor of Law
Widener University
School of Law, Health Law Institute

Jean Macchiaroli Eggen
Professor of Law
Widener University
School of Law, Health Law Institute

Diane E. Hoffmann, J.D., M.S.
Professor of Law
Associate Dean for Academic Programs and
Director, Law and Health Care Program
University of Maryland
School of Law

Wendy E. Parmet
Matthews Distinguished University Professor of Law
Northeastern University
School of Law

Vernellia R. Randall
Professor of Law
University of Dayton
School of Law

Evan Stark
Professor and MPH Program Director
Rutgers University
School of Public Affairs and Administration

Jon S. Vernick
Co-Director
The Johns Hopkins Center for Gun Policy and Research
Deputy Director, Johns Hopkins Center for Injury Research and Policy

Katherine A. Vittes
Johns Hopkins Center for Gun Policy and Research
The Johns Hopkins Bloomberg School of Public Health

Daniel W. Webster, ScD, MPH
Professor and Co-Director
Johns Hopkins Center for Gun Policy and Research

Elizabeth Weeks Leonard
Associate Professor
University of Kansas
School of Law

INTRODUCTION: BRINGING PUBLIC HEALTH TO BEAR ON CONTENTIOUS LEGAL AND SOCIAL ISSUES

John G. Culhane

Recently, I participated in a forum on same-sex marriage. The event was open to members of my law school community, but also in attendance were local citizens, media representatives, as well as audience members and participants from the local area. One question that I'd heard before came up again: "Where's the rights problem? Anyone can marry, including gays and lesbians. The same restriction – marry someone of the opposite sex – applies to everyone equally."

The standard law professor move at this point would have been to encourage the student to probe a bit more deeply into the notion of equality, asking whether the opposite-sex-only marriage rule duly respects the rights of same-sex couples to form state-sanctioned relationships with the person of their choice. But for some reason, that wasn't the point that occurred to me immediately. Instead, I wondered aloud whether it was good policy to encourage gays and lesbians to marry people of the opposite sex, given the social costs likely to be incurred: The marriage would likely be an unhappy one, possibly ending in divorce (with its documented effect on any children born to the couple); one or both of the parties might be drawn to more emotionally or sexually fulfilling liaisons outside of the marriage; and often such extramarital affairs are conducted in secret, with potentially grave health and emotional consequences for both the unfaithful spouse and his or her uninformed partner.

What is a law student – or a judge, or a legislator, or a member of the public, for that matter – to do with such a complex battery of arguments? They do not relate neatly to the language of rights, justice, and morality that often seem to define (and even polarize) discussion and debate. Part of the problem is that this consequential dimension of the problem is complex and multifaceted, so that even if it could be discussed with "rights" rhetoric, its effect on the discussion would be unclear. To return to our example, perhaps so few gay people, especially in an increasingly liberated society, are driven to marry members of the opposite sex that the dire outcomes catalogued above – which are, in any case, difficult to quantify – are minimal when balanced against some purportedly positive effect of denying marriage equality (for example, sending the message that children need two parents of opposite sexes). But maybe such sham marriages are real – and serious – consequences of the denial of marriage equality.

By raising such issues and questions, the law professor, judge, or lawmaker is knowingly or not turning to the language of public health and borrowing its population perspective. Public health is best known as a discipline that works to improve the health of communities and populations, most typically by preventing the spread of communicable diseases. More broadly understood, however, public health concerns itself with the preserving and improving the health of populations. In the expansive and influential definition suggested by the Institute of Medicine, "Public health is what we, as a society, do collectively to assure the conditions for people to be healthy."[1] Hence, public health seeks to benefit groups of people rather than simply individuals, and emphasizes the impact that policies and actions have across populations. Most importantly, it prizes a deeply contextual and empirically informed analysis. Thus in my marriage example, the information known about the impact of gay marriage on different populations is central – not peripheral – to any public health discussion of the issue.

Once the battle over public consequences and population-based outcomes is joined, it will rage far beyond the set of considerations put forth above. To stop short of overwhelming the reader at this early stage, let us cite just a few of the broadest examples of the population-based, or public health, dimensions of the marriage equality debate: What effect does allowing (or denying) marriage have on the physical and mental health and wealth of same-sex couples? On their children? On the welfare of society in general? What court – what mind, for that matter – can hold all of these questions before it?

Further, how could we even assess the competing public claims? Why make an already intractable problem even harder to resolve?

Often, those who favor a population-based approach to problems have compounded the difficulty, dropping the broad legal and moral authority of public health as a boulder that swamps other arguments and approaches. Thus, those who emphasize thinking about issues from this perspective are often frustrated at the unwillingness – perhaps inability – for others to simply "see" the benefit of their contribution. The unfortunate result is that it at times appears that legal rules and norms stand quite apart from public health, with neither gaining from the perspective of the other. The marriage equality debate is one of the most extreme examples of this tendency – the possible public benefits and costs of same-sex marriages, even when discussed, are almost never central.

This situation, however, is neither inevitable nor desirable, and this book is one effort to bridge this needless divide by focusing on a number of controversial and important debates in law and policy. In addition to the marriage equality debate already introduced, these include: reproductive rights; domestic violence; gun policy; racial justice and equality; compensation and punishment through the tort system; and decisions about death and dying. Before setting off on these compelling topics, a few words of background on the development of the public health, population-based perspective might be helpful.

Once upon a time, public health authorities had a comparatively modest goal: the eradication or reduction of contagious and infectious diseases. This uncontroversial aim reinforces the point that public health is concerned with populations, not individuals. This concern was well-founded, given that many of these acute diseases were quite serious – smallpox, bubonic plague, cholera, diphtheria, flu, and so on. Once it was discovered that basic hygienic and sanitary measures could reduce the incidence of these diseases, few quarrelled with public health's authority, under the state's police power, to enact laws for the health, safety, and welfare of the society, to pass basic sanitation laws. The advent of vaccinations to inoculate the populace against disease, beginning with the dramatic smallpox immunization and much later exploding to stem such diverse diseases as polio, measles, mumps, rubella, and varicella ("chicken pox") – to name just a few – has represented another vitally important advance in the struggle for sound public health outcomes. Antibiotics, widely available since the middle of the twentieth century, have also played a vital role in increasing life expectancy and decreasing the incidence of serious illness.

Even today, there are those who suggest that this basic infectious disease approach to public health should limit and define the field. In this view, the idea of using a public health approach to address difficult and complex social and political issues is anathema.[2] This misguided outlook overlooks the more recent history of public health, a history that reveals a now accepted – and vitally needed – broadening of public health's tools, scope, and mission.

Consider the case of tobacco. Unlike most of the diseases mentioned previously, those commonly resulting from the use of tobacco – according to Philip Morris USA itself, these include lung cancer, heart disease, and emphysema[3] – take years, often decades, to develop. But until quite recently – about the middle of the twentieth century – science was not equipped to demonstrate that chronic diseases resulted from long-term exposure. Laboratory science was dominant but was set up only to show the causal connections between exposure and acute illness. Indeed, much of the tobacco industry's success in long staving off responsibility for the damage caused by its products owed to a reluctance to accept that casual connections could be shown not only by laboratory proof, but also by population-based, epidemiological methodologies. As the science of epidemiology gained traction by the middle of the past century (in large part because of the interests in studying the effects of cigarette smoking itself), policy makers and eventually the public began to accept the probabilistic model of causation that has come to be the accepted "gold standard" in scientific inquiry and proof. In this way of looking at the relationship between exposure and disease, the causality is always contingent and subject to refutation; nonetheless, policy can be made and implemented based on the best available evidence. But note that this model of looking at public health problems is indeed more complex and indeterminate than the simpler cause-and-effect model long used in the case of infectious and contagious diseases.

To return to the example of smoking: A given smoker's lung cancer might have been caused by the cigarettes consumed over two decades, but also by genetic factors or other environmental exposures. Perhaps all of these possibilities were ingredients in the disease that developed. In short, epidemiology, which looks at populations, can establish that smoking is highly associated with lung cancer in general (a "risk factor"), but cannot by itself show that cigarettes caused our hypothetical smoker's cancer. As an epidemiologist might say, there are simply too many confounding factors. A population-based, public health approach attempts to reduce the number of smokers (and thereby the incidence of morbidity and mortality) through a complex mix of education, changes to the social and physical environment (most notably, by restricting the places and situations in which smoking is permitted), and legal rules and incentives (such as heavy taxation of cigarettes) discouraging tobacco use.

Once we see the complexity of assessing any outcome that is population-based in cases such as tobacco-related health issues, it becomes obvious that consideration of even those health outcomes seen as most clearly demonstrable through laboratory investigation can benefit from a broader look at causes and risks. Thus, even where vaccines are available, lack of access and information as well as religious, philosophical, and "health"-based beliefs can at times lead to an underprotected population. Recent outbreaks of measles in areas with unusually high concentrations of objectors makes the point,[4] as does recent public resistance to the polio vaccine in certain parts of India that is based, in part, on a distrust of public health authority itself.[5] In these cases, public health has taken a broader look at the deeper reasons – one might accurately say *causes* – of vaccination resistance.

Those opposing childhood vaccinations, for example, have cited such disparate reasons as religious doctrine,[6] a broad "natural philosophy,"[7] or discredited fears about a connection between inoculation and autism[8] in seeking (and usually obtaining) waivers for their children. A public health approach that does not take these social and behavioral factors into account compromises its own mission and risks irrelevance.

Thus, not only history but current public health problems continue to demonstrate the need for continuing to develop tools for assessing outcomes. The "old" public health model provides false clarity and risks real danger to the population. Complexity is often painful, but it is unavoidable. The population perspective can provide important lessons about issues that have long been thought beyond its purview, if indeed they were thought about at all. This book gathers some of the most contested and contentious issues currently in the public debate and then examines what insights and information might be imparted through this focus on the public's health and welfare. The chapters that follow offer a rich diversity of such topics, and the authors, drawn from both the law and public health fields, bring a wide range of views about the value and implications of a population-based, public health perspective to each of their subjects.

Violence is a good example of a problem that has traditionally been thought of, and dealt with, on the individual level. Criminal laws punish abusive spouses and those who use firearms to commit violence, but only recently have the various dimensions of the problem been viewed through the population-based lens. In the area of domestic violence, Evan Stark argues, the criminal law approach misses the most crucial effect of persistent, often "low level" violence by men against their spouses, namely the development of a host of physical, medical, psychosocial, mental health and behavioral problems. Professor Stark then situates his argument within a public health model, noting that these effects are seen among no other population of assault victims, including men abused by female partners or women abused by same-sex partners. Professor Stark then introduces and defends the concept of "coercive control" as the most probable explanation for this result: "the combination of social inequality and coercive and controlling strategies in personal relationships that has different effects on women than on men."[9] The chapter outlines the major dimensions of coercive control, identifies its principal harms as its effect on liberty, autonomy, and dignity in personal life, and concludes by calling on the law to address these complex problems by criminalizing not just the relatively infrequent episodes of violence, but also these coercive and controlling behaviors. The chapter shows that the choice of a public health model over the criminal law paradigm is not merely an academic exercise; as he demonstrates, the current approach has been an abysmal failure.

As for the well-documented problem of gun violence, the population-based perspective can support approaches that the polarized Second Amendment debate sets aside. For example, Jon Vernick and colleagues note that the problem of illegal gun trafficking can largely be traced to a tiny percentage of licensed dealers: Of more than 50,000 such dealers, about half of all guns used in crimes can be traced back to about one percent of them. Given the political difficulty of passing comprehensive gun legislation, the author's use of population-based, targeted results suggests that such an emphasis might be used in support of more modest laws and enforcement efforts to get at the problem dealers. They then use other research suggesting that cities that have employed strategies to address the bad dealers have seen a reduction in gun violence. Perhaps more than any other, this chapter shows what a public health and safety approach can achieve even in the face of daunting political obstacles.

Violence is an issue that, though often thought of in terms of criminal and victim, nonetheless has important public dimensions that are acknowledged, if not always fully appreciated. But so-called rights issues are even less likely to be considered through the broader, population-based perspective. My own contribution on marriage equality, introduced earlier, highlights the gain from such a major shift in emphasis. I advance the argument that the debate should cause us to reexamine the prerogatives and privileged status of marriage more broadly; probably not to abolish it, but to consider more critically the vast legal entitlements that go along with it. Professors Wendy Parmet and Diane Hoffmann achieve a similar shift in their pieces on reproductive rights and death and dying, respectively. Both chapters evince a subtle understanding of the complex and reciprocal relationship between individuals and populations.

In her chapter on reproduction, Professor Parmet moves the debate away from the focus on privacy that often dominates discourse. Focusing on the recent decision by the United States Supreme Court upholding the legislative ban on a certain method of late-term abortion (the so-called "partial birth abortion" issue) she notes that the anti-abortion forces have recently embraced the language of public health. Professor Parmet argues that public health claims should not be the subject of blind deference. Rather, public health outcomes must be rationally assessed based on sound epidemiological models. Even where such evidence suggests a particular approach or outcome, however, there is a complex interrelationship between the public's good and respect for individual rights, dignity, and autonomy that must be considered. Indeed, *respect* for public health can itself often serve public health goals. Thus, Professor Parmet concludes, a population-based approach to reproductive rights may move the law to where much of the American public already is: supportive of public programs enhancing access to reproductive education and contraception while leaving the ultimate decision of whether and when to reproduce to individual women.

Professor Hoffmann carefully dissects the various meanings we might attach to the question of "end of life care" and makes the case that the public health dimension of the problem will, to an extent, depend on which meaning we might choose. Do we mean the right to choose the care we want (or don't want) at the end of life? Is the problem in access to palliative measures? Or is it rationing of end of life care in cases of medical futility? Adding insights from a public health perspective might lead to further hard questions, which Professor Hoffmann then poses: Would we want government or lawmakers to take certain action as a result of using this lens? Would there be a danger that government might go too far? Would there be appropriate checks on government action? She specifies a range of interventions government might take to address problems of end of life care: from sanctions for physicians/hospitals that do not follow patient wishes, to making advance directives mandatory and changing the definition of death. Professor Hoffmann examines the benefits such interventions would bring to end of life care, the burdens they would impose on individual choice and decision making, and alternative mechanisms for achieving the same ends.

Professors Elizabeth Weeks Leonard and Jean Eggen tackle closely related topics that are seemingly even further from the office of public health, traditionally conceived: tort law and punitive damages awarded pursuant to tort judgments for egregious behavior. Professor

Weeks Leonard anticipates the reader's skepticism: "At first glance, it is perhaps difficult to see the overlap between tort law and public health." But, she notes, tort law does more than compensate injured victims of wrongful conduct. By imposing liability, the tort system also deters negligent (or worse) actors from similar conduct in the future. Yet, because it typically requires a showing of fault, tort law balances this need for the safety (and incidental regulation) achieved by deterrence with other values thought important: efficiency and productivity, and perhaps even education and aesthetic considerations. Similarly, public health must strike a balance, weighing individual rights and autonomy against the community's broader need to achieve good population-wide outcomes. But, she further argues, much additional work needs to be done to draw clear, principled lines between tolerable and intolerable intrusions onto individual rights. Perhaps the tort law approach to balancing, while it will always, to an extent, consider factors different from those involved in public health decision making, can provide valuable insights for making those resource allocation decisions in the public health arena.

Punitive damages, by their very nature and purpose, are not concerned with compensation, but with sending a message to both the defendant and those who might be tempted to emulate the reckless or intentionally harmful behavior that justifies the imposition of such damages. Such damages might also encourage defendants and others to invest in productive research-and-development initiatives. Thus, the public purpose of punitive damages is readily apparent. However, punitive damages have usually gone to the plaintiff, thereby blunting their potentially powerful public message. In Professor Eggen's view, they would be of greater service if diverted to the public treasury where they could be used in ways that might directly affect the public's health. For example, punitive damages obtained in a successful lawsuit against cigarette manufacturers might be directed toward a state's anti-smoking campaign. Thus, she recommends developing rules and mechanisms to achieve the diversion of punitive damages to these public health purposes. She acknowledges the obstacles inherent in trying to do this, and therefore begins the discussion of how we might designate appropriate agencies and proper purposes, to assure that the monies are spent appropriately.

Perhaps the reason that each of these authors struggles with the complex relationship between public health and individual rights is best captured by Professor Vernellia Randall. In her challenging article on the problems facing communities of color – she focuses especially on health care disparities and poor outcomes – she highlights the shortcomings of the medical and legal models for addressing these issues. The medical model ignores political, social, and communal contexts; specifically, for the most part, it is not able to address racism, problems with social support, stress, and other elements of an individual's lifestyle. It also does little to address the sociological causes of illness and disease. Similarly, the law and legal structure have proven inadequate. The Civil Rights Act of 1964 (Title VI) focuses almost exclusively on intentional discrimination. Case law limits access to the court and does not include physicians and other providers. Most importantly, the legal structure requires that individuals be aware of discrimination and injury.

In fact, the problem is even more deeply rooted, according to Professor Randall's sobering account. Even when policy makers focus on the health of the community rather than on individual medical or legal issues, they tend to miss much of the problem because of their strong tendency to identify with their own communities first (and sometimes solely). This affinity, she posits, is consistent with the theory of Maslow's hierarchy of need, which states that individuals must focus on and address their most basic needs before they have the luxury of concerning themselves with "growth needs," or their pursuit of personal fulfillment. Inasmuch as the life circumstances of most policy makers place them in the highest echelon, their concerns do not reflect those of people lower in the hierarchy.

This observation is likely applicable to the authors (including me), and we do well to remember, and to be humbled by, our own limitations of perspective in addressing these vital issues. But it is well past time to make the effort.

Notes

1. Comm. for the Study of the Future of Pub. Health, Inst. of Med., The Future of Public Health 19 (1988).

2. See, for example, Richard A. Epstein, *Let the Shoemaker Stick to His Last: A Defense of the "Old" Public Health*, 46 PERSP. IN BIOLOGY & MED. (SUPPLEMENT) S138 (2003).
3. From the company's website, this unequivocal statement: "PM USA agrees with the overwhelming medical and scientific consensus that cigarette smoking causes lung cancer, heart disease, emphysema and other serious diseases in smokers. Smokers are far more likely to develop serious diseases, like lung cancer, than non-smokers. There is no safe cigarette." See *Smoking and Disease in Smokers*, online at http://www.philipmorrisusa.com/en/cms/Products/Cigarettes/Health_Issues/default.aspx (accessed February 24, 2010).
4. See CDC, *Outbreak of Measles – San Diego, California, January – February 2008*, MMWR, Feb. 29, 2008, online at http://www.cdc.gov/mmwr/preview/mmwrhtml/mm5708a3.htm (accessed February 24, 2010) (describing an outbreak in San Diego among unvaccinated children).
5. Aravind Adiga, *What's Behind India's Outbreak of Polio Paranoia?* TIME, Sept. 28, 2006, online at http://www.time.com/time/health/article/0%2C8599%2C1540477% 2C00.html (accessed February 25, 2010) (attributing stubbornness of polio infection to views of influential fundamentalist Muslim clerics).
6. For a comprehensive discussion of religious and philosophical exemptions to vaccination, see Ross D. Silverman, *No More Kidding Around: Restructuring Non-Medical Childhood Immunization Exemptions to Ensure Public Health Protection*, 12 ANN. HEALTH L. 277 (2003).
7. *Sherr v. Northport-East Northport Union Free School Dist.*, 672 F. Supp. 81 (E.D.N.Y. 1987). The case demonstrates that those seeking the objection on such grounds often try to cast their objection in religious language, thereby to gain the protection of the exemption. In *Sherr*, the effort was unsuccessful because the court found the claim that the opposition was sincerely grounded in religion not to be credible.
8. Gardiner Harris, *Journal Retracts 1998 Paper Linking Autism to Vaccines*, N.Y. TIMES, Feb. 2, 2010, online at http://www.nytimes.com/2010/02/03/health/research/03lancet.html?partner=rss&emc=rss (accessed February 24, 2010) (discussing population-based studies refuting the link, and a recent retraction by British medical journal, *The Lancet*, of the one article that had purported to find such a connection).
9. Evan Stark, *Using Public Health to Reform the Legal and Justice Response to Domestic Violence, infra* at 125–152.

PART I BIRTH AND DEATH

1 BEYOND PRIVACY

A Population Approach to Reproductive Rights

Wendy E. Parmet

For at least forty years, Americans have debated whether women should have a legal right to safe abortions and effective contraception. This unusually contentious battle over "reproductive rights" has been waged in numerous arenas with arguments that reflect diverse worldviews as well as distinct disciplines, including theology, medicine, constitutional theory, sociology, and political theory. Among the arguments and perspectives that have at times been employed are those that purport to be based on public health. In recent years, such public health arguments have gained new prominence, especially among opponents of reproductive rights[1] and the Supreme Court.[2] This chapter considers the impact of this development on reproductive rights. I begin by exploring how each side in the reproductive rights debate has employed public health arguments and the impact of those arguments on the courts' recognition of reproductive rights. I conclude by contrasting the current use of public health arguments in the ongoing debate about reproductive rights to a fuller embrace of a public health perspective and ask what such an approach might bring to the table.

Public health focuses on the health of one or more populations.[3] In the debate over reproductive rights, the population that has generally been at issue is the population of women, especially women of childbearing age. Do reproductive rights advance or endanger their health? And in either case, what is the impact of that essentially empirical question on how we think about reproductive rights?

For many years, advocates of reproductive rights were the ones who were most likely to use "public health talk,"[4] arguing that the recognition of reproductive rights was not only conducive to but essential for protecting the health of women as well as their children. Thus in the early years of the twentieth century, Margaret Sanger and other birth control advocates claimed that access to birth control was "an integral part of public health"[5] and essential to ensuring the health of women and children. As scholars have noted, Sanger and other early birth control advocates often made arguments that echoed those of the eugenicists who sought to improve the human race by limiting the reproduction of people of supposedly inferior genetic stock.[6]

By the 1960s, as the fight for contraception and abortion began to make its way into constitutional law, proponents of reproductive rights continued to argue that the criminalization of contraceptives and abortion harmed women's health. For example, in 1966, prominent abortion activist Lawrence Lader cited studies estimating between 1,000 and 10,000 deaths occurred in the U.S. per year due to illegal abortions. Lader wrote:

> No study, moreover, could begin to measure the physical and psychological injury inflicted on women by quack abortionists, often virtual butchers. Nor could it encompass the damage women inflict on themselves in attempts at self-abortion.
>
> Into the emergency rooms of our city hospitals flow the grim products of this system.[7]

In effect, Lader argued that public health protection required the legalization of abortion.

In more recent years, advocates for legalized access to abortion and contraception have repeatedly pointed to the public health benefits ostensibly arising from such access. For example, proponents of over-the-counter access to Plan B, the so-called morning-after pill, claimed that it would "enhance the public health by reducing the risks of unintended pregnancies and the number of abortions."[8] Likewise, pro-choice advocates have repeatedly pointed to the dangers of so-called back-alley abortions. Often using the hanger as their visual symbol, reproductive rights advocates refer to studies showing that the legalization of contraception and abortion is associated with significant declines in maternal morbidity and mortality.[9]

In large measure, the claims of reproductive rights advocates have been supported by numerous studies and reports documenting the health risks that follow from the criminalization of abortion and the denial of access to safe contraceptives (including, of course, condoms that provide protection against HIV and other sexually transmitted infections). For example, a 2003 report by the World Health Organization (WHO) estimated that worldwide, 65,000 to 70,000 women die each year due to unsafe abortions (which they define as procedures not performed according to medical standards), and that 5 million women are hospitalized each year as a result of such procedures.[10] The WHO also reported that 1.7 million women are believed to develop secondary infertility due to unsafe abortions.[11]

A more recent paper by WHO and the Guttmacher Institute concluded that the "root cause" of induced abortion is unintended pregnancy, and that lack of access to contraception is critical to reducing unplanned pregnancies.[12] The paper added: "unrestrictive abortion laws do not predict a high incidence of abortion, and by the same token, highly restrictive abortion laws are not associated with low abortion incidence."[13] In effect, these reports contend that laws that impose barriers to abortion and contraception do not reduce the rates of abortion; they merely lead to more unsafe abortions and more maternal injuries and death.

Early abortion cases also stressed the health benefits of reproductive rights. For example, in *Roe v. Wade*,[14] Justice Blackmun's controversial opinion for the Supreme Court first discredited the state's claim that the prohibition of abortion protected the health of women by noting:

> When most criminal abortion laws were first enacted, the procedure was a hazardous one for the woman. ... Abortion mortality was high. ... Modern medical techniques have altered this situation. ... Mortality rates for women undergoing early abortions, where the procedure is legal, appear to be as low as or lower than the rates for normal childbirth. ... Of course, important state interests in the areas of health and medical standards do remain. The State has a legitimate interest in seeing to it that abortion, like any other medical procedure, is performed under circumstances that insure maximum safety for the patient.[15]

The Court then cited the opinions of both medical and public health organizations[16] to bolster its conclusion that the Constitution prohibited the state from banning abortions in the first two trimesters. The Court also noted:

> The detriment that the State would impose upon the pregnant woman by denying this choice [to terminate a pregnancy] altogether is apparent. Specific and direct harm medically diagnosable even in early pregnancy may be involved. … Psychological harm may be imminent. Mental and physical health may be taxed by child care.[17]

The *Roe* Court's emphasis on women's health was also evident in the limitations that it placed on the right to an abortion. Thus while the Court viewed the right to an abortion as supportive, if not essential, to protecting women's health, it acknowledged that the state had a legitimate interest in protecting a woman's health and that this interest became "compelling" and justified enhanced regulation at the start of the second trimester.[18] Indeed, even in the first trimester, when the *Roe* Court viewed the right to an abortion as at its zenith (in large part because abortion at this point in the pregnancy was as safe as or safer than childbirth), the Court clarified that states could require that abortions be performed only by state-licensed physicians.[19] Hence traditional and general regulations aimed at protecting public health could apply even during the first trimester. Finally, in the third trimester, when the state's interest in the potential life of a fetus also becomes, according to the *Roe* Court, "compelling," the state could not proscribe abortion "when it is necessary to preserve the life or health of the mother."[20] Thus throughout *Roe*, the Supreme Court viewed the constitutional right to choose an abortion as protective of women's health and also limited by the state's legitimate interest in women's health.[21]

In the years between *Roe* and the Court's watershed case in *Planned Parenthood v. Casey*,[22] arguments based on the health of women remained a salient, albeit background, factor that the courts as well as pro-choice activists used to support reproductive rights. For example, in *City of Akron v. Akron Center for Reproductive Rights*,[23] the Supreme Court struck down an ordinance that required all second-trimester abortions to be performed in a hospital. The City of Akron, not surprisingly, attempted to justify its ordinance using public health talk.

The city claimed that the regulation protected the health of women during the second trimester, an interest that the Court had found to be compelling in *Roe*. The Supreme Court rejected that claim not because it found that states could not protect women's health during the second trimester, but because it discredited the city's contention that the ordinance would indeed protect public health. According to the Court, "present medical knowledge" showed that abortions in the second trimester could be done just as safely in outpatient clinics as in hospitals.[24] In effect, the Court accepted that the state could enact regulations to protect the health of women during the second trimester but failed to accept the legitimacy of the city's rationale.

The dissenting justices were outraged. Justice O'Connor, writing for herself and Justices White and Rehnquist, declared that *Roe's* trimester approach was unsustainable: "the State's compelling interest in maternal health changes as medical technology changes, and any health regulation must not 'depart from accepted medical practice.' … [Thus] despite the Court's purported adherence to the trimester [framework from *Roe*], the lines drawn … have now been 'blurred'…."[25] Justice O'Connor went on to argue that the state always had an important interest "in the areas of health and medical standards" and that those interests justified regulation throughout pregnancy.[26]

In the years after *Akron*, the Supreme Court's approach to abortion began to shift, as did its perception of the relationship between state abortion regulations and public health. Most critically, in *Planned Parenthood of Southeastern Pennsylvania v. Casey*,[27] the decisive three-justice joint opinion (written by Justices O'Connor, Kennedy, and Souter) abandoned *Roe's* trimester framework and held that states could regulate abortion throughout pregnancy as long as they did not impose an "undue burden" on a woman's right to choose an abortion prior to viability.[28] Nevertheless, the Court followed *Roe* in viewing women's health as shaping the scope of a woman's right to an abortion. The Joint Opinion stated: "[a]s with any medical procedure, the State may enact regulations to further the health or safety of a woman seeking an abortion."[29] However, "[u]nnecessary health regulations that have the purpose or effect of presenting a substantial obstacle to a woman seeking an abortion impose an undue burden on the right" and are therefore unconstitutional.[30] Moreover, as in *Roe*, states were only permitted to limit postviability abortions if exceptions were made for those cases in which "appropriate medical judgment" concluded that an abortion was necessary for the preservation of the life or health of the mother.[31]

It was the latter holding from *Casey* that the Court relied upon in *Sternberg v. Carhart*, when a divided Court held that a Nebraska statute banning so-called partial birth abortions (known either as D & X abortions, for dilation and extraction, or as an intact dilation and evacuation, or D & E abortions) was unconstitutional in part because it did not include any exception for those times when the procedure might be necessary to protect a woman's health.[32] According to the Court, "a State may promote but not endanger a woman's health when it regulates the methods of abortion."[33] The Court added:

> Our cases have repeatedly invalidated statutes that in the process of regulating the *methods* of abortion, imposed significant health risks. They make clear that a risk to a women's (sic) health is the same whether it happens to arise from regulating a particular method of abortion, or from barring abortion entirely.[34]

To the majority, the fact that the state did not feel that there was a need for a health exception was unconvincing. Rather than deferring to the state's assertion that the banned procedure brought no health benefit, the *Sternberg* Court relied on the trial court's finding that "significant medical authority" asserted that the banned procedure was at times the safest for a woman. Thus once again the Court used health claims to shape the contours of both the woman's right and the state's regulatory powers.

The use of public health arguments by supporters of reproductive rights reflects the enormous influence that such arguments wield in American law and discourse.[35] Although particular actions and policies that states may undertake in the name of public health are frequently controversial, the importance of public health protection and the fact that the state should seek to further it via its laws and regulations is seldom contested.[36] Moreover, science also carries great weight and legitimacy in contemporary American culture.[37] By invoking public health arguments that sound in *science* in support of reproductive rights, reproductive rights proponents and the jurists who have recognized such rights have attempted to utilize the power and credibility of public health and science to support their cause.

Appeals to public health do not necessarily extinguish controversy, however. Most obviously, they do not quiet opposition that is based on theological or moral grounds. For those who believe that abortion constitutes the unjustified murder of innocent life, public health arguments showing that legalized access to abortion may save women's lives are unconvincing. Even within the domain of public health talk, public health arguments may not be able to secure reproductive rights. To the contrary, they may actually jeopardize such rights (at least as they are currently understood) by invoking a legal tradition in which state regulation has traditionally been granted broad deference.[38]

Although opposition to abortion has generally centered on moral claims about the life of the unborn fetus, since the 1980s, abortion opponents have also relied on public health claims, making what Reva B. Siegel calls "women-protective justifications."[39] These justifications are based on the claim that abortions (and sometimes contraception and other reproductive technologies) are harmful to women and therefore should be regulated as are other threats to population health, such as unwholesome food or dangerous drugs. To many feminists and reproductive rights proponents, these arguments are inherently "paternalistic" and hearken back to an era in which the law assumed that women could not make decisions for themselves.[40] But as public health law scholars know well, courts have traditionally permitted states to limit the autonomy of individuals (male as well as female), even in regard to very personal and intimate matters, in the name of public health.[41] Moreover, public health does not necessarily disdain paternalism.[42] To the contrary, public health values protecting the health of populations and the individuals within those populations even when those individuals do not appear to chose health-affirming choices. Thus, for example, public health supports reducing tobacco-related deaths even though such efforts may be viewed as paternalistic.

Opponents of reproductive rights have taken advantage of these attributes of public health talk and public health law to argue that access to abortion should be restricted not only for moral reasons but to protect women's health. Such use of public health talk by the pro-life movement goes back at least as far as the 1980s, when anti-abortion activists such as Vincent Rue began warning of the harm that abortion allegedly causes women.[43] In the late 1980s, anti-abortion leaders pressured President Reagan into asking Surgeon General C. Everett Koop, a strong abortion opponent, to issue official findings that abortion jeopardized women's health.[44] Koop refused to do so, concluding that there was insufficient scientific evidence to support such a finding and arguing that the case against abortion should be based on its morality.[45]

In subsequent years, opponents of reproductive rights have increased their reliance on public health arguments. Indeed, some vocal opponents of abortion have argued for what they call a public health strategy, suggesting that the pro-life movement should take a page from public health advocates' campaigns against tobacco.[46] David Reardon, a prominent proponent of the public health strategy against reproductive rights, has claimed that the public health evidence undermines the very foundation of *Roe* and hence a right to an abortion. According to Reardon, "pregnancy-associated deaths are actually two to four times higher for abortion women compared to delivering women."[47]

In recent years, abortion rights opponents have usually emphasized two different health risks that they claim are caused by abortion. One is breast cancer. Pointing to epidemiological studies going back as far as the 1950s, opponents of reproductive rights argue that epidemiological evidence firmly supports the so-called abortion-breast cancer link, known as the ABC link,[48] a linkage that, they hypothesize, occurs because exposure to hormones in early pregnancy leads to changes in breast tissue that make the tissue especially vulnerable to cancer.[49] These changes supposedly diminish at term, when the breast tissue completes the differentiation process and prepares to support lactation. According to biologist Joel Brind, one of the chief proponents of the ABC link, abortion's impact on breast cancer constitutes a major public health threat. Brind writes, "[w]e have estimated that upwards of 10,000 cases of breast cancer each year presently, and to 25,000 per year in twenty or thirty years hence, are or will be attributable to induced abortion."[50]

To be sure, the ABC link is widely disputed by most medical and public health researchers. In 2003, the National Cancer Institute convened a workshop on the issue, which concluded that "[i]nduced abortion is not associated with an increase in breast cancer risk."[51] Several more recent studies have also failed to support the claim,[52] though some scientists contend that the question warrants further research.[53] Opponents of abortion rights, however, discount studies and reports that reject the ABC link, arguing that mainstream medical societies and researchers are allowing ideology and their own economic interests in abortion to trump science.[54]

Opponents of abortion rights also argue that abortion (and sometimes even contraception)[55] causes psychological harm, and that women who have induced abortions have higher rates of depression, suicide, and emotional distress than other women.[56] They refer to what they call "postabortion syndrome," or PAS, a condition they liken to post-traumatic stress, which presumably arises from regret and guilt that women experience as a result of abortions.[57] (They seldom stop to ask, however, whether their own messages and advocacy help create an environment that may generate feelings of regret; rather they seem to assume that a woman's regret or guilt for an abortion is natural and not influenced by her cultural environment.) Again this claim is disputed by most mainstream authorities. For example, the American Psychiatric Association's Task Force on Mental Health and Abortion conducted a review of the empirical literature and concluded that there is "no evidence sufficient to support the claim that an observed association between abortion history and mental health was caused by the abortion *per se*, as opposed to other factors."[58]

Despite the fact that most mainstream researchers reject the public health claims made by abortion opponents, usually citing significant methodological flaws in the studies that find public health harms associated with or caused by abortion, these claims have gained traction in both state houses and the courts. For example, in 2005, the state of South Dakota convened a task force to study abortion.[59] The Task Force's Report began by listing the "incorrect assumptions" relied upon in *Roe v. Wade*, including the Supreme Court's failure to recognize that from "the moment of conception," a fetus is "a whole, separate human being."[60] But the Task Force did not rely simply on moral arguments or even what it claimed to be scientific facts about the fetus. It also emphasized the purported negative impacts of abortion on women's health. In particular, the Task Force found that abortion creates a wide range of physical risks for women, and that the Center for Disease Control and Prevention (CDC) statistics greatly underestimate the number of maternal deaths related to abortion.[61] The Task Force also reported on the testimony of 2,000 women who had had abortions and reported feeling wounded and guilty because of that fact.[62] Then, after summarizing the testimony of several well-known anti-abortion researchers about the negative mental health impacts of abortion (as well as women's limited ability to make informed decisions to have an abortion), the Task Force concluded that "it is simply unrealistic to assume that a pregnant mother is capable of being involved in the termination of the life of her own child without risk of suffering significant psychological trauma and distress."[63] This finding helped support the enactment of a South Dakota statute that, among other things, requires physicians to inform women seeking an abortion that the procedure causes an increased risk of suicide and suicide ideation.[64]

Courts have at times been sympathetic to such anti-abortion/public health arguments. Most strikingly, in 2007 in *Gonzales v. Carhart*,[65] the Supreme Court affirmed the federal "Partial-Birth Abortion Ban Act."[66] In upholding the law that criminalized what the Court called intact D & E abortions, Justice Kennedy, writing for the majority, first emphasized the differences between the federal ban and the Nebraska law struck down in *Sternberg*.[67] According to the Court, unlike the flawed Nebraska law, the federal statute was carefully written so as not to apply to the more commonly used method of late-term abortions, the so-called D & E procedure. Hence the federal law, the Court concluded, was not void for vagueness and did not impose an undue burden on a woman's right to obtain an abortion.[68]

More important, for our purposes, was the Court's discussion of Congress' rationale for banning the relatively rare intact D & E procedure. After all, if the ban would not prevent women from obtaining an abortion, what was its point? To this question the Court offered two illuminating answers. One was that the intact D & E procedure might have a detrimental impact on the sensibility of the "medical community."[69] In so doing, the Court invoked the traditional view that government may regulate the practice of medicine in order to protect the public's health.[70] Perhaps more telling, however, was the Court's second argument. The Court stated: "[w]hile we find no reliable data to measure the phenomenon, it seems unexceptional to conclude that some women come to regret their choice to abort the infant life they once created and sustained .... Severe depression and loss of esteem can follow," especially, the Court suggested, when women later learn that the procedure that was used to carry out the abortion was particularly gruesome.[71] In other words, Congress could ban intact D & E abortions to protect the mental health of women, even in the absence of *any* empirical evidence showing that the banned procedure threatened women's mental health.

A similar willingness to defer broadly to the legislature to protect the health of women was apparent in the Court's explanation of why the statute's failure to include a health exception did not render it unconstitutional. In *Sternberg*, the Supreme Court had followed *Roe* and *Casey* in requiring that a ban on intact D & E abortions have a health exception.[72] In many ways, this exception focused on the health of individual women and gave weight to the clinical judgment of their own physicians. In *Carhart*, the Court moved away from this *medical* stance and viewed the health issue from a broader, population perspective from which deference should be given not to individual physicians' thinking about the needs of their own patients, but to the legislature that, the Court concluded, was best positioned to make decisions about public health in the face of empirical uncertainty. The Court stated: "[t]he question becomes whether the Act can stand when this medical uncertainty persists.... The Court has given state and federal legislatures wide discretion to pass legislation in areas where there is medical and scientific uncertainty."[73] The Court then went on to cite several cases, including, most interestingly, *Jacobson v. Massachusetts*,[74] perhaps the seminal public health law case, that upheld the state's right to mandate vaccinations. In other words, as the Court saw the issue, when population health is at stake and scientific facts are contested, courts should defer to the superior fact-finding ability of legislatures, even if that means restricting access to a type of abortion and potentially endangering the health of particular women. Indeed, the Court was willing to defer to Congress even though the District Court found, and the Supreme Court did not disagree with its conclusion, that some of the Act's factual recitations were erroneous.[75]

From a public health *law* perspective, Justice Kennedy's reasoning does not appear all that exceptional.[76] Public health law 101 teaches that the states may use their police power broadly to protect public health.[77] In so doing, states frequently limit the liberty of individuals, even for their own good. Thus states may require motorcyclists to wear helmets[78] or prohibit individuals from driving without wearing a seatbelt.[79] When public health is claimed, as B. Jessie Hill has recognized, claims of individual autonomy frequently yield.[80] Moreover, when the health of a population is at stake, individuals may be forced to accept what they believe may jeopardize their own health,[81] although there may be limits to how much risk a particular person must bear.[82] Hence even in *Carhart*, the Court accepted that an as-applied challenge to the federal law brought by particular individuals who could show that the law had a deleterious impact on their own health might face a different fate.[83]

Carhart also followed public health law's tradition of granting the legislature great deference in determining so-called legislative facts that are relevant to population health policy. Indeed, in *Jacobson* itself, the Court stressed that deference should be given to public health officials in deciding whether or not vaccination was an effective intervention against smallpox. Writing for the Court, Justice Harlan stated: "It is no part of the function of a court or a jury to determine which one of two modes was likely to be the most effective for the protection of the public against disease. That was for the legislative department to determine in light of all the information it had or could obtain."[84] Thus when issues are presented as about public health, rather than about the clinical care of discrete patients, courts frequently defer to the state. Of course, such deference should not apply when fundamental rights are at stake; but by invoking public health talk and public health legal norms, the *Carhart* Court demonstrated the vulnerability of even those rights that have been recognized as fundamental to the leeway that legislatures are granted when they claim to act in the name of public health.

Perhaps more importantly, the invocation of public health arguments reveals a significant flaw in the efforts of reproductive rights activists to base reproductive rights on the concept of privacy. After all, by claiming that the state has an interest and is required to alter its law to protect the health of women, reproductive rights activists have in effect conceded a vital point: The health of any woman, indeed of any person, is not solely a private matter. The state has a legitimate, if not at times compelling, interest in enacting regulations to promote women's health. Thus if reproductive policy is viewed as presenting a contested question of public health, or as an empirical question about the best way to promote women's health, there may be no place for upholding reproductive rights as rights of *privacy* totally immune from state regulation. Hence the application of public health arguments to the reproductive rights debate may not curtail the controversy, nor may it secure such rights. Rather it would seem to put such rights at the mercy of the elected branches. Or must it?

The discussion thus far has explored the use and impact of public health talk and public health law in the battle over reproductive rights. But the use of public health arguments, however, is not necessarily identical or even faithful to the application of a public health *perspective.* In this section, I want to consider how the issue would appear if one went beyond making arguments based on conflicting epidemiological evidence and adopted what I have elsewhere called population-based legal analysis – that is, an approach to law that embraces not just public health claims but also its population perspective.[85]

According to Dan E. Beauchamp and Bonnie Steinbock, a population perspective refers to "the effort to understand the occurrence of disease from a group or community perspective."[86] As the Beauchamp and Steinbock definition makes clear, the population perspective focuses on the health of a "group or community" rather than the health of a single individual or patient. Therefore, the population perspective differs from the perspective that dominates medicine and medical ethics, which generally prioritizes the well being of individual patients. Finally, because of its emphasis on the health of groups of people, the population perspective values and relies on empirically derived epidemiological data rather than either the clinical examination of a patient or even legal precedent, and relies on such data to better understand what harms and what protects the health of groups.[87] As a result, a population perspective appropriately opens the door to empirically based debates about women's health.

Nevertheless, the population perspective does not necessarily support either the conclusions or the reasoning of either side in the abortion wars. To the contrary, by insisting that we consider the population health impact of our policies and laws on varied populations and that epidemiological evidence be taken seriously, the population perspective may point to some directions that may please neither side.

Consider first the use of public health talk by the Supreme Court in *Carhart*. At first glance, these arguments seem to comport with a population perspective. They emphasized the health of a population – women – rather than the health of any individual woman. For example, in *Carhart*, the Court accepted the absence of a health exception by deferring to the legislature's determination about women's health rather than the claims of physicians about the possible needs of individual patients. By so doing, the Court seemed to accept that the focus should be on the health of the larger group rather than the health of discrete individuals (although as noted earlier, the Court left open the door to the possibility that individuals could bring claims based on the application of the law in their particular case). Moreover the Court deferred to the legislature's power to determine the appropriate policy for the public's health. In all of these ways, the Court appeared to have adopted a population perspective and by so doing demonstrated the challenge that such perspective presents for reproductive rights.

In many other ways, however, the Court failed to truly embrace a population perspective. In fact, a population perspective leads to a far more nuanced appreciation of the relationship between the protection of population's health and individual rights than the *Carhart* Court's opinion evidences. First, precisely because the population perspective values epidemiological evidence, it would reject the *Carhart* Court's willingness to draw epidemiological conclusions in the absence of *any* data or other empirical support. Hence while the population perspective would undoubtedly counsel courts to give legislatures broad leeway to address pressing public health problems even in the face of uncertainty, perhaps adopting a "weak" version of the precautionary principle, it would not condone the open-ended deference, indeed blind credulity, that the Court displayed in *Carhart*. By permitting the legislature to reach any conclusion in the name of public health, even in the absence of *any* epidemiological evidence, the *Carhart* Court turned the population perspective upside down. Pretext prevailed over substance. Population health was used not as a valid concern of the law but as a label that could be employed to justify *post hoc* any policy, no matter its actual effect on health or other consequences.

Moreover, contrary to the views of many advocates on both sides of the abortion debate, a population approach does not insist that the law should simply tally up the deaths and illnesses associated with a particular practice and affirm a policy that, all other things being equal, leads to the lowest number of cases of a particular health problem, be that breast cancer or maternal deaths. In other words, although a population perspective places a very high value on the promotion and protection of public health – indeed it insists that the promotion of public health is one of the chief aims of law – it does not rely upon a crude form of act utilitarianism under which each legal decision is reached simply by looking at the discrete health impacts associated with the regulation under consideration. Thus a population perspective would not rely simplistically on a single study or even a multitude of studies that show that abortion is causally related to breast cancer to conclude that abortion should be outlawed. Nor would a population approach say that abortion must be made legal simply because it reduces abortion-related deaths. Rather a population perspective would, or should, recognize the complex and multi-factorial causality of human illness, as well as the overlapping and contingent shape of human populations. Hence a population approach is mindful not only of unanticipated and long-range consequences, including the health consequences that result from health regulations that protect short-term health by endangering the long-term well-being of a community, but also the fact that legal rules have different health consequences for different populations. After all, the abrogation of abortion rights to prevent breast cancer may have a very different impact on teenagers than it would on women over thirty. Moreover it is possible that even if abortion is causally related to breast cancer, the denial of legal access to abortion may not reduce the incidence of breast cancer, never mind improve the overall health of various subpopulations of women, because the total number of abortions may not, as the WHO study suggests, actually diminish. A population perspective would be sensitive to such nuances and complexity and avoid the knee-jerk conclusion that any particular action that may harm the health of any population in the short run must necessarily be met with a ban.

Likewise, a population perspective does not preclude the recognition of other important values such as equality, self-governance, and respect for individual dignity, values that, when followed, may themselves enhance the health of populations. Although a public health perspective places a high regard on public health, it does not insist that public health is the only value that lawmakers should consider. A society of long-lived and pain-free slaves would be neither just nor healthy. Adoption of a population perspective does not require, and should not prompt, the neglect of other important values and perspectives, especially when those values can help promote and secure a population's health.

Unfortunately in recent years, it has become far too common, especially among some policy makers and public health advocates, to view the struggle for public health in Manichean terms, as a struggle for the good of the many against the liberty of the individual. From this perspective, individual rights are viewed as being in opposition to the public's health, indeed as a luxury that cannot be afforded in the dangerous times. As a result, highly coercive policies such as quarantine and forced vaccination are being discussed and have been considered as part of a program of "preparedness."[88]

This Manichean view of public health protection has long influenced public policy regarding human reproduction. In the early 1900s, poor women such as Carrie Bell were viewed as threatening to the public's health for their reproductive potential. Then the Supreme Court in a memorable opinion by none other than Justice Oliver Wendell Holmes upheld Buck's mandatory sterilization to protect the health and vigor of the race, noting famously "three generations of imbeciles are enough!" He, too, cited *Jacobson*.[89]

In more recent years, pregnant women have been vilified for using alcohol or drugs while pregnant, for refusing HIV tests, or rejecting C-sections. In all of these cases, coercive actions have been taken against women on the theory that their rights had to be limited to protect the public's health. In all of these cases, the flag of public health has been used to justify harsh and often punitive treatment of women on the theory that this was required to protect the health of the many.

Today abortion opponents go further and argue that pregnant women endanger the public, as well as themselves, because the decisions they make increase their risk of cancer and lead to their own psychological trauma. Some advocates have even claimed that post-abortion trauma harms men and causes them to become violent.[90] In all of these arguments, there is a tacit assumption that the good of the individual and the well-being of the public are in conflict. From this the conclusion drawn is that the rights of the individual women must be restrained – or sacrificed as in time of war – for the greater good.

Now, it is of course true, as Justice Harlan stated in *Jacobson*, that life in society requires that limits be imposed on individual liberty.[91] It is also true that a population perspective leads us to value the health of populations and to question the belief that individual choices are made in isolation and hence can be wholly private.[92] Most fundamentally, a population perspective reminds us that we are all part of multiple communities and that the risks we face and the choices we make are all influenced by a host of social, cultural, economic, and environmental factors that operate upon the populations we inhabit. Law is, of course, one of those factors that influence our choices and decisions. To say that our choices must or can be private and hence apart from law is to ignore how law helps shape our choices in the first place.

But the recognition of population-wide influences does not and should not lead us to adopt laws that disempower individuals. Rather public health teaches that the common good is often strengthened by respecting individual liberty and enhancing the power given to historically disadvantaged groups. As a result, a population approach need not and should not overemphasize the opposition between individual rights and population health. Instead it should recall that the most effective public health interventions are often not those that prohibit individuals from making unhealthy choices but rather those that seek to restructure the environment to offer people healthier options.

For example, in the late nineteenth century, infectious diseases were controlled not primarily by quarantines or other liberty-limiting measures, but by providing people with clean food and water and sanitary sewage disposal.[93] More recently, public health practitioners have come to recognize the utility of interventions such as indoor smoking laws that alter the environment in which people make decisions affecting their health. Such broadly based, environmental interventions can often be more effective in promoting public health than are punitive, liberty-limiting measures.

In addition, a population perspective recognizes that populations are made up of individuals and that more often than not, populations are healthier when the people that comprise them are respected and empowered and are thereby able to care for themselves and their families. As a result, respect for individual agency and individual rights can enhance public health. Thus looking at the case of HIV, the late Jonathan Mann astutely and persuasively argued that respect for women's rights, including rights over their own sexuality and reproduction, was essential to containing the epidemic.[94] More recently, public health authorities have stressed the importance of respecting the rights of individuals for combating the global epidemics of HIV and TB.[95] In such cases, granting legal rights to individuals, even when that means granting them the right to undertake actions that may harm their own health or the health of others, may be more protective of a *population's* health than would be punitive laws seeking to restrict individual rights.

Similarly, the previously cited WHO study suggests that in developing countries, the recognition of reproductive rights does not increase the incidence of abortion; rather it lowers the incidence of abortion-related morbidity. Likewise, public health and development experts have emphasized the importance of increasing gender equality as well as the agency of women in order to decrease infant and maternal mortality, as well as rates of HIV/AIDS.[96] Hence even if it turned out, as abortion opponents claim, that abortion increases the risk of breast cancer or depression, granting women the right to make decisions about their own reproductive lives might still lead to greater overall improvements in the health of women and children, or at least in the health of some populations of women and children, than would laws impeding access to abortion. As a result, even if one accepts the epidemiological case against abortion currently being put forth by anti-abortion advocates, it does not necessarily mean that the law ought to restrict or abolish reproductive rights. Rather it may mean that legal resources should be devoted to influencing the social and environmental factors, including limited access to contraception, that result in unwanted pregnancies.

So what would a population perspective, rather than mere public health talk, bring to the wars over reproduction? Certainly it would accept that the empirical debate that has been raised about the safety of abortion, as well as any method of birth control, is critically important. The relationship, if any, between abortion and breast cancer, as well as between abortion and mental health, should be studied and when and if there is *credible* epidemiological evidence suggestive not merely of association but also causation, it should influence public policy. A population-based approach to reproductive law would not assume, a priori, that empirical facts are irrelevant or that new evidence that points in one direction or another should automatically be dismissed. In that sense, from a public health perspective, reproductive rights could not be either absolute or unchanging; they would always be open to new evidence and modification.

As was previously noted, however, valuing empirical evidence and recognizing its relevance to reproductive rights does not mean that the courts ought to defer reflexively to legislative findings of scientific fact, regardless of their scientific merit. To the contrary, because a population approach takes empirical evidence seriously, courts utilizing that approach would engage in and be capable of assessing empirical claims. Thus courts applying a population approach would neither demand unobtainable certainty from scientific studies nor accept results that lack scientific plausibility and that were performed using methodologies that significantly depart from widely accepted scientific methods. Junk science should and would receive no more credence in reproductive rights cases than it does in tort cases.[97]

In addition, because a population approach emphasizes the relationship between individuals and populations, it would likely eschew the rhetoric of privacy. It would look for and consider the social, not necessarily the private, determinants of reproductive health and construe the law in ways that facilitate positive social health determinants. Reproductive rights would be recognized to the degree that they would be not because reproduction is private, but because we value individual dignity and recognize the unique burden unwanted pregnancies place on women.[98] Likewise, reproductive rights would be respected not because individual rights trump the public good, but because empowering women and recognizing their dignity may provide a foundation for promoting their health as well as the health of their children.

Thus the recognition of the social and population context of reproductive health would not necessarily or even likely counsel for the significant evisceration of reproductive rights. Even if one accepts that certain reproductive choices, such as abortion, have some negative health consequences (and clearly that has hardly been proven), the question would remain whether the recognition of reproductive rights advances or thwarts the health of multiple populations. Moreover, a population approach would counsel us to ask whether the law would better advance the health of women and newborns by criminalizing abortion and restricting access to contraceptives, or by helping shape a social environment in which there are fewer unintended pregnancies. We would also want to ask whether restrictions on women's agency would promote their health, or whether women's health would be more firmly secured by empowering them to make decisions that are healthy for them and their families. In effect, a population approach requires us to ask whether reproductive rights are indeed helpful or harmful to the health of women broadly considered.

As the earlier discussion suggests, I suspect that a public health approach would support an altered but nevertheless robust role for reproductive rights. These rights might be less absolute and more contingent than they were under *Roe*. They would not be absolutes trampling on the power of the state, because the law would recognize that states have a legitimate role to play in shaping the social environment in which reproductive choices are made. But in other ways, these rights might be significantly broader because in recognizing the connections between an individual's reproductive choices and health and a community's well-being, a public health approach would embrace a more expansive, positive vision of rights – for example, by concluding that reproductive rights encompass positive rights to contraception, sex education, and prenatal care. Thus a population approach might well reject the Supreme Court's early rulings that government has no obligation to help indigent women effectuate their choice to have an abortion.[99]

True, many questions would remain. By being open to new empirical evidence, the population approach almost assures that the battle would continue as epidemiological studies, and their meaning, are debated. Indeed adoption of a population perspective would remind us that scientific facts, like social facts and ethical precepts, can be the subject of heated arguments. They do not end controversy, nor can we assume that claims made in the name of science are necessarily sound. Scientific claims themselves can be, as we have seen, hotly debated and highly contentious. But by emphasizing a goal that few reject – promoting the health of women and children – and by providing us with a tool – epidemiology, that we can use to measure that goal – even as we debate its findings, a population approach may alter the tone of the analysis and point the way to different, and perhaps more nuanced, understanding of reproductive rights.

Notes

1. Reva B. Siegel, *Dignity and the Politics of Protection: Abortion Restrictions under* Casey/Carhart, 117 YALE L. J. 1694, 1712–1733 (2008).
2. Gonzales v. Carhart, 550 U.S. 124 (2007).
3. For a fuller discussion of the multiple definitions of public health, see Wendy E. Parmet, POPULATIONS, PUBLIC HEALTH AND THE LAW, 7–13 (2009).
4. The term is Reva Siegel's. See Siegel, *supra* note 1, at 1724.
5. David M. Kennedy, BIRTH CONTROL IN AMERICA: THE CAREER OF MARGARET, SANGER 200 (1970).
6. Paul A. Lombardo, *Three Generations, No Imbeciles: Eugenics, the Supreme Court, and* Buck v. Bell, 156, 196 (2008).
7. Lawrence Lader, *Abortion*, 3 (1966).
8. Center for Drug Evaluation and Research Application Number 21–045/S011, Medical Review, 17 (August 2006), online at http://www.fda.gov/cder/foi/nda/2006/021045s00_Plan?B?MedR.pdf
9. NARAL Pro-Choice America Foundation, *Roe v. Wade* and the Right to Choose, online at http://www.prochoiceamerica.org/assets/files/Courts-SCOTUS-Roe.pdf (accessed August 19, 2009) (stating that by striking down abortion bans, *Roe v. Wade* "saved many women's lives").

10. World Health Organization, *Unsafe Abortion: Global and Regional Estimates of the Incidence of Unsafe Abortion and Associated Mortality*, 5 (2003).
11. *Id.*
12. Gilda Sedgh et al, *Induced Abortion: Estimated Rates and Trends Worldwide*, 370 LANCET 1338, 1343 (2007).
13. *Id.*
14. 410 U.S. 113 (1973).
15. *Id.* at 148–150.
16. *Id.* at 141–146.
17. *Id.* at 153.
18. *Id.* at 162.
19. *Id.* at 165.
20. *Id.* at 163.
21. Commentators have noted that the Court's opinion in *Roe* emphasized the role of the woman's physician. Linda Greenhouse, *How the Supreme Court Talks About Abortion: The Implications of a Shifting Discourse*, 42 SUFFOLK L. REV. 41, 44–48 (2008). The opinion also emphasized and relied in part on the opinions of medical and public health organizations. *Id.*
22. 505 U.S. 833 (1992).
23. 462 U.S. 416 (1983).
24. *Id.* at 437, *quoting* 410 U.S. at 163.
25. *Id.* at 452, 454–455 (O'Connor, J., dissenting).
26. *Id.* at 459, *quoting* 410 U.S. at 149–150.
27. 505 U.S. 833 (1992).
28. *Id.* at 872–874 (Joint opinion of Justices O'Connor, Kennedy, and Souter).
29. *Id.* at 878.
30. *Id.*
31. *Id.* at 879.
32. 530 U.S. 914 (2000). The Court also found that the statute was so vague as to impose an undue burden on a woman's ability to obtain an abortion.
33. 530 U.S. at 931.
34. *Id.*
35. Parmet, *supra* note 3, at 1, 37–45.
36. In contrast, the state's role in supporting or deciding upon medical care for individuals has been highly contested for decades, as is evident by the continuous political volatility of health care reform.
37. Dean M. Hashimoto argues persuasively that the Court often uses science rhetorically, calling upon its mythic power rather than relying upon it analytically to resolve questions. See Dean M. Hashimoto, *Science as Mythology in Constitutional Law*, 76 OR. L. REV. 111 (1997).
38. B. Jesse Hill, *The Constitutional Right to Make Medical Treatment Decisions: A Tale of Two Doctrines*, 86 TEX. L. REV. 277, 296–304 (2007).

39. Reva B. Siegel, *The New Politics of Abortion: An Equality Analysis of Women-Protective Abortion Restrictions*, 2007 U. Ill. L. Rev. 991 (2007).
40. *Id.* at 1000–1005.
41. Hill, *supra* note 38, at 303–304.
42. Ronald Bayer and Amy Fairchild, *The Genesis of Public Health Ethics*, 18 BIOETHICS 473, 485–492 (2004).
43. For a longer discussion, see Ronald Turner, Gonzales v. Carhart *and The Court's "Women's Regret" Rationale*, 43 WAKE FOREST L. REV. 1, 22–31 (2008).
44. Siegel, *supra* note 39, at 1016.
45. *Id.*
46. Justin D. Heminger, *Comment, Big Abortion, What the Antiabortion Movement Can Learn From Big Tobacco*, 54 CATH. U.L. REV. 1273, 1290 (2005).
47. David C. Reardon et al, *Deaths Associated with Abortion Compared to Childbirth - A Review of New and Old Data and the Medical and Legal Implications*, 20 J. CONTEMP. HEALTH L. & POL'Y 279, 281 (2004).
48. *E.g.*, Joel Brind et al, *Induced Abortion as an Independent Risk Factor for Breast Cancer: A Comprehensive Review and Meta-Analysis*, 50 J. OF EPIDEMIOLOGY AND COMMUNITY HEALTH 481 (1996).
49. Angela Lanfranchi, *The Science, Studies and Sociology of the Abortion Breast Cancer Link*, 21 ISSUES L. & MED. 95, 98–101 (2005).
50. Joel Brind, *The Abortion-Breast Cancer Connection*, 21 ISSUES IN LAW & MED. 109, 135 (2005).
51. National Cancer Institute, Summary Report: Early Reproductive Events and Breast Cancer Workshop (2003), at http://www.cancer.gov/cancerinfo/ere-workshop-report (accessed August 20, 2009).
52. See, for example, Karin B. Michels et al, *Induced and Spontaneous Abortion and Incidence of Breast Cancer Among Young Women: A Prospective Cohort Study*, 167 ARCH. INTERN MED. 814 (2007); Katherine DeLellis Henderson et al, *Incomplete Pregnancy is Not Associated with Breast Cancer Risk: The California Teachers Study*, 77 CONTRACEPTION 391 (2008).
53. See, for example, A.J. Kitchen et al, *Is There a Link Between Breast Cancer and Abortion: A Review of the Literature*, 50 FERTILITY 267, 270 (2005).
54. For example, Joel Brind et al, *supra* note 48, at 481; Lanfranchi, *supra* note 49, at 98–101.
55. For example, J. Kilkarni, *Depression as a Side Effect of the Contraceptive Pill*, 6 EXPERT OPINION ON DRUG SAFETY 371–74 (2007).
56. Heminger, *supra* note 46, at 1290; Turner, *supra* note 43, at 25–31.
57. Siegel, *supra* note 39, at 1016.
58. APA Task Force on Mental Health and Abortion, Report of the APA Task Force on Mental Health and Abortion, Aug. 13, 2008.
59. See Siegel, *supra* note 39, at 1026–1036.

60. Report of the South Dakota Task Force to Study Abortion, December 2005, 10, available at http://www.voteyesforlife.com/docs/Task_Force_Report.pdf (accessed August 25, 2009).
61. *Id.* at 49.
62. *Id.* at 33.
63. *Id.* at 47–48.
64. South Dakota House Bill 1166 (2005), codified at S.D.C.L. § 34–23A-10.1. The statute has been the subject of significant litigation. See Planned Parenthood of Minnesota v. Rounds, 530 F.3d 724 (8th Cir. 2008) (en banc) (vacating preliminary injunction); Planned Parenthood of Minnesota v. Rounds, Civ. 05–4077 KES (D.S.D. Aug. 20, 2009). In 2009, the federal district court struck down the provision cited in the text while affirming other parts of the state's informed consent law. See *id.*
65. Gonzales v. Carhart, 550 U.S. 124 (2007).
66. 18 U.S.C. §1531.
67. Stenberg v. Carhart, 530 U.S. 914 (2000).
68. 550 U.S. at 147.
69. *Id.* at 157.
70. See West Virginia v. Dent, 129 U.S. 114 (1889).
71. 550 U.S. at 159.
72. 505 U.S. 833, 872 (1992) (Joint Opinion of O'Connor, Souter, and Kennedy, JJ).
73. 550 U.S. at 163.
74. *Id.* citing 197 U.S. 11, 30–31 (1905).
75. 550 U.S. at 165–166.
76. See Hill *supra* note 38, at 318–324.
77. Lawrence O. Gostin, Public Health Law: Power, Duty, Restraint 91 (2d ed. 2008).
78. For example, Abate of Georgia v. Georgia, 137 F. Supp. 2d 1349 (N.D. Ga. 2001).
79. For example, State v. Hartog, 440 N.W.2d 852 (Iowa 1989).
80. Hill, *supra* note 38, at 295–304. It should be noted, however, that they generally do not yield quite so readily to fundamental rights of the sort that are at issue here.
81. Jacobson v. Massachusetts, 197 U.S. 11, 36–37 (1905); Abigail Alliance for Better Access to Developmental Drugs v. Von Eschenbach, 495 F.3d 695, 708–710 (D.C. Cir. 2007)(en banc)(rejecting a fundamental right to take experimental drugs in order to try to save one's life).
82. 197 U.S. at 38–39.
83. 550 U.S. at 167. The dissent noted the impracticality of such a challenge. 550 U.S. at 169, 189–190 (Ginsburg, J., dissenting).
84. 197 U.S. at 30.
85. Parmet, *supra* note 3, at 51–59.

86. Dan E. Beauchamp & Bonnie Steinbock, New Ethics For The Public's Health 25 (1999).
87. Parmet, *supra* note 3, at 58–59.
88. Wendy E. Parmet, *Dangerous Perspectives: The Perils of Individualizing Public Health Problems*, 30 J. Leg. Med. 83, 96–99 (2009).
89. Buck v. Bell, 274 U.S. 200, 207 (1927).
90. Reclaiming Lost Fatherhood Conference – The Conversation Over Men and Abortion Begins, 35 National Right to Life News 20 (Jan 2008).
91. 197 U.S. at 26.
92. See Parmet, *supra* note 3, at 141–161.
93. Wendy E. Parmet, *Quarantine Redux: Bioterrorism, AIDS and the Curtailment of Individual Liberty in the Name of Public Health*, 13 Health Matrix 85, 100–104 (2003).
94. Jonathan M. Mann, *Medicine and Public Health, Ethics and Human Rights*, 27 Hastings Ctr. Rep. 6, 61–14 (1997).
95. For example, UNAIDS, *International Guidelines on HIV/AIDS and Human Rights, 2006 Consolidated Version*, 16 (noting the complementary relationship between human rights and HIV prevention); World Care Council, Patients' Charter for Tuberculosis Care, (2006 Edition), http://www.worldcouncil.org/node/12 (charter of rights for TB patients).
96. United Nations Development Programme, En Route to Equality: A Gender Review of National MDG Reports, 2005, at http:www.undp.org/women/docs/en-route-to-equality.pdf (accessed August 23, 2009); See also Nicholas D. Kristof and Sheryl Wu Dunn, *Saving the World's Women, The Women's Crusade*, New York Times Magazine, Aug. 17, 2009, at 28.
97. See Daubert v. Merrell Dow Pharms., Inc., 509 U.S. 579 (1993); Parmet *supra* note at 231–235.
98. See Siegel, *supra* note 1, at 1736–1790.
99. Harris v. MacCrae, 448 U.S. 297 (1980); Maher v. Roe, 432 U.S. 464 (1977).

2 STRETCHING THE BOUNDARIES OF PUBLIC HEALTH:

Should We Consider End-of-Life Care a Public Health Issue?

Diane E. Hoffmann

INTRODUCTION

The nature of dying today differs markedly from dying 100 or even 60 years ago, and the debates surrounding end of life care – for example, when to stop life-sustaining treatment of a terminally ill patient – are unquestionably a product of the modern era of dying. During the nineteenth century, dying and care of the dying moved from the sphere of religion to that of medicine. Some have termed the evolution as "art to technique," wherein the art of death refers to dying as a public or community event and technique to the modern institutions and machinery of dying.[1] In the 1800s, death for most took place in the presence of "immediate relatives, the physician, ... the local preacher, ... [and] friends and relatives."[2] The priest or minister and the doctor both played significant roles – one administering to spiritual pain, the other to its physical counterpart. Over the next 200 years, the role of the physician expanded and that of the religious counselor diminished, resulting in the "medicalization" of death.

Prior to the 1950s, there were few controversies regarding end of life care simply because medical technology had not reached a point where it could extend life considerably for terminally ill patients. As a result, most people died at home, outside of hospitals or other health care institutions. Today, over 80 percent of individuals die in health care institutions.[3] Advances in medical technology, including mechanical ventilators, chemotherapy and radiation, artificial nutrition and hydration, and organ transplants, have allowed individuals who as recently as forty years ago would have died sooner to live an additional ten, twenty, or more years. In medicine, two notable advances have significantly contributed to extending the lives of chronically and terminally ill individuals. One such advance is medicine's ability to diagnose diseases more accurately and earlier. This has led to earlier interventions that can prolong life. The other advance has been in "rescue medicine," allowing physicians to remove and replace major organs and bring individuals "back" after a heart attack or stroke. Thus, the "way that we both perceive death and the circumstances in which we die" have changed considerably over the last fifty years.[4]

For at least the last half-century in the United States, care of the dying has been a clinical matter, shrouded in the framework of the doctor-patient relationship and the protective constructs of individual rights, patient autonomy, and privacy. Since the case of Karen Ann Quinlan,[5] decided by the New Jersey Supreme Court in 1976, in which the parents for a young woman in a persistent vegetative state won the right to have her disconnected from a ventilator, individuals and their families have fought for the right to control their deaths or the deaths of their loved ones. Often they have battled a medical establishment that seeks to extend life regardless of the quality of that life. While in some cases physicians acted out of concerns about potential liability, more often they were acting consistent with their training to treat and cure, to not give up on their patients. The courts, however, recognized the rights of individuals to refuse life-sustaining treatment and legislatures enshrined that right by codifying laws recognizing advance directives and the ability of family members to refuse life-sustaining treatment for a loved one, if such refusal was consistent with the individual's wishes or, if those wishes were not known, in the individual's best interest.

More recently in the United States, we have seen the dynamics of the debate change in some cases, although the focus on individual rights has remained intact. Rather than having a desire to extend life and use expensive, life-prolonging therapies, doctors may view continued medical care as futile or unjustified by the limited benefits and disproportionate costs. There is also considerable concern as a matter of health policy and national health expenditures that the costs of health care at the end of life may not be justified. Patients subject to decisions to deny them desired care, however, view those decisions as an infringement on their "right" to treatment that would sustain their life.

The suggestion that end of life care be treated as a public health issue stands somewhat counter to this relatively recent legal trend, at least in the United States, to view decisions about medical treatment of dying patients as highly individual, autonomous choices. But, considering the question – what, if anything, might be gained by treating end of life care as a public health issue – is intriguing. The question invites contemplation of a series of preliminary questions about the nature of the "end of life care problem," the boundaries of public health, and the goals of classifying end of life care as a public health issue.

Whether end of life care should be considered a public health issue may also depend on a specific cultural and geographic setting – that is, arguments for conceptualizing end of life care as a public health issue may be more salient, for example, in developing countries than in more developed regions of the world. The characterization of dying set forth above primarily describes end of life care in the United States and other developed countries. The difference between the medical services provided to terminally ill patients in the developed world and developing world is enormous. Terminally ill patients in less developed regions, where medical resources are scarce and policies deter adequate pain treatment, suffer tremendously in the last days of their lives. In those regions, arguments to classify end of life care as a public health issue are compelling. While this chapter primarily addresses end of life care in the United States, I devote the end of the chapter to end of life issues in less developed regions of the world.

DEFINING THE "END OF LIFE CARE" PROBLEM

Asking the question whether end of life care should be considered a public health matter implies a problem with end of life care that a public health approach might identify, correct, or ameliorate. It also implies some agreement as to what the end of life care problem is. How the problem is defined will undoubtedly influence whether end of life care should be considered a matter for public health.

There are several ways one might define the "end of life care problem." One perspective is that people who are dying do not receive the care that they want. In most cases, at least in the United States, this means they receive too much care, that is, their wishes to terminate life support are not honored. These individuals are often kept alive in intensive care units, tethered to numerous life support systems, with tubes in every orifice. Some have equated these conditions with torture.[6] In some cases, though, those who wish to receive more care and life-prolonging medical treatments are denied them. These individuals often lack health insurance and are unable to access all but emergency medical treatment.

A second perspective on the problem is that many dying individuals do not obtain access to appropriate palliative care and undergo unnecessary pain and suffering before they die. While the first view takes as its starting point a mismatch between individual preferences and receipt of medical services, this second framing of the problem shifts from one of autonomy to one of beneficence, and is shaped by medical judgment of patient needs rather than patient desires. According to this view, too many dying individuals do not obtain appropriate access to hospice or palliative care programs that administer morphine for pain relief and other medications for symptom relief such as shortness of breath. Hospice is often considered the "gold standard" for palliative care, and there is considerable literature indicating that for those who lack access to hospice, dying is not well managed:

> Patients receive care from multiple providers in a variety of separately governed and poorly communicating settings. Many are forced to endure futile therapies and procedures they do not want in an environment which takes away their sense of control and neither acknowledges nor meets their individual needs. Distress from pain and other symptoms often goes unrelieved, and spiritual anguish is neither diagnosed nor treated. Fear of being a physical and financial burden to families is common.[7]

Hospice, in contrast, delivers palliative care via a multidisciplinary team of trained professionals and volunteers. These individuals provide care both to the dying patient and to the patient's family members.

In contrast to the previous two definitions of the problem, a third perspective is that the problem is one of justice, where many people are requesting and receiving "too much" end of life care; that is, they are utilizing valuable health care resources with little benefit to themselves but which could be put to greater benefit if used for other patients. Those who criticize end of life care from this vantage point argue that a disproportionate amount of our health care budget is spent on care for the last six months of life for elderly patients.[8] They cite estimates of health policy experts that individuals who execute advance directives and receive hospice care "could save up to 10 percent of the cost of care" in the last year of life, "10 to 17 percent in the last six months, and 25 to 40 percent in the final month."[9] This view of the end of life care problem clearly stems from a public policy perspective in contrast to one based on individual rights.

THE BENEFITS OF A PUBLIC HEALTH APPROACH TO END OF LIFE CARE

In contemplating whether we should consider one or more end of life care problems as a public health issue, it seems appropriate to ask two separate questions: First, what gains or insights might we obtain by looking at care of the dying through the lens of public health; and, second, what are the implications of actually classifying end of life care as a public health issue for purposes of legal and regulatory authority? The former deals with the question of what benefits "public health analysis," that is, the tools of public health, can bring to a problem. The latter goes to whether the state or lawmakers might take certain actions as a result of emphasizing the public health dimension of end of life care, and whether there is a danger that the state might go "too far," that is, might take actions that would significantly curtail individual autonomy in ways that would lead to greater public harm than public good. Mark Hall has argued that we need to be clearer in our discussion of public health issues, clarifying whether we are referring to public health analysis or public health authority.[10] I address both aspects of public health but devote most of this chapter to the question of whether we should or would want to classify end of life care as a public health issue for purposes of the use of state authority.

At its core, taking a public health approach implies taking a population-based approach to an issue, in other words, emphasizing the impact of the problem on a group, or looking at the behavior of a group, rather than an individual. Public health uses the tools of epidemiology and biostatistics to assess the effect on a population of a practice or behavior or an environmental exposure. The field of end of life care has indeed been the subject of epidemiological studies. For example, there is the well-known SUPPORT study, published in the *Journal of the American Medical Association* in 1995, which recorded the end of life care of over 9,000 adults hospitalized with one or more of nine life-threatening diagnoses.[11] Phase I of the study revealed significant inadequacies in the care of these patients, ranging from failure of communication between physicians and patients to over-aggressive treatment and to failure to appropriately treat pain.[12] Other epidemiologic studies have found disparities in the writing of "Do Not Resuscitate" ("DNR") orders[13] and in the provision of adequate pain medication.[14] Such studies can lead to changes in treatment patterns and improvements in access to care. These benefits arise from the domain of public health analysis.[15]

While such studies and the use of public health "techniques" can have beneficial effects on treatment, there is a caveat to this positive assessment. Public health methods also include cost-effectiveness analyses in order to make tradeoffs among investments in various public health approaches. Such analyses may incorporate concepts such as Quality-Adjusted Life Years, which give more weight and priority to interventions or activities that extend life and reduce morbidity. This presents a problem for palliative care, which does not aim to increase life expectancy or reduce morbidity, but rather aims to make the dying individual more comfortable. The application of this conceptual tool may tend to undervalue palliative care when compared to other curative or preventive interventions.

Taking a public health approach to end of life care might also lead to state actions that would improve end of life care. Typical government approaches to dealing with public health problems include public education, monitoring of care or diseases, reporting of quality or outcome measures, changes in health care delivery, incentives to change individual behavior, and mandates to change the behavior of individuals and practices of other actors, such as polluters and manufacturers of harmful products. Perhaps most significantly, categorizing an issue as a public health problem may result in more resources being devoted to address the problem. Government actions to improve end of life care could result in more individuals executing advance directors, more individuals receiving palliative or hospice care, and/or reducing unnecessary expenditures on life-sustaining treatment. These benefits stem from the use of the state's public health authority.[16]

SHOULD WE INCLUDE END OF LIFE CARE AS A PUBLIC HEALTH PROBLEM FOR THE PURPOSE OF EXERCISING PUBLIC HEALTH AUTHORITY?

There is probably little debate about whether end of life care should be considered a public health problem for purposes of applying public health tools to analyze end of life care data. However, there is likely to be much more controversy about whether we should consider end of life care a public health issue for purposes of using "public health authority."

Determining what constitutes a public health problem for purposes of asserting public health authority is not clear-cut. Gostin has written that definitions of public health "vary widely" and that answering the question of what we mean by public health is "not easy because the field of public health is highly eclectic and conflicted."[17] He observes that:

> Most definitions share the premise that the subject of public health is the health of populations – rather than the health of individuals – and that this goal is reached by a generally high level of health throughout society, rather than the best possible health for a few. The field of public health is concerned with health promotion and disease prevention throughout society. Consequently, public

> health is less interested in clinical interactions between healthcare professionals and patients, and more interested in devising broad strategies to prevent, or ameliorate, injury and disease.[18]

Thus, a hallmark of a public health problem is that it affects a significant proportion of a population. Legislatures and government agencies are unlikely to use the power of the state unless they are convinced that the problem is large. Unfortunately, and perhaps because we have traditionally not viewed end of life care as a public health problem, we do not have precise data on the numbers of individuals who are kept alive longer than they wish, who do not receive adequate palliative care, or who receive more care than is "medically appropriate." However, we do have some indications of the potential scope of these problems. For example, we know that only about 18–36 percent of the population has completed an advance directive,[19] and that individuals without an advance directive are at higher risk of not having their wishes complied with at the end of their life than those who have completed such documents.[20]

Regarding access to palliative care, while individuals can receive palliative care outside of hospice, they are much less likely to do so. As a result, the numbers of dying individuals receiving hospice care may be a good proxy for those receiving palliative care. Over the last decade, there has been very significant growth in the number of hospice programs nationwide. In 2005, "approximately one-third of all [non-sudden] deaths in the United States were under the care of a hospice program."[21] In 2008, approximately 40 percent of Medicare decedents used hospice.[22] While these numbers are encouraging, there is also evidence that many terminally ill individuals do not access hospice care until it is too late, that is, they do not receive hospices services when they would have benefited from them.[23] In 2007, the median length of stay in hospice was 20 days; however, approximately 30 percent of hospice patients die or are discharged in seven days or less.[24] According to experts in the field, "patients need to be enrolled in hospice for at least 60 days to maximize its benefits, in terms of pain and symptom management and psychological and spiritual support."[25] We also know that individuals who do not enroll in hospice may experience significant untreated or inappropriately managed pain at the end of their life. Studies from a dozen years ago also found that more than half of dying patients reported being in serious pain.[26] Yet, the medical profession has placed significant emphasis on improving pain treatment during the last decade, and it is highly likely that the percentage of patients dying in pain has declined.

Although we do not have exact numbers regarding individuals who are kept alive "too long," in the sense that continued medical care is no longer medically appropriate or effective, a 2002 report by Last Acts, a national coalition to improve end of life care, funded by the Robert Wood Johnson Foundation, looked at "overaggressive" treatment for dying persons. Such treatment was defined as spending more than a week in intensive care. The authors of the report found that the numbers varied significantly from state to state. In Oregon, for example, only 3.4 percent of dying individuals spent over a week in the intensive care unit ("ICU"), whereas in New Jersey, the figure was 17.3 percent. The mean figure across all states was 10.1 percent.[27]

The number of individuals affected is only one criterion for considering an issue as a public health problem, although some critically assert that it has become the only criterion.[28] The traditional conceptions of what constitutes a public health problem seem to focus on causation, that is, whether the problem is caused by a pathogen, individual behavior, or the environment. Clearly, problems in end of life care are not infectious, nor are they caused by the classic environmental pollutants that lead to illness in a large population. However, some end of life care problems, especially those in which patients do not receive the care that they want or demand too much care, can be attributed to individual behavior. Individuals are more likely to receive care that they wish or to have care withheld or withdrawn in accordance with their preferences if they execute an advance directive. The fact that a significant majority of the population in this country has not executed such documents is in large part a matter of individual behavior. Similarly, the fact that some individuals request or demand care that is of very little benefit and of great cost is largely a behavioral issue.

Other conceptions of end of life care problems do not fit neatly into the classic causal-related definitions of public health but may fit into a more current, expanded view of the concept. Recent characterizations of public health problems have moved beyond concepts of infection, environment, and behavior. The trend in public health practice and scholarship has been to broaden the reach of public health to include all social determinants of health status. The Institute of Medicine's *The Future of Public Health*, for example, took a very expansive view of public health, defining it as "what we, as a society, do collectively to assure the conditions for people to be healthy."[29] Advocates of this broad view have included under the public health tent such social problems as "war, violence, poverty, economic development, income distribution, natural resources, diet and lifestyle, health care infrastructure, overpopulation and civil rights."[30] This extensive reach has been criticized by a number of academics who have described this unbridled expansion as the "public healthification" of social problems.[31]

The growth of what constitutes public health appears in part a result of our response to, and understanding of, diseases. Initially, public health focused on communicable diseases. Public health responses included improvements in water quality and sanitation and vaccinations. Medical responses included antibiotics. When chronic diseases began to overtake infections as the leading cause of death, the public health focus switched to behavioral changes individuals could make to improve their health. These included smoking cessation, exercising, and eating more healthfully. Soon, however, it became clear that there were limits to what individuals could do – "not everyone was capable of changing his or her environment or habits," and public health advocates began to call for social approaches to public health.[32] In a debate over whether end of life care should be considered a public health issue, the modern public health advocate would argue, for example, that individual failures to execute an advance directive or to demand "excessive" end of life care are not necessarily issues that individuals control. These public health advocates would take into account the social, cultural, and institutional reasons why some individuals do not execute an advance directive or why some individuals continue to demand life-sustaining treatment.

The comprehensive perspective is certainly broad enough to include each of the articulated end of life care problems, yet this broad view seems a stretch. Gostin has argued that an all-encompassing definition of public health dilutes the field of any precision, moves it beyond its core area of expertise, and depending on the area it claims, may highly politicize the field.[33]

The question of whether matters of clinical medicine should be deemed public health issues is perhaps at the heart of whether we should consider end of life care a public health matter. Many end of life care problems can be traced to inadequacies in clinical medicine and the doctor-patient relationship, that is, physicians who fail to discuss end of life care preferences with patients or ignore advance directives (because of religious or cultural perspectives and/or fear of lawsuits, or because they are unskilled at talking about dying or providing palliative care). Gostin admits that the "dividing line between health care and public health is exceedingly difficult to draw."[34] While he argues that the "quintessential feature of public health is its concentration on communal well-being, and that this feature separates public health from medicine,"[35] he also states that "public health subsumes personal medical services as one of many conditions necessary to preserve the population's health."[36] From this last statement, one might assert that when one sums up the health improvements for each individual treated clinically, the cumulative effect is an improvement in the health of an entire community. As a result, many clinical health problems could be considered matters for public health.[37]

Even if we were to concede that problems related to clinical medical practice were matters for public health, not all of the obstacles to good end of life care are attributable to the doctor-patient relationship or the practice of medicine. Some are actually policy driven or are matters relating to the health care system and health care financing. For example, some individuals are denied hospice services because of the narrow definition of the Medicare hospice benefit or because of reimbursement rates that may, in some cases, be a disincentive for institutions, such as nursing homes, to refer patients to hospice. While these policy issues affect a large number of individuals at the end of life, we might ask whether we should use "public health authority" to address them when we have other tools, such as conditions of insurance coverage, that could be employed.

ECONOMIC AND LEGAL ARGUMENTS LIMITING THE REACH OF PUBLIC HEALTH

While public health advocates have sought to expand the umbrella of public health,[38] those external to the field have expressed concerns in large part based on fears of the inappropriate use of the state power of coercion. This perspective is grounded in the widely accepted view that deeming an issue a "public health problem" is a way of signaling that the government may – or must – address it. Critics of a broad view of public health have relied on economic and legal constructs to put some boundaries around what constitutes a public health issue. They define a public health issue as one that warrants state or collective action because "individuals acting in their own self-interest, even if fully informed and rational, will not effectively address the problem because they do not internalize some of the major costs or benefits of action or non-action. …"[39] Alternatively, they may agree that public action is appropriate if a centralized response is much more cost-effective than individual action, or a solution to the problem cannot be individualized.

Under this economic perspective of what constitutes a public health issue, some end of life care problems may warrant state action, but others would not. Individual patients whose wishes are not followed arguably can effectively address the problem by executing an advance directive or making sure others know about their wishes. (This assumes, however, that they know about these instruments and how to execute them.) If they have an advance directive and it is not being followed, they or a member of their family (on their behalf) may bring a lawsuit seeking to enforce the directive. Courts have enforced such documents through declaratory judgments or injunctive orders.

In contrast, individuals who do not have access to appropriate palliative care or hospice care may be limited in their ability to obtain such access. The Medicare hospice benefit limits the availability of hospice to those over sixty-five with a "terminal condition," which is often narrowly defined by physicians. In addition, many people do not know about hospice services and may not be informed by their health care providers of the hospice option. Nursing home patients, for example, may have difficulty obtaining access to hospice because nursing homes, for a variety of reasons, including concerns about fraud charges and reimbursement disincentives, often do not contract with hospices to provide services to their residents.[40]

The strongest argument for a need for state action can be made in the context of individuals receiving too much care at the end of life. Such overutilization of care is in large part a result of economic incentives to continue care, which occurs when individuals are shielded from the true cost of their care because they have health insurance coverage. Such overutilization has significant negative externalities. Thus, under a view of public health that focuses on the need for collective action to fix the problem, it would not be appropriate to label lack of advance directives, which individuals can execute and enforce individually, a public health problem, but it might be appropriate to label lack of palliative care and spending too many resources on end of life care as matters appropriate for public health action.

GOVERNMENT ACTIONS TO IMPROVE END OF LIFE CARE

To the extent that government action is deemed warranted, legislators and government agencies can take a variety of actions to improve end of life care with different degrees of coerciveness. Government actors can simply encourage a voluntary response or educate individuals about the problem and actions they might take to mitigate it or prevent the problem from occurring or expanding. In the area of end of life care, as in other areas, there is a range of interventions legislatures or government agencies might take to address identified problems. For example, if we define the problem as individuals not having their wishes followed, government actors could implement public education programs for physicians and health care workers, informing them about the need to discuss end of life care wishes with their patients. Ratcheting up the government responses, state legislatures might establish mandatory registries for advance directives. A state might also require mandatory reporting by hospitals and nursing homes indicating whether they have complied with patients' end of life care wishes. In addition, states could establish and enforce sanctions for physicians, hospitals, and long-term care facilities that do not follow patient wishes. State legislatures could even make it easier for patients to bring lawsuits against health care providers who do not follow their wishes, or increase damage awards, for example, award treble damages in cases where patients successfully challenge a physician's failure to comply with an advance directive. At the federal level, using its authority as a health insurer, Congress or the Centers for Medicare and Medicaid Services ("CMS") could require that individuals execute an advance directive in order to receive Medicare benefits.

With respect to the problem of inadequate palliative care, public health agencies could establish a public health education program targeting patients and educating them about the benefits of hospice care. In addition, Congress could revise the Medicare hospice eligibility rules making it easier for individuals to access the Medicare hospice benefit. This might be done by eliminating the requirement that individuals waive the option of curative care. (Individuals who elect the Medicare Hospice benefit must waive coverage of all Medicare-funded curative care related to the patient's terminal illness.) Congress and/or CMS might also change reimbursement incentives so that nursing homes would be more likely to refer residents to hospice. Currently, nursing homes are sometimes reluctant to refer patients to hospice if those patients also qualify for the skilled nursing home benefit. A nursing home resident who is eligible for both the skilled nursing benefit and the Medicare Hospice benefit must choose one or the other. Nursing facilities "may prefer that the resident receive the [skilled nursing benefit] as it would be financially advantageous to the facility."[41] Other potential government actions to increase the use of palliative care might include relaxing laws regarding the administration of opioids or allowing physician-assisted dying. In Oregon, where physician-assisted suicide has been legal for over a decade, there is some empirical evidence that palliative care in the state has improved.[42]

If the problem were considered to be one of overutilization of medical treatment at the end of life, government actors might consider additional interventions. This conceptualization of the problem arguably would require a more heavy-handed government approach, such as making advance directives mandatory. Alternatively, states could be encouraged to adopt laws such as the Texas Advance Directives Act, which allows physicians, with ethics committee approval, and over the objection of a patient or his/her family members, to withhold or withdraw life-sustaining treatment they deem "medically inappropriate" ten days after the ethics committee's decision.[43] While such a law arguably protects the clinical decision-making domain of physicians, one could envision a similar law that, as a matter of hospital licensure, limited the number of days in an ICU for certain diagnoses or set across-the-board standards for termination of life-sustaining treatment rather than permit physicians to make case-by-case determinations for end of life care. More states could follow in the steps of Oregon, Washington, and Montana, which have legalized physician-assisted dying. Or even more extreme, states could change the definition of death by, for example, including such conditions as persistent vegetative state or other conditions closer to the margins of what is currently included under the definition of death. Some medical ethicists, for example, have argued for a change to the definition of death to include infants with anencephaly (where part or all of the higher brain does not develop).[44]

THE RISKS OF AND NEED FOR A PUBLIC HEALTH APPROACH

Despite the potential benefits that a public health approach might bring to end of life care, critics of an expanded view of public health would caution against labeling any of the end of life problems as public health issues. This reaction is based largely on fears of government overreaching and overregulation, as well as an argument that government has other means to achieve its goals. Richard Epstein, for example, asserts that designating something as a public health issue is "designed to signal that state coercion is appropriate."[45] Mark Rothstein argues that "[t]he key element of public health is the role of the government – its power and obligation to invoke mandatory or coercive measures to eliminate a threat to the public's health."[46] Mark Hall, in an article on *The Scope and Limits of Public Health Law*, similarly concludes that "[c]lassifying problems as public health problems tends to invoke public health legal principles. …"[47] He argues that government actors may start "with less intrusive, more innocuous measures, such as information, education, or taxation, but if these fail, then the case is even stronger for pursuing a panoply of more aggressive and coercive strategies, including mandates and bans, closures and seizures, quarantine, and criminal sanctions."[48] Each of these scholars contends that an overly broad view of public health can lead to overregulation. Such overregulation can sap "the social resources and focus to deal with public health matters more narrowly construed"[49] and arguably more pressing.

Others have made the point that when a state asserts that its actions are grounded in response to a public health problem, that justification has great weight in the courts, even in reaction to constitutional challenges. Parmet and Smith, for example, have observed that even when the courts "were especially solicitous of individual autonomy, attempts by the state to protect public health prevailed more often than not."[50] This was true for state efforts to mandate motorcycle helmets, close gay bathhouses, and ban physician-assisted suicide.[51]

In considering the range of interventions that the state might pursue to improve end of life care, however defined, some would surely argue that there is a risk of government overreaching and inappropriate infringement on individual autonomy. This is especially true for interventions that would put pressure on individuals to reject life- sustaining treatments or health care providers or institutions to prematurely withhold or withdraw life support. Such interventions would bump up against the beliefs of some religious groups regarding the sanctity of life and the need to maintain life despite the costs and would be vigorously opposed. This was the case in the most recent round of U.S. efforts to expand health insurance coverage to the nation's population. One of the proposals considered by lawmakers in an effort to improve end of life care and control health care costs of the terminally ill was to pay physicians who discuss end of life care options, including how to prepare advance directives, with elderly patients. The proposal would have allowed Medicare to reimburse doctors for "advance care planning consultation" once every five years.[52] The sessions would have been voluntary. Opponents immediately began to describe the provision on blogs and radio talk shows as "'an ORDER from the Government to end your life,' promoting 'death care' and ... an attempt to 'kill Granny.'"[53] The provision was not characterized as a public health initiative but was an effort to use Medicare payment to increase the execution of advance directives. It was alternatively described by *proponents* as an effort to improve the quality of end of life care and help ensure that health care providers comply with their patients' wishes, and by *opponents* as a cost-cutting strategy that would prematurely end life.

It is not clear whether the power of the state to implement these end of life care initiatives would trump individual rights if end of life care were considered a public health issue. This would depend on the specific action contemplated by the state, but a cursory constitutional analysis of several possible government actions indicates that the government's actions would largely go unchecked by constitutional challenge. Voluntary educational interventions would certainly be permissible under any constitutional analysis. Other interventions might provoke legal challenges, but their success would be questionable. For example, a consumer group could challenge a state law mandating that all adults complete an advance directive and file it with a state registry. As long as the law did not mandate that an individual adopt a certain response (e.g., no life-sustaining treatment if terminally ill), it is very likely that the law would withstand legal challenge. Assuming the law simply required individuals to execute a document and file it, not to make a decision one way or the other, the level of scrutiny applied to such a requirement would likely be relatively low – a rational basis – so that the state action would need only be a reasonable means to achieve a "legitimate" government interest. The government interest in ensuring that health care providers know of an individual's wishes for life-sustaining treatment and carry them out is certainly legitimate. Moreover, the requirement to execute an advance directive would seem reasonable and not unduly burdensome.

Challenges to other laws, such as those that would limit the number of days hospital patients could spend in an ICU if terminally ill, might also have difficulty. If tied to hospital licensure, such a law would constitute state action, but arguing that the law violates substantive due process would unlikely be successful because there is no fundamental right to continued medical treatment. Supreme Court cases have made clear that "the Due Process Clauses generally confer no affirmative right to governmental aid, even where such aid may be necessary to secure life, liberty, or property interests of which the government itself may not deprive the individual."[54]

Legislative action to change a state's definition of death, for example, by including persistent vegetative state, would likely meet with significant political resistance, but whether opponents would be successful in a constitutional challenge is also uncertain. A plaintiff might try to argue that because one has a fundamental right to the "life" contemplated by the Fourteenth Amendment, a statute that defines "death" so as to encroach upon the constitutional meaning of "life" is a deprivation of life that can be sustained only if there is compelling state interest. In addition, one might argue that under the Equal Protection Clause of the Fourteenth Amendment, patients in a persistent vegetative state (if that were to be a condition that the state considered dead) are as alive, within the meaning of the Fourteenth Amendment, as other brain-injured people. Thus, to deprive them of medical care through the device of declaring them dead would violate the Equal Protection clause. Whether such arguments would be successful would depend not only on the Court's view of these arguments but also its view of whether the state's purpose in expanding the definition of death was sufficiently compelling.

This cursory analysis indicates that, in many cases, a state's actions to improve end of life care through "public health" laws would not likely be checked by a constitutional challenge. Thus, giving the state's actions the imprimatur of a response to a *public health* problem might give the state the political clout it would need to pass and implement some of these ideas. However, such heightened import to the issue seems misguided and could lead to the passage of laws that would be unduly intrusive of individual autonomy. For example, states could increase physician sanctions or damages in a lawsuit against a physician for failure to comply with a patient's advance directives. This might lead to physicians prematurely terminating life support in order to avoid sanctions or legal actions. Or, as mentioned above, states could change the definition of death to include persistent vegetative state. Such a change would be a radical departure from our current laws allowing individuals to decide whether they wish to be kept alive in such conditions.

Perhaps more important than whether or not a state could implement these types of laws is the question of whether the purported benefits of these laws would outweigh their harms. Would they, for example, significantly improve the quality of end of life care or save significant health care dollars? The answer is not obvious.

Finally, there is also a question about the necessity of using the power of public health to address the problem of end of life care. Many of the possible government responses to the different conceptions of the end of life care problem, such as mandatory execution of advance directives as a prerequisite to receipt of Medicare benefits, mandatory reporting by health care institutions of compliance with advance directives, revision of the Medicare hospice eligibility rules, and reimbursement rates for hospice care, could be addressed via insurance laws, state licensure laws, and/or other quality of care laws and regulations. The recent proposal to pay physicians for discussing end of life care options with patients, for example, came out of the federal government's role as a health insurer for the elderly. Richard Epstein, in his article *Let the Shoemaker Stick to His Last: A Defense of the "Old" Public Health*, discusses efforts of public health advocates to expand public health regulation via government insurance and argues that "[t]he government is surely in a position to impose restrictions in its role as an insurer that it could not impose simply as regulator acting to defend public health. The only restriction on its power to act is the germaneness of the restriction to the objectives of the insurance plan."[55] The state also has other alternatives at its disposal to implement some of the suggested interventions. For example, the requirement for individuals to execute an advance directive could be tied to the ability to obtain a driver's license. Politically, whether these alternative approaches would be more feasible is open to debate, but legally, these approaches may be more defensible.

The potential for overreaching on the part of the state through the use of its public health powers to improve end of life care is not an insignificant problem. The fact that there are other mechanisms that the state can use to achieve the same objectives reduces the need to raise the specter of public health to add weightiness to the government's goals. In addition to state actors, there are also a number of private actors that have been and continue to be motivated to improve end of life care. These include insurers, health care institutions, professional societies, and medical schools. In 1999, for example, the AMA implemented the EPEC (Education of Physicians for End of Life Care) project, an effort to educate all practicing physicians with the "knowledge and skills to provide the best possible care for dying patients." The project included educational materials for physicians on palliative care, ethical decision making, symptom management, communication, and psychosocial aspects of care at the end of life. Also, in 2000, the American Bar Association (ABA) "adopted a resolution urging state, federal and territorial governments to remove legal barriers to high-quality pain and symptom management."[56]

Foundations have also devoted considerable resources to the improvement of end of life care, most notably the Robert Wood Johnson Foundation, which funded the decade-long Last Acts campaign. The campaign established a coalition of more than 800 national and consumer groups that worked to "[i]mprove communication and decision making for consumers about their own death[; c]hange the culture of health care institutions[; and c]hange American culture and attitudes toward death."[57] The campaign published numerous resources for the public and professionals about end of life care.

Given these alternative mechanisms to improve end of life care, it is not at all clear that we would want to give the state a public health justification for taking on end of life care. If we were to do so, we might have trouble reining in the government and preventing it from implementing increasingly more coercive measures. While education on advance directives might be helpful, it is not clear that the issue warrants more heavy-handed measures.

A MORE GLOBAL PERSPECTIVE

The analysis in the preceding section and the cautionary admonition about treating end of life care as a public health issue is premised on end of life care practices in the United States. A different response might be more appropriate in less developed countries where the problem is greater and the causes are different. In many developing countries, the problem is not that dying individuals do not have their wishes to terminate life-sustaining procedures followed or that too many resources are devoted to keeping individuals alive at the end of their lives. Rather, the issue is one of many people dying without palliative care – more specifically, without pain medication. Recent news reports have highlighted this horrendous problem.[58] The problem is more significant now than in earlier periods, because in many less developed countries people are no longer dying of diseases like malaria, infections, or even AIDS. Due to the wider availability of vaccines and antibiotics, they are now living long enough to develop cancer. Often the diagnosis is made very late in the spread of the disease, so that death is inevitable. Even if the cancer is diagnosed earlier, for many, treatment in the "form of surgery, chemotherapy and radiotherapy" is not available.[59] Doctors in these countries see tumors the likes of which are rarely seen by western physicians any more. The tumors are often very large and may protrude through the skin. Many of those afflicted suffer severe pain. Doctors from African countries have reported cases of "patients whose pain is so bad that they have chosen other remedies: hanging themselves or throwing themselves in front of trucks."[60]

The problem is not confined to Africa. In India, "[a]bout 1.6 million [people] endure cancer pain each year. Because of tobacco and betel nut chewing, India leads the world in mouth and head tumors, and has high rates of lung, breast and cervical cancer."[61] Less than 1 percent of these individuals receive any type of pain medication. Clinics where morphine is dispensed are extremely scarce – "some patients live 500 miles from the nearest. Calcutta, a city of 14 million, has only one."[62]

The World Health Organization (WHO) estimates that about 80 percent of all cancer patients suffer from severe pain and that "4.8 million people a year with moderate to severe cancer pain receive no appropriate treatment."[63] The lack of pain treatment, however, is not limited to cancer patients. WHO further estimates that 1.4 million people each year with late-stage AIDS do not have access to pain medication.[64] For other causes of chronic pain, such as "burns, car accidents, gunshots, diabetic nerve damage, sickle-cell disease," WHO issues no estimates but believes that "millions go untreated" for their pain.[65] This is in stark contrast to the U.S. where in 2004, "consumption of morphine per person … was about 17,000 times that in Sierra Leone."[66] Globally, the share of morphine consumed by the developing countries is approximately "6 percent, although these countries account for almost 80 percent of the world's population."[67]

Although in many of these countries poverty can affect access to pain medication, it is not always the obstacle. A recent report by Human Rights Watch concludes that "[t]he poor availability of pain treatment is both perplexing and inexcusable. Pain causes terrible suffering yet the medications to treat it are cheap, safe, effective and generally straightforward to administer. Furthermore, international law obliges countries to make adequate pain medications available."[68] The three major impediments to adequate access to palliative care in developing countries have been identified as "lack of government commitment, opioid availability and limited education."[69] While morphine can easily be made from opium, which is in significant supply in Africa and other developing nations and is inexpensive to make, drug companies often "preferentially supply more expensive opioid formulations and drug types to developing countries rather than cheap, generic morphine."[70] Moreover, morphine is not available in many poor countries because of an intense fear of diversion and use for illicit purposes. Doctors in these countries are taught that morphine inevitably leads to addiction and premature death. In virtually all countries, handling of morphine is limited to physicians and pharmacists, but many developing countries have insufficient physicians to treat the dying. In Sierra Leone, for example, "there are only about 100 doctors – one for every 54,000 people, compared with one for every 350 in the United States."[71] Laws meant to curb drug trafficking are also complex and harsh; even minor infractions can lead to lengthy prison sentences. In India, after the passage in 1985 of the Narcotic Drugs and Psychotropic Substances Act, which established penalties for narcotics distribution, legal morphine use in the country fell by 97 percent.[72]

The WHO has recognized the need for improved palliative care in the world's developing nations. The organization has recommended that every country have a "national policy for implementing palliative care services which could be integrated into the existing health system and the country's cultural and social context."[73] Initially, WHO's focus was the treatment of cancer-related pain and symptoms. Recommendations included that countries make available opioid and non-opioid analgesics to patients experiencing significant pain. Specifically, the recommendations state that:

Governments should ensure that their drug legislation makes full provision for:

- regular review, with the aim of permitting importation, manufacture, prescribing, stocking, dispensing and administration of opioids for medical reasons;
- legally empowering physicians, nurses, pharmacists and, where necessary, other categories of healthcare workers, to prescribe stock and administer opioids;
- review of the controls governing opioid use, with a view to simplification, so that drugs are available in the necessary quantities for legitimate use.[74]

Few countries have successfully implemented the recommendations.[75] Any adoption of such recommendations must take into account each country's specific socio-economic, cultural, and medical system characteristics.

In light of the suffering and pain that millions of people in developing countries are experiencing as they die and the unwillingness of their governments to produce more morphine and use it domestically for medical purposes, classifying end of life care as a public health issue in these regions would be highly appropriate. Human Rights Watch argues, in its report, *"Please Do Not Make Us Suffer Any More ..."*, that "[u]nder international human rights law, governments must address a major public health crisis that affects millions of people every year. They must take steps to ensure that people have adequate access to treatment for their pain."[76] Clinicians alone cannot achieve the necessary changes in practice without changes in laws and public policy. Classifying end of life treatment and palliative care as a public health problem in these countries would help elevate the issue, increase awareness of the problem, and might motivate the appropriate legislative body or government agency to take actions to improve the care of the dying.

Notes

1. See Shai J. Lavi, The Modern Art of Dying: A History of Euthanasia in the United States 9–13 (2005).
2. *Id.* at 29.
3. Kant Patel & Mark E. Rushefsky, Health Care Policy in an Age of New Technologies 29 (2002).
4. *Id.*
5. *In re* Quinlan, 355 A.2d 647 (N.J. 1976).
6. Carol D'Onofrio & True Ryndes, *The Relevance of Public Health in Improving Access to End of Life Care*, Hastings Center Rep., Mar.–Apr. 2003 (Supp.), at S30, S31.
7. *Id.* at S31.
8. Ceci Connolly, *Talk Radio Campaign Frightening Seniors*, Wash. Post, Aug. 1, 2009, at A1.
9. Last Acts, Means to a Better End: A Report on Dying in America Today 16–17 (2002), online at http://www.rwjf.org/files/publications/other/meansbetterend.pdf
10. Mark A. Hall, *The Scope and Limits of Public Health Law*, 46 Persp. in Biology & Med. (Supplement) S199 (2003).
11. SUPPORT Principal Investigators, *A Controlled Trial to Improve Care for Seriously Ill Hospitalized Patients*, 274 JAMA 1591 (1995).
12. *Id.* at 1593–94.
13. Neil S. Wenger et al., *Epidemiology of Do-Not-Resuscitate Orders*, 155 Archives Internal Med. 2056 (1995).
14. Carmen R. Green et al., *The Unequal Burden of Pain: Confronting Racial and Ethnic Disparities in Pain*, 4 Pain Med. 277 (2003).
15. Hall, *supra* note 10 at S205.
16. *See id.* at S202–04.
17. Lawrence O. Gostin, *Public Health, Ethics, and Human Rights: A Tribute to the Late Jonathan Mann*, 29 J. Law, Med. & Ethics 121, 121 (2001).
18. *Id.* at 122.
19. Office of Disability, Aging & Long-Term Care Policy, U.S. Dep't of Health & Human Servs., Advance Directives and Advance Care Planning: Report to Congress (2008), online at http://aspe.hhs.gov/daltcp/reports/2008/ADCongRpt.pdf
20. However, executing an advance directive is not a guarantee that one's wishes will be followed. See, for example, Angela Fagerlin & Carl E. Schneider,

Enough: The Failure of the Living Will, HASTINGS CENTER REP., Mar.–Apr. 2004, at 30.

21. National Hospice & Palliative Care Organization, NHPCO's Facts and Figures – 2005 Findings (Nov. 2006), online at http://www.allhealth.org/BriefingMaterials/NHPCO-NHPCOsFactsandFigures-2005Findings-760.pdf
22. See Kim Neuman, "Assessing Payment Policy: Hospice," online at www.medpac.gov/transcripts/hospice_December2009_for%20public.pdf
23. See Gail Gazelle, Perspective, *Understanding Hospice – An Underutilized Option for Life's Final Chapter*, 357 NEW ENG. J. MED. 321 (2007).
24. National Hospice & Palliative Care Organization, NHPCO FACTS AND FIGURES: HOSPICE CARE IN AMERICA 5 (2008), online at http://www.nhpco.org/files/public/Statistics_Research/NHPCO_facts-and-figures_2008.pdf
25. LAST ACTS, *supra* note 9, at 17.
26. *Id.* at 34 & 93 n.52 (citing Russell K. Portenoy, *Opioid Therapy for Chronic Nonmalignant Pain: A Review of the Critical Issues*, 11 J. PAIN & SYMPTOM MGMT. 203 (1996)).
27. *Id.* at 27, 29.
28. See Richard A. Epstein, *Let the Shoemaker Stick to His Last: A Defense of the "Old" Public Health*, 46 PERSP. IN BIOLOGY & MED. (SUPPLEMENT) S138 (2003) (maintaining that the modern public health establishment wrongly views certain noncommunicable conditions, such as obesity and diabetes, as "epidemic" because more people than ever are overweight).
29. INST. OF MED., THE FUTURE OF PUBLIC HEALTH 19 (1988), online at http://books.nap.edu/catalog.php?record_id=1091
30. Mark A. Rothstein, *Rethinking the Meaning of Public Health*, 30 J. LAW, MED. & ETHICS 144, 144 (2002).
31. *Id.* at 145 & 149 n.5 (quoting Ilan H. Meyer & Sharon Schwartz, *Social Issues as Public Health*, 90 AM. J. PUB. HEALTH 1189, 1189 [2000]).
32. See Allan Kellehear, COMPASSIONATE CITIES: PUBLIC HEALTH AND END-OF-LIFE CARE 12 (2005).
33. See Gostin, *supra* note 17.
34. Lawrence O. Gostin, PUBLIC HEALTH LAW: POWER, DUTY, RESTRAINT 12 (2000).
35. *Id.*
36. *Id.* at 17.
37. See Rothstein, *supra* note 30, at 146 ("[I]t is unclear at what point cumulative individual health measures become population health [or public health].").
38. See, for example, Lawrence O. Gostin, Jo Ivey Boufford & Rose Marie Martinez, *The Future of the Public's Health: Vision, Values, and Strategies*, HEALTH AFFAIRS, Jul.–Aug. 2004, at 96.

39. Hall, *supra* note 10, at S204.
40. See Diane E. Hoffmann & Anita J. Tarzian, *Dying in America – An Examination of Policies that Deter Adequate End-of-Life Care in Nursing Homes*, 33 J. LAW, MED. & ETHICS 294 (2005).
41. Hoffmann & Tarzian, *supra* note 40, at 298.
42. See Kathryn L. Tucker, American Constitution Society for Law & Policy, Choice at the End of Life: Lessons from Oregon 9–10 (June 2008), online at http://www.acslaw.org/files/Kathryn%20L.%20Tucker%20Issue%20Brief.pdf
43. Texas Advance Directives Act, TEX. HEALTH & SAFETY CODE ANN. §§ 166.001-.009, .031-.051, .081-.101, .151-.166 (Vernon 2001 & Supp. 2008).
44. See, for example, Peter Singer, RETHINKING LIFE AND DEATH: THE COLLAPSE OF OUR TRADITIONAL ETHICS 47 (1994).
45. Epstein, *supra* note 28, at S154.
46. Rothstein, *supra* note 30, at 146.
47. Hall, *supra* note10, at S203.
48. *Id.*
49. Epstein, *supra* note 28, at S139.
50. Wendy E. Parmet & Jason A. Smith, *Free Speech and Public Health: A Population-Based Approach to the First Amendment*, 39 LOY. L.A. L. REV. 363, 372 (2006).
51. *Id.*
52. America's Affordable Health Choices Act, H.R. 3200, 111th Cong. § 1233(a)(1) (2009).
53. Connolly, *supra* note 8.
54. Webster v. Reprod. Health Servs., 492 U.S. 490, 507 (1989) (quoting DeShaney v. Winnebago Co. Dep't of Social Servs., 489 U.S. 189, 196 (1989)).
55. Epstein, *supra* note 28, at S155.
56. LAST ACTS, *supra* note 9, at 34 & 94 n.56 (citing Memorandum from F. Wm. McCalpin, Chair, ABA Comm'n on Legal Problems of the Elderly to the ABA House of Delegates: Proposed ABA Policy on Legal Obstacles to Effective Pain Management [Apr. 2000]).
57. Robert Wood Johnson Foundation, Assessment of Last Acts(R) Program Provides Recommendations for Future Direction (Oct. 2002), online at http://www.rwjf.org/reports/grr/038049.htm
58. See, for example, Donald G. McNeil, Jr., *In India, a Quest to Ease the Pain of the Dying*, N.Y. TIMES, Sept. 11, 2007, at F1 [hereinafter McNeil, *In India*]; Donald G. McNeil, Jr., *Drugs Banned, Many of World's Poor Suffer in Pain*, N.Y. TIMES, Sept. 10, 2007, at A1 [hereinafter McNeil, *Drugs Banned*]; Donald G. McNeil, Jr., *Japanese Slowly Shedding Their Misgivings About the Use of Painkilling Drugs*, N.Y. TIMES, Sept. 10, 2007, at A15.

59. Ruth Webster, Judith Lacey & Susan Quine, *Palliative Care: A Public Health Priority in Developing Countries*, 28 J. PUB. HEALTH POL'Y 28, 29 (2007).
60. McNeil, *Drugs Banned*, *supra* note 58.
61. McNeil, *In India*, *supra* note 58.
62. *Id.*
63. McNeil, *Drugs Banned*, *supra* note 58.
64. *Id.*
65. *Id.*
66. *Id.*
67. Webster, Lacey & Quine, *supra* note 59, at 31.
68. HUMAN RIGHTS WATCH, "PLEASE, DO NOT MAKE US SUFFER ANY MORE ...": ACCESS TO PAIN TREATMENT AS A HUMAN RIGHT 2 (2009), online at http://www.hrw.org/sites/default/files/reports/health0309web_1.pdf
69. Webster, Lacey & Quine, *supra* note 59, at 34.
70. *Id.* at 32 & 38 n.52 (citing L. De Lima, C. Sweeney, J. L. Palmer & E. Bruera, *Potent Analgesics Are More Expensive for Patients in Developing Countries: A Comparative Study*, 18 J. PAIN & PALLIATIVE CARE PHARMACOTHERAPY 59 [2003]).
71. McNeil, *Drugs Banned*, *supra* note 58.
72. McNeil, *In India*, *supra* note 58.
73. Webster, Lacey & Quine, *supra* note 59, at 31; see also Jan Stjernswärd, Viewpoint, *Palliative Care: The Public Health Strategy*, 28 J. PUB. HEALTH POL'Y 42 (2007).
74. Stjernswärd, *supra* note 73, at 45.
75. *Id.* at 44–46; see also Webster, Lacey & Quine, *supra* note 59.
76. HUMAN RIGHTS WATCH, *supra* note 68, at 2.

PART II THE LIMITS OF CIVIL RIGHTS

3 DYING WHILE BLACK IN AMERICA:

Maslow's Hierarchy of Need and Racial Policy Making

Vernellia R. Randall

Inequality is killing Black Americans!

Higher morbidity and mortality in the African-American population is not caused by income, education, or lifestyle. Rather, these health deficits are the continuing legacy of slavery and segregation, and sustained even today by the impact of living in a racialized society and the chronic stress of racism. The situation is complicated by ineffective efforts to reduce racial health disparities. The ineffectiveness of policy making is related to the unmet needs of the White majority and the inability of Congress, the White House, and the Supreme Court to pass and enforce strong anti-discrimination laws. However, without such laws, people will continue dying while Black.

DYING WHILE BLACK IN AMERICA

Blacks are sicker than Whites and are dying at a disproportionately higher rate. Each year, 87,000 Black Americans die who would not die if they had the same death rates as White Americans.[1] The death rate for Black Americans is 1,039 per 100,000 population.[2] This is the equivalent of one jumbo jet filled with Black Americans crashing every day of every year. The death rate for White Americans is 797 per 100,000.[3] Another way to think about the problem is not just the excess deaths of Black Americans, but the prevented deaths of White Americans. That is, White Americans avoid 500,000 deaths per year by having a lower death rate than Black Americans.[4] The fragile condition of Black Americans is borne out by international health indicators such as life expectancy, maternal mortality, infant mortality, and low birth weight.

Life Expectancy

Life expectancy is the predicted number of years of life remaining from birth. The World Health Organization (WHO) uses life expectancy at birth because "[it] reflects the overall mortality level of a population. It summarizes the mortality pattern that prevails across all age groups – children and adolescents, adults and the elderly."[5] Black men's life expectancy at birth is six years less than that of White men.[6] The life expectancy of White American males is 76 years; that of Black American males is 69 years.[7] Black American males' life expectancy is the same as Jamaica's and behind Chile, Barbados, the Bahamas, and Antigua and Barbuda. The life expectancy of Black American women at birth, 77 years, is an average of four years shorter than that of White American women, 81 years.[8] Internationally, that places Black American females' life expectancy on a par with that of Maternal the Bahamas and behind Cuba, Barbados, and Bosnia and Herzegovina.[9]

Table 3.1. *Life expectancy, in years*

Males			Females		
Rank	State	Years	Rank	State	Years
1	San Marino	80	1	Japan	86
2	Japan	79	4	Switzerland	84
9	Canada	78	9	Canada	83
18	United Kingdom	77	18	Netherlands	82
30	Cuba	76	29	United Kingdom	81
	White American Male	**76**		**White American Female**	**81**
35	Chile	75	33	Cuba	80
44	Barbados	72	39	Barbados	79
57	Bahamas	71	46	Bosnia and Herzegovina	78
66	Antigua and Barbuda	70	55	Bahamas	77
	Black American Male	**69**		**Black American Female**	**77**

Maternal Mortality

Maternal deaths are deaths that occur during pregnancy, childbirth, and the postpartum period. Th. major direct causes of maternal mortality are hemorrhage, infection, high blood pressure, unsafe abortion, and obstructed labor. The WHO uses maternal mortality as a measure of health of a population because "complications during pregnancy and childbirth are a leading cause of death and disability among women of reproductive age in developing countries."[10] The number of maternal deaths among Black American women (31.7) is almost four times as high as it is among White American women (9.1).[11] Internationally, the rate of maternal deaths of Black American women is fifty-seventh, behind Bulgaria, the Bahamas, Barbados, and Costa Rica. Maternal mortality among Black American women is closer to that of developing countries like Costa Rica (30 per 100,000) than to developed countries like Sweden (3 per 100,000).[12]

Table 3.2.[13] *Maternal deaths per 100,000 live births*

Rank	State	Deaths
1	Ireland	1
2	Sweden	3
15	Switzerland	5
21	Canada	7
25	United Kingdom	8
30	New Zealand	9
	White American	9.1
34	Bulgaria	11
45	Bahamas	16
45	Barbados	16
56	Costa Rica	30
	Black American	31.7

Infant Mortality

Infant mortality rate, measured by deaths per 1,000 live births, is the probability of a child dying before its first birthday. The WHO uses infant mortality as a measure of health of a population because "... infant mortality rate[s] are leading indicators of the level of child health and overall development in countries."[14] The number of infant deaths among Black Americans (13.6) is more than twice as high as it is among white Americans (5.7).[15] Internationally, infant mortality rate among Black Americans is sixty-sixth, behind the Bahamas, Barbados, and Antigua and Barbuda.[16]

Low Birthweight in Newborns

A low-birthweight infant weighs less than 2,500 g. The WHO uses low birthweight as a measure of health of a population because "At the population level, the proportion of babies with a low birth weight is an indicator of a multifaceted public-health problem that includes long-term maternal malnutrition, ill health, hard work and poor health care in pregnancy. On an individual basis, low birth weight is an important predictor of newborn health and survival."[17] The percentage of low birthweight Black American babies (13.6 percent) is almost twice the percentage of White American babies with low birthweight (7.2 percent).[19] Black Americans have a higher percentage of low birth weight infants than women in Rwanda, Ghana, and Tanzania.[20]

Table 3.3.[18] *Infant Health: Mortality and Birthweight*

Infant Mortality Rate (per 1000 live births)			Low Birthweight Newborn (percentage) per 1000 Live Births		
Rank	State	Rate	Rank	State	percentage
1	Iceland	2	1	Albania	3
2	Japan	3	3	Sweden	4
17	Switzerland	4	21	Cuba	6
27	Cuba	5	40	Bahamas	7
	White American	**5.7**		**White American**	**7.2**
36	Belarus	6	75	Rwanda	9
44	Chile	8	90	Barbados	10
52	Antigua and Barbuda	10	103	Ghana	11
58	Barbados	11	114	Uganda	12
65	Bahamas	13	123	Tanzania	13
	Black American	**13.6**		**Black American**	**13.6**

Summary

On March 21, 2008, conservative commentator Pat Buchanan commented that Black Americans should be grateful for being in the United States.

> . . . America has been the best country on earth for black folks. It was here that 600,000 black people, brought from Africa in slave ships, grew into a community of 40 million, were introduced to Christian salvation, and reached the greatest levels of freedom and prosperity blacks have ever known ... no people anywhere has done more to lift up blacks than white Americans.[21]

He fails to appreciate that when it comes to health, Black Americans are more like the inhabitants of a developing country than like their white fellow Americans. This health disparity is not the result of genetic differences between the races, but of simply being black in America.

RACISM AND SOCIAL DETERMINANTS OF HEALTH

Being Black in America means a life time subject to racism in all areas considered social determinants of health. The social determinants of health are the conditions under which people live: wealth/income, education, physical environment, health care, housing, employment, chronic stress, and racism/discrimination. Social determinants of health are the primary factors in the inequality in health status between Blacks and Whites. In fact, for blacks racism is a primary chronic stress factor and thus a health disparities factor. Middle-class Blacks have poorer health than middle-class Whites. The stress of living in a racist society accounts for racial health inequalities.

In health and in health care, race matters. As Professor Ian F. Haney Lopez explains, race is a "vast group of people loosely bound together by historically contingent, socially significant elements of their morphology and/or ancestry."[22] Race is not a genetic concept. The notion of genetic differences based on race has never rested on a firm scientific foundation and has, in fact, been thoroughly refuted.[23] Still, race matters because social privileges and advantages are distributed on the basis of race. In addition, race matters because it is a proxy for racism and racial discrimination.

For black Americans, slavery, segregation, and racism have resulted in health disparities. Between 50 to 100 million Africans were captured, enslaved, and transported in the transatlantic slave trade.[24] Africans who were captured and brought first to the Caribbean islands did not get off the slave ships in a healthy condition. Half of them died before reaching their destination.[25] The survivors were sick. Thus, today's health disparities began with the transatlantic slave trade. During slavery, blacks suffered physical and mental abuse, emotional and physical violence, and medical neglect. It should be no surprise that by 1865, there were significant differences in health between White and Black Americans.

Professor Joe Feagin argues that based on the theory of internal colonialization, many people continue to view blacks as slaves.[26] As a colonized population in the United States, Blacks suffered the effects of racism, were dominated by outsiders, much as colonial subjects in the Third World, and had their values and ways of life destroyed. The history of blacks in North America shows that his theory has merit. Slavery was translated into institutionalized racism and discrimination. Institutional racism and discrimination affect health through racial inequality and discrimination.

Racial health inequality persists largely because racial discrimination persists in the United States. Institutional and structural discrimination persist because our civil rights law does not adequately address twenty-first-century discrimination. Most twenty-first-century discrimination is based on unconscious stereotypes and biases – unintentional discrimination. Unfortunately, Title VI of the Civil Rights Act of 1964 only prohibits intentional discrimination. Unfortunately, no law addresses reckless or negligent discrimination. Reckless discrimination occurs when someone knows that there is a high risk of discrimination and proceeds with the behavior that results in discrimination. Negligent discrimination occurs when someone should have known that his or her behavior would result in discrimination and failed to prevent or minimize that discrimination. Most discrimination today takes the form of reckless or negligent discrimination. Eliminating racial discrimination is essential to closing the health gap in America. Congress, however, has failed to pass strict antidiscrimination laws. The Supreme Court has narrowly defined discrimination, and enforcement of discrimination law is lax.

MASLOW'S HIERARCHY OF NEED AND RACIAL POLICY MAKING

The question is why discrimination in American law is so narrowly defined when other areas of the law, like torts and criminal law, are not. The answer may come from psychology and need-based decision making. It also requires an understanding of racial policy making. In particular, Maslow's hierarchy of need may provide insight.[27] Abraham Maslow's research was related to human motivation. Prior researchers had focused on biology, achievement, or power in explaining what motivates human behavior. Maslow created a hierarchy of human needs based on two groupings: deficiency and growth. Maslow's argument was that lower needs must be satisfied before higher needs can be. Once each of these needs has been satisfied, if a deficiency is later detected, the individual will act to compensate for that deficiency. In this sense, humans are motivated by their unmet needs. Just as Maslow defined the needs for individuals, every community has a sociological explanation of its needs and consequently of its behavior.

Every community has several levels of needs. The first needs in Maslow's Hierarchy are physiological: food, clothing, housing, and the like. The second needs are for safety: security, protection, stability, structure, law and order, and freedom from fear and chaos. The third community need is the need to belong. "Belongingness" orients the person toward affectionate relations with others and a sense of place in family and groups. According to one contemporary viewpoint, all people need regular and satisfying social interactions.

The fourth community need is the need for esteem. There are two kinds of esteem needs. The first is a desire for adequacy, mastery, competency, achievement, confidence, independence, and freedom. The second type of esteem needs is the desire for respect, attention, recognition, appreciation, status, prestige, fame, dominance, importance, and dignity.

The fifth need is the need for actualization – the desire for fulfillment. In other words, actualization is the need for people to reach their potential. This need is met as a person becomes the person that he or she is capable of becoming. In order for a community to actualize itself, the majority must have its deficiency needs gratified. The majority of the members show positive use of their capacities and have motivations linked with that of betterment of society. The fulfillment of the lower basic needs is necessary for actualization of the person or the community. However, for a community striving for actualization, its direction is one of growth and the motivation is positive. As one becomes more actualized and transcendent, one becomes wiser and knows what to do in a wide variety of situations. Thus, the motivation for actualization, unlike most of the other basic needs, is not based on deficiency but on the need to grow and improve.

A significant minority of people in a community can determine the functional level of that community. The functional level of a community is based on the lowest level of need that a significant portion of the community is still struggling to meet. Thus, where a significant portion of a community is still struggling to meet its need for food, shelter, and clothing (i.e., the homeless community), the functional level of the community is at the physiological level. When a significant portion of the community is struggling with violence, drugs, illness, and death (i.e., inner city communities), the functional level of the community is at the safety and health level.

Community needs are hierarchical, and the community's pursuit of a higher need is impaired until a lower need has substantially been met. However, once lower needs are met, the higher unmet needs become the basis for motivation.

The ultimate need that every individual and every community has is "actualization." Community actualization is the community's efforts to maximize its talents and resources – its striving to become all that it can. However, a community cannot focus on actualization if its needs for food, clothing, shelter, safety, or health have not been met. Rather, communities, like individuals, will focus on their "lesser" unmet needs.

In a class-based society, communities function and compete on different need attainment levels. Many middle-class and upper-class communities' unmet needs are esteem and actualization. Individual rights and interests are necessary for a people and community to become self-actualized and to develop strong esteem. Thus, for many middle- and upper-class communities, protecting individual rights and interests is a prerequisite for their community's needs fulfillment.

Underclass communities that are struggling for food, clothing, housing, safety, and health, and middle-class communities that are struggling for acceptance may have little interest in the rights and interests arguments advanced by those seeking esteem and actualization. This is a very significant fact when considering the impact of needs fulfillment on policy making in medicine, law, and community health. Since most of the policy makers and providers are middle-class, and many of their communities are striving toward self-esteem, much of the discussion of problem-solving is centered on the protection of rights or interests. The result is that the policy makers and providers filter the potential policy, law, or intervention through their own community need for esteem and actualization.

The word *motivation* has the same root as the word *motion*. It is the process by which organisms advance toward their goals. A behavior, thought, or feeling may result from multiple motivations. Maslow's hierarchy provides only one way of understanding legislative policy making. Needs are universal, but the methods used to satisfy them may be specific to the person's culture. Everyone has a need for esteem. However, Maslow's hierarchy fails to recognize the complicating factor of the need for the maintenance of superior white societal advantage and how that need alters the hierarchy and policy making. A look at American racial lawmaking, from the failure to outlaw slavery in the Constitution, to the immigration laws that required a determination of whiteness in order to immigrate to the United States, to the internment of Japanese Americans in concentration camps, to the limitation of discrimination to intentional conduct – reveals a consistent pattern of racial subjugation of minority interests.

Congress, the Supreme Court, and the Justice Department make or enforces laws to protect the interest of their community of identification. A community of identification is the community to which an individual feels personally connected to or responsible for. In the United States, the primary community of identification for most lawmakers is the White middle class. This includes lawmakers of color who are elected and live in White communities. As a result, lawmaking and policy making is designed to protect the interest of those communities. For example, even as the Congressional Black Caucus has used its status as a civil rights organization to become a fundraising power in Washington, the caucus has ties to companies whose business is seen by some as detrimental to its black constituents. These include cigarette companies, Internet poker operators, beer brewers, and the rent-to-own industry, which has become a particular focus of consumer advocates for its practice of charging high monthly fees for appliances, televisions, and computers.[28]

The history of racial policy making is one in which the needs of the Black community are only met when doing so serves the White majority; even then, the meeting of the need will be compromised. This problem can be traced all the way back to the formation of the Constitution where the framers, even as they declared liberty and freedom for all men, included protection of slave owners' property interest in slaves. A century later, the same impulse surfaced in the repeal of the Freeman's Bureau Act.[29] Passed in 1866 to build schools and hospitals for recently emancipated free people of African descent, the Freeman's Bureau Act was repealed the following year to appease the South. The subjugation of black need in racial policy making even occurred after the landmark Supreme Court decision in *Brown v Board of Education*, where the Court held that separate schools were unequal.[30] Because the Court held that schools only need to integrate with "all deliberate speed," and thirteen years after *Brown* many schools were still not integrated, I graduated from a segregated high school. In fact, communities and schools in the United States continue to be separate and unequal in 2010. The fact is, "contemporary sacrifices of black rights and interests underlie policies on death penalty, drugs, penalty sentencing rules, and reliance on standardized test scores and college and graduate school admissions procedures."[31] There is a "pattern of pandering for white votes by asserting the dangers to whites' well-being."[32]

Many Whites see any gains made by Blacks as a threat. As a consequence, there is a backlash to any advances. This opposition makes racial policy making based on the needs of the Black community extremely difficult. As Professor Bell has pointed out, there are two rules of racial policy making:

> Rule one. The interest of blacks in achieving racial equality will be accommodated only when that interest converges with the interests of whites in policymaking positions. This convergence is far more important for gaining relief then the degree of harm suffered by blacks or the character of proof offered to prove that harm.

> Rule two. Even when interests convergence results in an effective racial remedy, that remedy will be abrogated at the point that policymakers fear the remedial policy is threatening the superior societal status of whites, particularly those in middle and upper middle class.[33]

Translated into the hierarchy of community needs language, policy makers will only make laws and policies to eliminate racial inequality when White communities have an unmet need. Furthermore, the usefulness of remedies will be small because any remedy must not threaten the need for "superior societal status of whites."[34] Higher social status helps meet Whites' need for self-esteem and belonging by providing them "with a sense of belonging based on neither economic nor political well-being, but simply on an identification with the ruling class determined by race and a state – supported and subsidized belief that as whites they were superior to blacks."[35] This seems to be true; even though many Whites oppose welfare programs that they think primarily benefit Blacks, they miss the fact that many low-income Whites have similar employment, education, health care, economic, and social service needs and that most people accessing welfare programs are White. The need to maintain white superior societal status is so great that it causes many Whites to ignore their most basic needs based on Maslow's hierarchy (safety, food, shelter, health) in order to maintain that illusion. For example:

> When I lived in Alaska, one day I was driving from downtown Juneau to the Mendenhall Valley – about 13 miles. It was the middle of winter; dark, cold and raining ice and sleet. It was weather that no person should be walking in. I saw a woman standing on the side of the road with two small children. With my own two small children in the car, I had immediate empathy and pulled over to give her and her children a ride. She ran to the car, opened the door, and as she leaned into the back seat to put her children in she got a good glimpse of me and my family. She saw that we were Black and I saw she was White ... She hesitated for a second, backed up and said – with great disdain as she slammed the door shut – "I'd rather walk." I've never forgotten that. Her racial superiority need was more powerful than her need for safety for herself and her children.

That same attitude plays out on a larger level in health care policy making, where weak antidiscrimination laws are passed in lieu of stronger ones, which would ultimately benefit both people of color and Whites.

HEALTH CARE DISCRIMINATION AND RACIAL POLICY MAKING

Compounding societal racial discrimination is the institutional racism in health care. Despite efforts to eliminate discrimination and reduce racial segregation over the past thirty years, little improvement in the quality of or access to health care for many minorities has occurred. According to the U.S. Commission on Civil Rights:

> Despite the existence of civil rights legislation equal treatment and equal access are not a reality for racial/ethnic minorities and women in the current climate of the health care industry. Many barriers limit both the quality of health care and utilization for these groups, including ... discrimination.[36]

Racial discrimination in health care delivery, financing, and research continues, and racial barriers to quality health care manifest themselves in lack of economic access to health care, barriers to hospitals and health care institutions, barriers to physicians and other health care providers, racial discrimination in medical treatment, discriminatory policies and practices, lack of culturally competent care, disparate impact of the intersection of race and gender, inadequate inclusion in health care research, and rationing through managed care.

Lack of Economic Access to Health Care

More than 43 million Americans are uninsured. As access to health insurance in the United States is most often tied to employment, racial stratification of the economy stemming from other forms of discrimination has resulted in a concentration of racial minorities in low-wage jobs. These jobs are almost always without insurance benefits. As a result, disproportionate numbers of the uninsured are racial minorities. In fact, a disproportionate number of racial minorities have no insurance, are unemployed, or are employed in jobs that do not provide health care insurance, are ineligible for government assistance programs, or fail to participate because of administrative barriers. Disparities in health status and the absence of health information are directly related to access to health care.[37]

Barriers to Hospitals and Health Care Institutions

The institutional/structural racism in hospitals and health care institutions manifests itself in (1) the adoption, administration, and implementation of policies that restrict admission; (2) the closure, relocation, or privatization of hospitals that primarily serve the minority community; and (3) the continued transfer of unwanted patients (patient dumping) by hospitals and institutions. Such practices have a disproportionate effect on racial minorities, banishing them to distinctly substandard institutions or to no care at all.[38]

Barriers to Physicians and Other Providers

Areas that are heavily populated by minorities tend to be medically underserved. Few White physicians practice in minority communities. Minority physicians are significantly more likely to practice in minority communities, making the medical education and training of minorities extremely important. Yet, due to discrimination in post-secondary education, racial biases in testing, and quality of life issues affecting school performance, minorities are seriously underrepresented in health care professions. The shortage of minority professionals affects not only access to health care but also access to the power and resources to structure the health care system, leaving its control almost exclusively in the hands of White Americans. The result of this situation is an inadequate, ineffective and marginalized voice on minority health care issues.

Racial Discrimination in Medical Treatment

Differences in health status reflect inequities in preventive care and treatment. Black Americans are more likely to require health care services but are less likely to receive them. Disparity in treatment has been well documented in studies done on AIDS, cardiology, cardiac surgery, kidney disease, organ transplantation, internal medicine, obstetrics, prescription drugs, treatment for mental illness, pain treatment, and hospital care.

Discriminatory Policies and Practices

Discriminatory policies and practices can take the form of medical redlining, excessive wait times, unequal access to emergency care, deposit requirements as a prerequisite to care, and lack of continuity of care, all of which have a negative effect on the care received.

Lack of Language and Culturally Competent Care

A key challenge has been to get the government to establish clear standards for culturally competent health care. Culturally competent care is "sensitive to issues related to culture, race, gender, and sexual orientation."[39] Cultural competency would ensure that all health care providers can function in a culturally diverse setting; it involves understanding and respect for cultural differences. In addition to recognizing the disparities in health status between White Americans and minority groups, we must recognize differences within groups as well. Ethnic and racial minority communities include diverse groups with diverse histories, languages, cultures, religions, beliefs, and traditions. This diversity is reflected – often negatively, unfortunately – in the health care they receive and the experiences they have with the health care industry. Without understanding and incorporating these differences, health care cannot be provided in a culturally competent manner.

Disparate Impact of the Intersection of Race and Gender

The health care system has largely ignored the unique experiences of women of color. Racial discrimination and sex discrimination often intersect to magnify the difficulties minority women face in gaining equal access to quality health care. In addition, restrictions on access to health care for racial/ethnic minorities and other barriers to care predominantly affect minority women. There are also gender differences in medical use, provision of treatments, and inclusion in research. This is partly the result of men's and women's different expectations of medical care and the gender bias of health care providers.

Inadequate Inclusion in Health Care Research

Despite volumes of literature suggesting the importance of race, ethnicity, and culture in health, health care, and treatment, there is little information on the racial, ethnic, and biological differences that affect the manifestations and treatments of certain illnesses. These biological differences are not based on meaningful genetic differences, but rather represent the impact of chronic stress from racism and racial inequality on health. In response to years of exclusion of minorities and women, several statutory requirements have been enacted to ensure that research protocols include a diverse population. The health of women and minorities will continue to suffer until they are included in all types of health research.

Rationing through Managed Care

The health care financing system has been steadily moving to managed care as a means of rationing health care. Without oversight – oversight that does not currently exist – managed care will place increasingly stringent requirements on providers. They may fail to develop more expensive but culturally appropriate treatment modalities, and they may refuse or minimize the expenditures to develop an infrastructure for minority communities. The potential for discrimination, particularly racial/ethnic discrimination, to occur in the context of managed care is significant and is recognized as such by the United States Commission on Civil Rights and leading commentators and advocates for civil rights in health care services, financing, and treatment. However, little has been done to protect minorities from this risk of discrimination.

ELIMINATING RACIAL DISCRIMINATION IN HEALTH CARE

While the factors just discussed contribute to disparities in health care, one that should be relatively easy to address is discrimination in medical treatment, but it has proven one of the most difficult. Racial inequality in health care persists in the United States despite laws against racial discrimination, in significant part because of the limited view of *mens rea*, or state of mind, in discrimination law. The law recognizes several states of minds:

> Intentional: Intentional harm occurs when the actor actually desires for the harm to occur or is substantially certain that the harm will occur.
>
> Reckless: Reckless harm occurs when the actor desires a harmful consequence, foresees the possibility, and consciously takes the risk; alternatively, it is a state of mind in which a person does not care about the consequences of his or her actions.
>
> Negligent: Negligent harm occurs when the actor knew or should have known that there was a risk of harm from the conduct.
>
> Strict Liability: Strict liability occurs when regardless of the actor's state of mind, the actor is held responsible based on conduct alone.

Thus, in criminal law, there is Murder (Intentional), Negligent Homicide (Negligence) and Felony Murder (Strict liability). A similar array of states of mind exists in tort law, but not in discrimination law.

The courts have gone to great lengths to limit Title VI,[40] the primary federal antidiscrimination law, to intentional conduct. According to Section 601 of Title VI:

> No Person in the United States, shall, on the grounds of race, color, or national origin, be excluded from participation in, be denied the benefits of, or be subject to discrimination under any program or activity receiving federal financial assistance.

The Supreme Court reaffirmed in *Alexander v. Choate* that Title VI applies only to intentional discrimination.[41] However, the reliance on intent is problematic for health care, where most discrimination is "unthinking or unconscious."[41]

Thus, limiting liability to acts that meet the requirement of intent does not reflect the fact that decisions about racial matters are largely influenced by factors that can be characterized as neither intentional – in the sense that certain outcomes are self-consciously sought – nor unintentional – in the sense that the outcomes are random, fortuitous, and uninfluenced by the decision maker's beliefs, desires, and wishes. The problem confronting the legal system is that someone who holds a negative stereotype about a group is more likely to discriminate and that such discrimination, which is a form of stereotype-linked bias, is both automatic and unconscious. Furthermore, it occurs even among people who are not consciously prejudiced against the group in question. According to Professor David Williams, several factors contribute to discrimination in health care:

> Healthcare providers and institutions are a part of the larger society that views racial and ethnic minorities negatively on multiple social dimensions ... Second, research on stereotypes indicates that encounters in the healthcare setting contain ingredients that enhance the likelihood of the use of stereotypes .... Stereotypes are more likely to be activated under time pressure, the need to make quick judgments, cognitive overload, task complexity and when anger or anxiety are present ... Third, ... [physicians view their Black patients] ... more negatively than their white counterparts .... Physicians viewed Black patients (compared to their white counterparts) as less likely to adhere to medical advice, less likely to be kind, intelligent and educated, more likely to lack social support, and more likely to abuse alcohol and drug.[42]

In an effective health policy, state and federal laws must prohibit discriminatory practices in health care. Thus, the crux of the problem, given managed care, the historical inequity in health care, and "unthinking discrimination," is that the laws do not address the barriers faced by minorities. Because of the needs of their community of identification and the limitation of racial policy making, the executive branch, Congress, and the courts are reluctant to hold health care institutions and providers responsible for unconscious or unthinking discrimination. This is evidenced by the failure to correct the Supreme

Court's decision in *Sandoval*, which limited the enforcement of agency regulations that outlaw disparate impact discrimination. As the U.S. Commission on Civil Rights found: "There is substantial evidence that discrimination in health care delivery, financing and research continues to exist. Such evidence suggests that Federal laws designed to address inequality in health care have not been adequately enforced by federal agencies ... [Such failure has] ... resulted in a failure to remove the historical barriers to access to quality health care for women and minorities, which, in turn has perpetuated these barriers."[43]

Racial inequity in medical treatment rarely occurs because of overt, intentional discriminatory behavior. Most race discrimination that occurs in health care is probably the result of subconscious bias, disproportionate impact of policies and practices, and disparate impact. Effective policy making on health care discrimination would at a minimum define discrimination in a way that included not only intentional discrimination but also reckless discrimination and negligent discrimination. Thus, negligent discrimination in health care would occur when health care providers fail to take reasonable steps to avoid discrimination based on race when they knew or should have known that their actions would result in discrimination. An example of this would be decisions to close inner city hospitals and to move them to the suburbs.

Many factors can be attributed to the 87,000 unnecessary deaths that occur among Black Americans each year. Ineffective antidiscrimination policies are among the most significant. If people were held more responsible for nonintentional discrimination, they would take immediate action to eliminate the disparities that are evidence of that discrimination. However, the racial need to maintain the superior social status and self-esteem of Whites has resulted in ineffective racial policy making. Thus, African Americans will continue to experience Dying while Black.

Notes

1. Vernellia R. Randall, DYING WHILE BLACK 43–45 (2009).
2. U.S.DEPT. OF HEALTH AND HUMAN SERVICES, HEALTH, UNITED STATES, 2008, US NATIONAL CENTER FOR HEALTH STATISTICS, Table 27 and Table 28 219–24, online at http://www.cdc.gov/nchs/data/hus/hus08.pdf (hereinafter Health, United States, 2008).

3. *Id.*
4. *Id.*
5. World Health Organization [WHO], *Life expectancy at birth (years)*, WHO Statistical Information System [WHOSIS], online at http://www.who.int/whosis/indicators/compendium/2008/2let/en/index.html
6. Health, United States, 2008, *supra* note 2, at 203 (Table 26).
7. *Id.*
8. *Id.*
9. *Id.*; 2008 World Health Statistics, *supra* note 5.
10. World Health Organization, Maternal Mortality, WHO Statistical Information System [WHOSIS], Oct. 19, 2009, online at http://www.who.int/whosis/indicators/compendium/2008/3mrf/en/index.html
11. Health, United States, 2008, *supra* note 2, at 249 (Table 42).
12. *Id.*; 2008 World Health Statistics, *supra* note 10.
13. Health, United States, 2008, *supra* note 2 at 249 (Table 42, 00); 2008 World Health Statistics, *supra* note 10.
14. World Health Organization, *Infant Mortality Rate*, WHO Statistical Information System [WHOSIS], Oct. 19, 2009, online at http://www.who.int/whosis/indicators/compendium/2008/3mr5/en/index.html
15. Health, United States, 2008, *supra* note 2, at 188–89 (Table 18).
16. Health, United States, 2008, *supra* note 2.
17. World Health Organization, *Low Birthweight Newborns (percentage)*, WHO Statistical Information System (WHOSIS), Oct. 19, 2009, online at http://www.who.int/whosis/indicators/compendium/2008/2bwn/en/index.html
18. Health, United States, 2008, *supra* note 2, at 203 (Table 26). World Health Organization, World Health Statistics 2008 38–58, online at http://www.who.int/whosis/whostat/en/ (accessed Nov. 08, 2009) (hereinafter, 2008 World Health Statistics).
19. Health, United States, 2008, *supra* note 2, at 174 (Table 12).
20. Health, United States, 2008, *supra* note 2.
21. Posting of Patrick J. Buchanan, *A Brief for Whitey*, to http://buchanan.org/blog/pjb-a-brief-for-whitey-969 (Mar. 21, 2008).
22. Ian F. Haney Lopez, *The Social Construction of Race: Some Observations on Illusion, Fabrication, and Choice*, Harv. C.R.-C.L. L. Rev., Winter 1994, at 1, 7.
23. James M. Jones, Prejudice and Racism 342–47 (1997); David R. Williams, *Race and Health: Basic Questions, Emerging Directions*, 7 Annals of Epidemiology 5, 322–33 (1997).
24. W. Michael Byrd & Linda A. Clayton, An American Health Dilemma: A Medical History of African Americans and the

Problem of Race, Beginnings to 1900 (2000); James Oliver Horton & Lois E. Horton, Slavery and the Making of America 14–16 (2005); Hugh Thomas, The Slave Trade: The Story of the Atlantic Slave Trade: 1440–1870(1997).

25. *Id.*
26. Joe Feagin, *Slavery Unwilling to Die: The Background of Black Oppression in the 1980's*, 17 J.Black Stud. 173 (1986).
27. See generally Abraham Maslow, *A Theory of Human Motivation*, 50 Psychol. Rev. 370, 380–83 (1943).
28. *In Black Caucus, a Fund-Raising Powerhouse*, The New York Times, Feb. 14, 2010, online at http://www.nytimes.com/2010/02/14/us/politics/14cbc.html?pagewanted=all (accessed Feb. 21, 2010).
29. An American Health Dilemma, *supra* note 22, at 322; Randall, *supra* note 1, at 66–67.
30. Brown v. Board of Education of Topeka et al, 347 U.S.483 (1954).
31. Derrick Bell, Silent Covenants: Brown v. Board of Education and the Unfulfilled Hopes for Racial Reform 29–48 (2004)(hereinafter Silent Covenant).
32. *Id.* at 42.
33. *Id.* at 69–76.
34. *Id.*
35. *Id.* at 77–86.
36. United States Commission on Civil Rights, The Health Care Challenge: Acknowledging Inequity, Confronting Discrimination, and Ensuring Equality, Volume I, The Role of Governmental and Private Health Care Origframs Initiatives, 287 No. 902–00062–2 (Sept. 1993).
37. Randall, *supra* note 1, at 76.
38. *Id.* at 77–80.
39. Vernellia Randall, *Does Clinton's Health Care Reform Proposal Ensure [E]Qual[ity] of Health Care for Ethnic Americans and the Poor?*, 60 Brook. L. Rev. 167, 205–12 (1994).
40. Title VI of the Civil Rights Act of 1964, 42 U.S.C.S. §2000d (1982).
41. Alexander v. Choate et al., 469 U.S. 287 (1985).
42. Randall, *supra* note 1, at 66–67.
43. United States Commission on Civil Rights, The Health Care Challenge: Acknowledging Inequity, Confronting Discrimination, and Ensuring Equality, Vol. I, The Role of Governmental and Private Health Care Origframs Initiatives, 287 No. 902–00062–2 (Sept. 1993).

4 PUBLIC HEALTH AND MARRIAGE (EQUALITY)

John G. Culhane

Until quite recently, one could have accurately stated that the public debate about same-sex marriages was almost entirely focused on rights and morality: Must the law treat same-sex couples the same way it treats their opposite-sex counterparts? What messages, positive or negative, are we sending by allowing gay couples to marry? Are gay unions morally equivalent to straight ones? As anyone who's read a newspaper, watched television, or scanned the internet is well aware, this loud national conversation has played out – at times viciously – in a charged political context. Even the terms of engagement have been a bone of contention. Those favoring marriage rights for same-sex couples have coined the term "marriage equality" to make the point that basic principles of fairness and treating like cases alike compels recognition of same-sex couples' unions, whereas the most virulent opponents place the word marriage into alarmed and ironic quotation marks – homosexual "marriage" – to signal that, in their worldview, such unions can never be true marriages, even if the law deems it otherwise.

This debate is vital and continues at an almost breathless pace. In 2009 alone, only the most fervent of partisans could have kept up with the seemingly endless developments, as the nation (and the world) continued to lurch forward – and backward – on the matter of marriage. On the judicial front, the California Supreme Court upheld the momentous Proposition 8,[1] the voter-approved initiative that stripped gay couples of the right that the court had the year before deemed fundamental, and the Iowa Supreme Court unanimously held that the state's constitution demanded that gay couples be issued marriage licenses.[2] The marriage equality forces have now shifted focus to the federal courts, with two high-profile cases centered in Massachusetts and California.[3] The cases might end up in the United States Supreme Court and could provide answers to constitutional questions about Proposition 8, the federal Defense of Marriage Act, and the bans on same-sex marriages more generally.

Matters were, if anything, more breakneck at the legislative level. In the spring of 2009, New England states took the lead, with state houses in Vermont,[4] New Hampshire,[5] and Maine[6] granting same-sex couples the right to marry. Washington, D.C. followed suit by enacting a similar bill at the end of the year.[7] Yet the pro-equality forces ended the year mostly on a down note. In November, Maine voters issued an electoral rebuke to the legislators and to their gay neighbors, repealing the measure passed earlier in the year.[8] And legislatures in two states thought to be among the most progressive – New York and New Jersey – soundly voted down marriage equality bills that earlier had been thought to stand a strong chance of approval.[9]

The Year 2010 has been equally tumultuous. The Proposition 8 trial wrapped up in California, and the case is seen as having the potential to reach the U.S. Supreme Court. Meanwhile, legislatures in both New Mexico and Hawaii wrestled with civil union laws, with the negative outcome in Hawaii under judicial challenge.[10]

Every development has also occasioned a cacophony of commentary, and positions have not broken down along easily identified lines: Conservatives are split on gay marriages, with many of the most prominent favoring the idea as a way of strengthening the institution through the assimilation of gay couples, while others continue to fear the long-term consequences to heterosexual marriage.[11] On the left, the liberal consensus favoring marriage equality has been challenged by a more radical critique that questions the energy devoted to an issue of formal legal equality over more substantive issues of social justice.[12] Queer theorists and others have deconstructed marriage itself as a subordinating, privileging institution that gay people should want no part of. Perhaps nothing showcases the complexity of the issue as much as the "strange bedfellows" California case challenging Proposition 8 with erstwhile foes Ted Olson and David Boies, opposed on the (in)famous *Bush v. Gore*[13] case, now aligned – conservative and liberal – on one side of what they see as history, and justice. Others, of course, disagree.

This focus on rights and temporal politics had long obscured another, vital piece of the discussion: Would granting marriage rights to same-sex couples improve public health and welfare? It has been challenging to get people to focus on this dimension of the issue. When I first mentioned to a colleague the value of focusing on the population-related impact of marriage equality, he looked at me askance and then allowed that such considerations might be "the fourth or fifth most important" consideration. I hope to prove him wrong. In this chapter, I advance the argument that a focus on public health and welfare can refresh the national discussion about marriage equality. Indeed, I think that considering the issue of marriage equality naturally opens up, even if it does not demand, the focus on these broader issues of public health. Rights do not exist in a vacuum; no matter what the claim, the plaintiff must show that the state has exceeded its legal authority in denying equality. Such authority, in turn, is closely tied to the societal costs and benefits of the suggested expansion of rights. Once that discussion begins, we are in the realm of population-based health and policy.

First, a disclaimer: It's too simple to say that these broad issues about the effect of gay unions on society have not been raised at all. They have been. Until recently, however, the issue was often cast as whether same-sex marriages would have a negative effect on opposite-sex ones. Thus, some have explored whether societies that pass laws recognizing the equal legal status of gay and lesbian couples have seen any change in the occurrence and stability of heterosexual marriages. Some evidence is coming in on the question, and it suggests that gay unions have been a boon, not a challenge, for the institution of marriage.[14] Because the evidence is based on experiences in European countries with vastly different social, historical, and political backdrops, however, it has limited predictive value for the U.S. model. Further complicating matters, the unions studied have mostly been gay partnerships that were not the full equivalent of marriage.

Even these efforts fail to fully address a constellation of broader issues that the marriage equality movement invites – indeed, compels: Will couples in same-sex marriages realize the same benefits of marriage that have often – but controversially – been ascribed to heterosexual marriages, including improved emotional and physical health, as well as the financial advantages that come from both economies of scale and social support? If they do, is that an argument only for marriage equality, or does it also compel reassessment of the enormous privileges and benefits that government bestows on married couples?

My conclusion is that we should recognize the public, population-based good of granting marriage equality to gay, lesbian, and bisexual couples, but also be mindful of broader issues relating to marriage. Is state-sponsored marriage justified, particularly in its present form? If so, does that mean all (or even most) of the government-conferred benefits are necessary, or even desirable? And how might we assess the effect of such benefits?

It is best to begin with a bit of legal background on the marriage equality movement, a discussion that will provide a foundation for the analysis that follows.

THE MARRIAGE EQUALITY MOVEMENT

Although cases challenging state bans on same-sex marriages were brought as early as the 1970s,[15] it was not until the 1990s that what has become known as the marriage equality movement took firm root. A decision by the Hawaii Supreme Court in 1993 that laid the groundwork for same-sex marriages in that state set off a political shockwave,[16] memorably causing the United States Congress to step into the *state* issue of marriage as it had not done before. Under the Defense of Marriage Act ("DOMA"), passed in 1996 and signed by the then-President Bill Clinton, states would not be required to recognize same-sex marriages performed in other states. DOMA also defined marriage, for federal purposes, as the union of a man and a woman.[17] At that time, marriages between two people of the same-sex were an even more frightening prospect to politicians than they are today, and the legislation passed by overwhelming margins in both chambers. At that point in the history of the marriage equality movement, members of Congress felt at liberty to make a variety of unsupported pronouncements: "Same-sex unions do not make strong families."[18] "Out of same-sex relationships … emotional bonding oftentimes does not take place …."[19] "[S]ame sex 'marriages' demean the fundamental institution of marriage. They legitimize unnatural and immoral behavior."[20] Only a few dared speak to the contrary.[21]

After that, Congress stepped aside. DOMA is still law and likely won't be repealed any time soon (although its fate in the courts is less clear), but the calls for Congress to propose to the states an amendment to the U.S. Constitution that would define marriage as the union of one man and one woman seem to have receded. Matters are back in the state courts and legislatures, where the results have been mixed and unpredictable. After Hawaii voters amended their state constitution to allow the legislature to ban gay marriages, there ensued a cascade of events that has been exhaustively chronicled. In the 1999 case *Baker v. State*, the Vermont Supreme Court held that denying gay couples the benefits of marriage was unconstitutional but left to the legislature how best to remedy the problem.[22] In 2000, the legislature took both the command and the hint, passing the nation's first civil union law, which purported to grant same-sex couples all of the benefits of marriage – except the name.[23] Far more states, however, ran in the other direction – first, by passing *statutes* against same-sex marriages, and then, in some cases, by impaling the prohibition into their state *constitutions*. Recently, some state legislatures have moved in the other direction, following the compromise course born in Vermont by enacting laws – sometimes called civil unions, sometimes domestic partnerships – that provide all of the state-conferred benefits of marriage but pointedly withhold the term "marriage", reserving it solely for opposite-sex couples. And, as noted earlier in the chapter, by 2009, three states and the District of Columbia had enacted marriage equality legislation.[24]

As the Vermont decision suggests, matters in the states' courthouses have been no less complicated. On balance, though, these judicial developments have been more favorable to the marriage equality movement. While state high courts in Washington,[25] New York,[26] and Maryland[27] turned away challenges to prohibitions on same-sex marriages, courts in Massachusetts,[28] California (until compromised by Proposition 8),[29] Connecticut,[30] and Iowa[31] came to the opposite conclusion: Bans on same-sex unions violated the state constitution's promise of equal protection under the law and, in California and Massachusetts, the constitutional commitment to the fundamental freedom to marry. For those with a legal focus, the California, Iowa, and Connecticut decisions are especially noteworthy, because those courts broke ground by subjecting discrimination based on sexual orientation to a heightened level of scrutiny. Before the California Supreme Court's decision in *In Re Marriage Cases*, no state supreme court had so held. Rather, such laws were reviewed under the much more state-friendly "rational basis" test. Once that dam had been ruptured, both Iowa and Connecticut quickly followed suit. Usually, laws reviewed under this heightened standard fail, and the marriage bans in all three states suffered exactly that fate.

These decisions came several years after the Massachusetts Supreme Judicial Court had held, in *Goodridge v. Department of Public Health*, that the state's prohibition against gay marriage could not withstand even rational basis review. I want to focus on that 2003 decision here, but not (much) on the court's legal analysis, which has been much dissected. Often overlooked, though, has been the court's understanding and articulation of the public health justifications for marriage. Developing these will bring us from marriage equality, which the court eloquently defended, to broader points about marriage and the arguments for (and against) its justification.

MARRIAGE, FROM A PUBLIC HEALTH PERSPECTIVE

Where does the state get the authority to regulate marriage in the first place? Why not simply leave the matter to religious institutions, for example? What is the state's interest in marriage? The state's principal legal authority to regulate public health and welfare is through the police power, which is the state's most general type of authority, limited in its reach only by constitutional safeguards against unwarranted incursions into personal liberty. In *Goodridge*, the Massachusetts Supreme Judicial Court defined the police power as "the Legislature's power to enact rules to regulate conduct, to the extent that such laws are 'necessary to secure the health, safety, good order, comfort, or general welfare of the community.'"[32]

The state's regulation of marriage is clearly an exercise of this police power and is manifested in licensure and solemnization requirements for entry, and in providing the means of legal exit. But why does the state license marriages in the first place?

First, such licenses are tied to a host of benefits. In that way, they are similar to uncontroversial grants of state permission, such as a driver's license. In each case, the "aim of licensure generally is preservation of public health, safety, and welfare by extending the public trust only to those with proven qualifications."[33]

In the case of a license to drive, the connection between qualification and public health and safety is clear; licenses are issued only to those whose ability to pass written and "field" tests provides evidence that they will navigate the roadways with skill and care. Those who drive without licenses deprive the state of the ability to assess their capacity, and unlicensed drivers therefore risk hefty penalties. Oddly, though, a license to marry is easier to obtain than a license to drive. "The state is not a bit choosy about who can marry."[34] All adults (and some older minors, depending on the jurisdiction) are free to marry anyone of their choice, provided that neither party is already married and that the parties are not too closely related.

In most states, however, there is the additional requirement that the parties be of opposite sexes. Why? From the state's perspective as an issuer of marriage licenses, and given the otherwise permissive view on the right to marry, what justifies this blanket exclusion? Asked another way, why does the state grant marriage licenses, tied to so many benefits, in the first place? Only by understanding the justification for state-sanctioned support of marriage can restrictions on membership be critically assessed. There is therefore a clear, if seldom articulated, connection between the marriage equality movement and the broad, population-based justification for state-sanctioned marriage.

The state recognizes and licenses marriage because of the contribution that institution is thought to make to the reservoir of public good. According to the *Goodridge* court: "Marriage is a vital social institution. The exclusive commitment of two individuals to each other … brings stability to our society."[35] The court later expanded on this insight, noting that "civil marriage enhances the 'welfare of the community.' It is a 'social institution of the highest importance.' Civil marriage anchors an ordered society by encouraging stable relationships over transient ones."[36]

Unfortunately, the court did not much develop the ways in which stable relationships bring order to society, but did offer at least one weighty elaboration: "[Marriage] is central to the way the Commonwealth identifies individuals, provides for the orderly distribution of property, ensures that children and adults are cared for and supported whenever possible from private rather than public funds, and tracks important epidemiological and demographic data."[37]

Many vital characteristics of marriage are packed into the court's statement. First, identifying someone as married relieves the state of many practical difficulties in determining and vindicating all sorts of rights and obligations. The difficulties routinely faced by gay couples in seeking recognition for their relationships in the absence of this state-created status are well known and were summarized sympathetically by the Washington State Supreme Court: "[M]any day-to-day decisions that are routine for married couples are more complex, more agonizing, and more costly for same-sex couples, unlike married couples who automatically have the advantages and rights provided to them in … laws and policies such as those surrounding medical conditions … probate … and health insurance."[38] Stories in the popular press and economic studies have supported this obvious point.[39]

The court's statement about the value to society of having both children and adults supported by private rather than public sources is a seed for developing a deeper exploration of the public health and policy benefits of marriage. In that respect, at least, *Goodridge* advanced the discussion of the public function of marriage in a way that other courts have largely failed to do.

Thus, on the way to recognizing the state's obligation to recognize the full equality of same-sex couples who wish to marry, the court addressed broader questions about the purposes of marriage. Of course, the two issues are inextricably linked from the perspective of public health and populations. The *Goodridge* court's analysis of the state's purported justifications for excluding same-sex couples therefore serves two purposes here: By considering the broad policy arguments for and against the rights of gay and lesbian couples to marry, we also and unavoidably connect up with the more global question of whether marriage (at least in its current, highly privileged form) is justified. My aim is to turn the conventional legal analysis upside down – instead of considering the sources and guarantees of legal rights the primary material and the public health and policy questions as subordinate, I look at the societal, population-wide benefits of marriage equality as the central issues to which the legal analysis should be in thrall.

So, can the state justify the exclusion of gay couples from the rights, benefits – and title – of marriage? If excluding same-sex couples from marriage were independently defensible, the difficulties faced by gay couples compared to their straight counterparts might be justified. However, none of the proffered justifications can withstand even rational basis analysis, and they melt completely under the glare of heightened scrutiny.

EXCLUDING SAME-SEX COUPLES FROM MARRIAGE

On the terms on which the marriage equality battle is being waged, same-sex unions should be the clear winner. If we take for a moment the argument that marriages are good for the couples that are in them, it seems likely that these benefits would also extend to same-sex couples, at least to a degree. This much has been admitted even by virulent opponents of marriage equality.[40] Same-sex spouses would gain health and financial benefits from marriage, at least to some degree; and their children would also realize financial, social, and emotional benefits from the ability of their parents to marry.[41] These gains are important from a nuanced view of public health that pays particular attention to populations within the broader society, and that recognizes that respecting individual rights, dignity, and esteem also serves public health goals.

As with opposite-sex couples, the benefits from marriage would not be limited to the couples themselves; they have important effects on the broader society in which the couple abides. A couple with legal and related social support for their union can be expected to form an efficient economic unit that will reduce the government's burden of social welfare, especially to the extent that their finances become intertwined. Most studies show that married couples are likelier than cohabitating opposite-sex couples to have interdependent finances.[42]

Whether this intermingling of finances is as true of same-sex couples is unclear, because the side-by-side comparison groups are not available; gay couples can't marry. My suspicion, supported not by empirical studies[43] – which are in their infancy – but by my own experience as a parent who can barely keep track of my kids' gloves and hats (much less separate finances), is that parenting is the greater spur toward interdependence. Certainly the evidence suggests that this is true for opposite-sex couples, and the same sort of dynamic might (at least to an extent) be expected for same-sex couples.[44] So perhaps we should enact laws and policies that support parents – whether straight or gay, married or not – and thereby encourage their interdependence.

This observation leads naturally to the related question of whether same-sex unions are good for children. States defending laws that bar same-sex couples from marrying have often argued that they are not, or at least that the evidence isn't in. They express the fear that a "social experiment" should not prematurely cause the abandonment of the "traditional" marriage rule that has existed in so many (although, it must be acknowledged, not all) societies, and relatedly, that the essential purpose of marriage is procreation and child rearing. Note again the connection between rights and the public good.

The procreation argument has by now been thoroughly discredited, and its death throes have led to increasingly convoluted, baroque, and counterintuitive arguments. None of these make sense from a perspective that is attentive to the health of the population of parents who do not procreate in the "traditional" way, or to couples that marry for other reasons. The most basic version of the assertion has been refuted by, of all people, Justice Scalia. Fearing that the Supreme Court's decision in *Lawrence v. Texas* (which requires only that the state leave same-sex couples' intimate, consensual conduct to themselves) leads inexorably to marriage equality, he wrote that, under the majority's rationale, "the encouragement of procreation" was a weak argument for excluding gay couples, "since the sterile and the elderly are allowed to marry."[45] Also, certainly in the twenty-first century, "procreation" is not unavailable to same-sex couples, at least not in any way that is not also used by many opposite-sex couples. Both use surrogates, and (presumably) no court would dream of denying an opposite-sex couple a marriage license because they relied on this method of reproduction.

A variant of this "natural procreation" argument has had some success, however. Perhaps seized by a collective madness that was in the air in the summer of 2006, the high courts in both Washington and New York States found that the state could have a rational basis for restricting marriage to only those couples who might "accidentally" procreate. The decisions, written only three weeks apart, made this argument: Since sex sometimes leads to unintentional procreation (even in the age of birth control), it makes sense to have in place an institution that will support the couple in its difficult effort to remain together and raise their accidental child.[46] This may well be true, and might be *one* purpose of marriage. But there are many others, among the most obvious of which is providing a stable environment even for children whose birth is planned, and for adopted children. Only a selective, almost claustrophobic view of population health could have caused the court to miss this point, which was drilled home by Chief Judge Kaye of the New York Court of Appeals, who noted that the state's "legitimate interest in the welfare of children" was in fact "undermined" by "excluding same-sex couples from marriage."[47] Depriving the many thousands of children "currently being raised by same-sex couples" of the "tangible legal protections and economic benefits to married couples and their children," she wrote, "is antithetical to their welfare."[48]

The related argument that marriage provides the optimal setting for child rearing fares no better. In fact, it too is self-defeating. If marriage is the best institution for children, then why would the state not want to invite same-sex parents into this ideal environment? As court after court has recognized, especially in the many states that allow same-sex couples to adopt children, the argument makes no consistent sense. By recognizing that a child's best interest is served by having two committed parents – even when those parents are of the same sex – the state is validating the very practice that it then tries to deem a "social experiment" in the context of marriage equality litigation.

Given that these arguments are so weak, what explains the continued popular, legislative, and (to a lesser extent) judicial reluctance to extent marriage rights to same-sex couples? As the Iowa Supreme Court explicitly recognized in *Varnum v. Brien*, much of the opposition is grounded in religion.[49] While this has clearly motivated voters and even legislators, it is inadmissible in a court of law; thus, other arguments are invoked by both state attorneys general in defending the law and by courts in papering over the true source of the problem. But this approach skews and distorts the proper, public approach that should be taken. By making such disingenuous arguments, states are doing a kind of perverse public miseducation that can have the long-term effect of compromising the trust in government that public health relies on. Admittedly, the issue is difficult because state attorneys general are supposed to defend the laws, even if they might personally disagree with them. Legal scholars divide over whether this duty extends to laws that are plainly in violation of constitutional principles, but state officials should in any event avoid making arguments that needlessly demonize a class of citizens, or that stem from unsupported assumptions that then become an acceptable part of the public discourse. Again, one of the central pillars of the modern view of public health is that respect for equality contributes to population health, and we should therefore reject arguments that compromise this value without strong, clear reasons that the party discriminated against can see as justified.

WHAT JUSTIFIES MARRIAGE IN THE FIRST PLACE?

Allowing same-sex couples into the club is only one part of "the marriage issue" and not even the hardest one. Inasmuch as marriage enforces obligations, it does to that extent serve a kind of social welfare function, albeit in millions of discrete silos (each separate couple). Of course, we might choose to create and enforce obligations in other ways, so the question becomes: What public benefits of marriage might support the preferential treatment afforded it by law?

This question should be taken seriously, not sidestepped by the tautological statement that "the State has a compelling interest in regulating and preserving the institution of marriage as that institution has been defined by the State."[50]

Indeed, it can be difficult even to see the need to question the state's "compelling interest." We should start by recognizing that the state need not even *need* to officially sanction marriages in the first place. This conclusion may seem odd in light of the Supreme Court's consistent position that the right to marry is fundamental. But that right has been developed in federal and state cases involving the exclusion of certain groups – interracial couples, prisoners, deadbeat parents, and now same-sex couples[51] – not the more existential question of whether the state is obliged to confer official recognition, much less any particular benefit or set of benefits, on marriages at all. The California Supreme Court addressed the issue in its decision striking down the state's law against same-sex marriages, but (wisely) declined to decide the question.[52] The *Goodridge* court went further, opining that the state need not confer a legal right to marry.[53] Note that we are not talking about one's right to a religious marriage here; those matters are, and must be, left up to the tenets and beliefs of the religions themselves. The question is whether the *government* need recognize the institution of marriage.

The question is more theoretical than real, at least for the foreseeable future. Despite some academic proposals to the contrary, no one believes that the state is going to abolish marriage any time soon.[54] Yet raising the issue has the beneficial effect of inviting questions about the extent to which those in marriages enjoy privileges not given to other couples – or indeed to anyone else at all, whether single or in relationships of any kind or size. After all, recognizing and supporting marriages is a political choice, one that entails both costs (to the government in the subsidies conferred) and covert distributional decisions: By channeling money to married couples, the amount available for other purposes is reduced. Through taxation, the unmarried subsidize the married. The *Goodridge* court confronted this point, but indirectly: One of the state's arguments was that recognizing same-sex couples would deplete the state's limited resources.[55] This argument was seen, rightly, as a makeweight: If the state is going to privilege marriage, it cannot then turn around and exclude people based on their claim to those very same benefits. Presumably, resources would also be conserved by denying the benefits of marriage to people with red hair, but that is hardly a sufficient reason for doing so. One needs an independent reason for excluding certain couples from marriage, and the court had already considered and rejected the state's other arguments.

A broader point lurks within this seemingly throwaway discussion of the economic benefits given to married couples. While few would deny that the state's support of marriage has (largely intended) social and emotional consequences for both those inside and outside of its protective umbrella, it is vital to ask: How much of this state sponsorship is justified from the population perspective?

The short answer is that *no one knows* whether the government's recognition, much less its substantial support, of marriage is justified. Social science evidence suggests that married couples do better than their cohabitating, unmarried counterparts, but this conclusion has not escaped the criticism it deserves.[56]

There have been efforts to correct for the selection bias – the fact that those already doing well tend to be the ones who choose marriage – but the problem is intractable. It might be that we could do away with at least the state-recognized version of marriage, but the positive effects would remain. Perhaps the religious commitment and social support for committed, long-term unions that would remain in place would be sufficient to confer on couples the benefits now attributed to marriage. Indeed, in her important work taking a closer look at the many subcategories of cohabitating couples, Cynthia Grant Bowman suggests that legally recognized marriage might not be important for some populations within the United States (such as Puerto Rican couples living on the mainland).[57] Thoughtful scholars have recognized the indeterminacy of the evidence while arguing that, on balance, state support – even encouragement – of marriage is proper and in the best interests of a stable society that supports and nurtures children.[58]

Marriage can also be criticized from a different perspective. Marriage is the legal recognition and support of a status, and such status-based relationships are in decline, and for a good reason. As with master-slave, the husband-wife relationship has supported the comprehensive subordination of women; and the parent-child relationship has similarly enabled the worse kind of mistreatment and neglect of children. The law of coverture – under which married women's rights disappeared under their spouses' protective "cover" – has long since disappeared, but marriage remains tied to this subordinating, gender-identified setting of roles and social expectations. One of the more interesting but underdeveloped criticisms of the exclusion of gay couples from marriage has been that the state thereby engages in a kind of vestigial sex discrimination, based on lingering perceptions of the proper roles of men and women; roles that same-sex unions inherently upend.[59] But if marriage continues to support this kind of gender subordination, we should seriously think about the cost of the institution to the emotional health of the female population.

Some of those making what I might term the "continuing subordination" argument then try to rehabilitate marriage, and have gotten rather existential about it. These scholars begin by observing that we live in a postmodern society where status is disintegrating and where people then become (and might fear becoming) "just" the sum total of their discrete actions and choices. In this reality, a modern reimagining of marriage might create a foundation of meaning from which some might find emotional support and even identity – but now freely chosen.[60] To the extent that this observation is valid, it might lead to two further claims. First, same-sex marriages should be supported, because gay and lesbian couples are not anchored to the subordinating history of marriage; their unions are the true products of choice, and those same-sex couples who find marriage an attractive option will be forced to define their roles for themselves. Indeed, one might optimistically imagine that same-sex couples would offer something of value to the ongoing project of defining marriage by providing an example of true equality unmoored in essentialist role-modeling that (still) diminishes both the dignity and therefore the creative potential of those in opposite-sex marriages. Second, this critical reconstruction of the purposes and value of marriage might be supported from a population-based perspective: By giving legal recognition to marriage, the state nourishes the emotional health of a substantial number of its citizens.

But what about the flip side? Can the state support marriage without sending the message that being *unmarried* is a lesser state, and thereby damaging the emotional well-being of this "other" population? The answer to this question for same-sex couples seems clear in a society that excludes them. The negative signals in this context are devastating for many: Studies show that anti-gay policies and rhetoric, including laws and arguments related to the denial of basic marriage equality, have serious mental health consequences for those in the lesbian, gay, bisexual, and transgender (LGBT) community.[61] These costs demand consideration in any responsible discussion of marriage policy, but they are often ignored by those who focus solely on the entirely speculative (and unlikely) costs that marriage equality would visit on the institution. As Jonathan Rauch has memorably stated: "A one-eyed utilitarian is a blind utilitarian."[62]

Nor can this enforced subordination be solved by the "virtual equality" of the civil union, which is in part explicitly designed to confer upon such same-sex couples a lesser status than that afforded opposite-sex couples. The irony is inescapable. By granting all of the benefits of marriage without the label, the state has made its point more clearly than it could have by failing to consider the question at all, and the message is this: "Get your meaning somewhere else. You're not married." Of course, many same-sex couples have developed their own rituals and commitment ceremonies, and many consider themselves married despite the state's disapproval. But the message of second-class citizenship remains and will have psychological effects ranging from subtle to devastating on many couples. A population-focused approach regards these costs as substantial.

For opposite-sex couples, matters are more difficult to determine. Surely some are content in their unmarried state. Some cohabitating couples truly do not care about the "signals" of marriage; others likely do but have practical or philosophical objections to marriage (including, for some, an unwillingness to marry as long as marriage equality is denied same-sex couples) that overwhelm their concern about "official messaging." Yet there is a cost to others who might wish to marry but have not done so because they are unable to find a suitable partner, or who do not want to marry but are negatively affected by hearing constant messages (even today) that they *should* do so. As for single (non-cohabitating) people, again the cases will vary along a wide spectrum. For many senior citizens who are widowed, their single status may create practical problems but no feelings of inferiority, given the widespread social acceptance of those married and left widowed. For younger singles who once were married but have divorced, the message is less clear and may be especially sensitive to personal predilection, confidence, political views, and a host of other hard-to-quantify (or even to name) variables. Those unable to find a suitable partner for marriage may feel themselves somehow "apart," as well, in a society that even today so values marriage.

What then, on balance, should be done about marriage? Does it further public health or compromise it?

Unfortunately, no one knows or can even be confident in defending a "best policy." There are simply too many complex variables at play to definitively decide on an optimal state marriage policy, even where we take as a given that the state will continue to license marriages for the foreseeable future. We should be wary, however, of any government-sponsored "marriage promotion" effort, such as the one endlessly trumpeted during the administration of George W. Bush; not because supporting and promoting marriage is (necessarily) a bad idea, but because marriage has been used as a simplistic fix for deeper problems of poverty and the lack of economic and educational opportunity.

Should the government be encouraging a couple that has borne a child together to marry? No matter the circumstances? Even if doing so provides an excuse not to do anything else for the child? If the evidence shows that kids born to young, unwed mothers are often in poverty, would not the more direct approach be to assist the child and (more controversially) the mother, rather than to assume that marriage to a partner whose own prospects might be dismal will magically improve the situation? Such assistance, especially to the mother, has its own problems – including the often overemphasized "moral hazard" that the availability of assistance will discourage initiative – but my point here is only that matters are more complex than the marriage promotion forces often acknowledge. At most, such efforts are one modest part of a more thoughtful and comprehensive approach; one that would include, at the very least, counseling about the responsibilities, challenges, and benefits of marriage for the couple and for any child(ren) they might have. Now *that* could lead to positive, population-wide health outcomes.

Beyond the often-clumsy efforts at marriage promotion, what rules should the federal government and the states establish for the regulation and the subsidization of marriage? We need to begin with two related – though contested – assumptions, borrowed from *Goodridge*: Marriage should be designed to support and encourage stable relationships, and such stability is a societal good. Always bearing in mind that the support of marriage comes with a cost – in dollars and to the self-esteem of at least some of those not within its societal embrace – the discussion that follows is meant to stimulate further thought, conversation, and action on the kinds of steps that can be justified in support of marriage. I begin here with laws that support existing marriages. I then discuss how marriage privileges children of married couples, and how the law of marriage dissolution is designed to protect and therefore encourage the expectations of couples who choose to enter into stable, long-term relationships.

LAWS THAT SUPPORT EXISTING MARRIAGES

An embarrassment of state-conferred riches awaits the married couple. These have been endlessly dissected and described, especially in articles criticizing the inability of gay and lesbian couples to marry, and no point is served by exhaustively cataloguing them here. But the mention of just a few of the most significant ones will situate the discussion that follows. At the federal level, married couples enjoy numerous tax advantages (including a different rate of taxation and the ability to file a joint return),[63] Social Security protection (survivorship benefits),[64] the right to sponsor spouses under immigration law,[65] and many others. State laws confer additional tax advantages (such as exclusions from estate taxes and real estate transfer taxes),[66] an infeasible right under the law of intestacy,[67] rights to sue for wrongful death and personal injury to the spouse,[68] and medical decision making and hospital visitation rights. Local governments can also provide health benefits to their workers' spouses and relieve them of local tax burdens. Moreover, private parties often continue to take their cue from government, granting benefits based on marital status, the most significant of which are health insurance benefits.

All of these benefits can be criticized for granting benefits and legal advantage based on marital status, not upon any notion of distributional need or fairness. Consider, for example, the survivorship benefits granted to spouses under Social Security law. It might be that, in a given case, the person most reliant on the decedent was an unrelated person, such as a cohabitant, or someone related but ineligible, such as an adult sibling who relied on the deceased sibling financially in exchange for other kinds of support (transportation, housework, and companionship, for example). Moreover, the surviving spouse might have many other sources of income available, so that the government subsidy comes under question given the limited pool of resources and their source: taxpayer funding. The same might be said about the favorable tax treatments, or even about the right to sue in tort for the wrongful death of a spouse: Why tie the right to recover to legal status rather than to reality? Since the tort action is designed to compensate for a loss of expected support, why should state laws assume that only spouses might have received such continued support?

Note that the laws just discussed provide for no "work around" – people in other kinds of mutually supporting relationships cannot contract themselves "into" the statutory scheme. Other legal rules, such as the presumption that one spouse has the right to make medical decisions for the other, can be overcome but only by preparing, executing, and paying for legal documents that are, in any case, often unavailable, unclear, or ignored when needed. How could the law better define or adjust these rights?

One size will not fit all. Just as marriage is a clumsy proxy for reality, so too any other inflexible, marriage-based approach to all cases will fail to reflect reality and run the risk of misallocating scarce resources. The underlying goal of a particular law or policy should determine eligibility for a given benefit or presumption. In many cases, that goal will be to recognize the benefit to society and overall public health and welfare in supporting and encouraging those relationships that, in turn, create benefit to society through private, "familial" support.

There is, of course, a *cost* to moving away from these bright-line rules that privilege marriage. Efforts to assess qualification for a particular benefit from a functional perspective might be expensive and time-consuming. It might therefore be possible to justify the "marriage required" rule in certain cases, such as the right of U.S. citizens to sponsor their spouses for citizenship. (For the moment, we overlook the obvious unfairness to gay couples who cannot marry.) Given the limited resources available to federal authorities and the indeterminacy of a ruling that an unmarried couple was sufficiently "close" – and how would that be defined? – perhaps one can defend the requirement of marriage as a proxy for a long-term, committed relationship. Yet even the government recognizes that the ease of entering into marriage and the incentives to gain U.S. citizenship will lead some to enter into marriages purely of convenience. These "fraudulent" marriages will result in the deportation of the sponsored spouse where the immigration authorities determine that the couple isn't "really" married, but attempting to use the spouse-sponsorship law to gain citizenship.[69] So it turns out that, even in the case of immigration, a marriage license does not work perfectly as a determinant of eligibility for a valuable benefit.

Maybe, though, marriage is a good default rule in some cases: A married couple qualifies for benefit or presumption X automatically, whereas those choosing not to marry can qualify by showing that the underlying "good" (here defined as a benefit to those in the relationship and less directly to the overall society) would be served by extending the law's protection to them. For example, a tort plaintiff in a wrongful death action should have standing to sue in either of two classes of cases: (1) If they stand in the kind of legal relationship that creates requirements or expectations of support, such as spouse, parent, or child (even adult child); (2) If they can make a preliminary showing that they were, in fact, dependent on the deceased person for support. In either case, though, actual recovery would depend on demonstrating to a fact finder (court or jury) that the deceased had provided, and would have continued providing, sufficient support. One does not typically think of the right to sue in wrongful death as a "government-conferred benefit." But it surely is. Wrongful death laws are statutory and set the terms of a valuable legal entitlement. Even the related law allowing recovery for "loss of consortium," which is usually judicially and not legislatively created, places the authority of the government behind those in formal legal relationships only, leaving out many others who have suffered obvious harm.

The same argument about government involvement cannot be made of private health insurance benefits; both insurance companies and the companies that buy their policies may define classes of eligible beneficiaries as they choose. Increasingly, benefits have been opened up to those in other kinds of relationships, such as domestic partnerships.[70] In so doing, these bottom-line entities are often doing a better job than government in recognizing the real needs of today's families, defined not exclusively by legal status but by relationships of affinity. Using the private insurance model as an example to be followed, more flexibility in legal rules defining "close relationship" or "family" might be expected to result in a greater benefit to public health and welfare. There is one crucial difference, though: Government-conferred benefits and advantages should be means-tested and limited, because overall distributional fairness should be a concern, as it is not in the case of private parties.

LAWS THAT BENEFIT THE CHILDREN OF MARRIED COUPLES

"When a law's purpose is to protect children, marriage is never an appropriate dividing line."[71] This line, written by Professor Nancy Polikoff, is just about right. Indeed, tying benefits to marriage severs the government's direct connection to the child and thereby risks attenuating or even defeating the purpose of child protection. Note that this is *not* to say that recognizing and privileging marriage might not cause more people to marry, and that marriages might not then themselves be beneficial to children; some have argued strenuously, and with some support, for this conclusion. But here we are investigating whether benefits specifically directed toward the children of married couples – and only to them – are justified. To see why they are not, let us consider just a few examples from each side of the ledger: laws that require marriage as a condition of benefits to children, and those that do not.

Until relatively recently, the law greatly penalized illegitimacy by tying legal status and entitlements to the marriage of the child's parents. But for decades now, such distinctions have been receiving their overdue interment. A telling example can be found in Louisiana's wrongful death law, which prevented mothers from recovering for the death of their illegitimate children, and reciprocally denied recovery to such children in cases where their mothers had died. In a pair of cases decided on the same day in 1968, the United States Supreme Court struck down both of these laws, focusing on the facts of the relationship rather than the status of illegitimacy. In *Levy v. Louisiana*,[72] the Court raised all of the right questions about the line the state had drawn:

> The rights asserted here involve the intimate, familial relationship between a child and his own mother. When the child's claim of damage for loss of his mother is in issue, why … should the tortfeasors go free merely because the child is illegitimate? Why should the illegitimate child be denied rights merely because of his birth out of wedlock? [L]egitimacy or illegitimacy of birth has no relation to the nature of the wrong allegedly inflicted on the mother. These children, though illegitimate, were dependent on her; she cared for them and nurtured them; they were indeed hers in the biological and in the spiritual sense; in her death they suffered wrong in the sense that any dependent would.[73]

Thus, the reality of financial and emotional dependency, *not* the mother's marital status, gives rise to the right of recovery. This is simple common sense. In some cases, moreover, granting a benefit to a surviving spouse but ignoring the deceased spouse's children can also work a hardship on them. In these situations, privileging marriage makes a distributional choice that is hard to justify from the point of view of supporting family structures that are, in fact, responsible for the raising of children. Consider the military death benefit, which goes to surviving spouses, not to those who are actually raising the deceased military member's child(ren). In one prominently reported case, a military woman's spouse received the $100,000 death benefit, while the woman's parents, who would be raising her son (from a previous relationship) received nothing.[74] This policy values marriage over children, at least in some cases.

On the other hand, where the law recognizes reality rather than formal status, it better approaches a sensible result that should appeal to those concerned with population-wide outcomes. A good example is the Family and Medical Leave Act (FMLA), which allows time off (but not pay) for family members to care for each other in cases of illness, injury, or the parenting of infants. Of relevance here, the FMLA grants the right to care for sick children not only to "parents," but to anyone who stands in loco parentis to a child.[75] The regulations then define "in loco parentis" by reference to reality, granting the right to anyone who has "day-to-day responsibilities to care for and financially support a child."[76] Further regulations then make explicit what the foregoing definition implies, stating that a "biological or legal relationship is not necessary."[77] The child's need for an involved caregiver is valued over any other consideration; the one providing care might be the cohabitating partner – of the same or opposite sex – of the child's biological (or adoptive, for that matter) mother or father. Inasmuch as legal rules should support relationships likely to support population health, the FMLA's approach is sound.

We can insert a small caveat here. It might be possible to defend the ancient legal presumption that a man whose wife bears a child is the father of that child.[78] Such a presumption of paternity might be justified in such cases; if the goal is in the best interest of the child, a good starting place for assessing that interest would be the stability often associated with an intact marriage (and a family unit), especially when compared to the disruption that could emerge from allowing a third party – here, the potential biological father – to intrude on that unit. Here we find that protecting children and privileging marriage through a specific legal rule might coalesce in a beneficial way, but our conclusion even here must be qualified: Making the presumption of paternity *rebuttable* – as some states have done – better serves the goal of child welfare.[79] Neither biology nor legal status should be determinative in all cases. While defensible in choosing the legal relationship over the biological one in the first place, the law would be better constructed were it to allow a legal advocate for the child to argue, in an appropriate case, that hardship to the child could only be avoided by holding the biological father legally and financially accountable.

In general, though, the law errs when it ties children's rights to benefits to their parents' marital status. This consideration of children's best interests again highlights the importance of a critical consideration of the exalted position that marriage holds. It turns out that marriage's special prerogatives are most justified in the legal rules that apply to their dissolution. More than other laws, the legal regime that creates and enforces the end of marriage can contribute to the public's health and welfare.

LAWS THAT PROTECT THE INTERESTS AND EXPECTATIONS OF THE PARTIES UPON DISSOLUTION OF MARRIAGE

Here I think one can make a strong case for positioning the formal, legal commitment that marriage entails over other, less formal arrangements. Often marriage involves a decision to divide labor in a way that best accommodates couples' mutual skills, interests, and goals. As noted earlier, historically (and, to an extent, even today), these "choices" were not decisions at all, but rather legally and socially coerced or mandated rules of gender-oppressing status. To the extent that marriage is now (or is becoming) a freely chosen partnership, one expectation of that union is that it will endure, or that, if it fails, the law will protect the assumption of permanence. Accordingly, spouses can forego their own economic gain and other immediate goals in favor of the greater good of the marital unit and of their children. Thus, for example, one spouse might pay for the other's higher education, with the expectation that the investment will pay off for the couple later. Or the couple might "invest" (in a different sense of that word) in their children's long-term welfare by having one spouse remain at home for a few years while the other works. Economic and emotional support are (arguably) optimized in a legal regime that honors expectations while providing for a means of escape that are not too onerous – hence, no-fault divorce.

The few community property states best reflect these expectations through the rule that most property acquired by either spouse during the course of the marriage belongs to the couple as a "community," and is therefore properly the subject of equitable division upon dissolution.[80] Even in the majority of states, the consequences of the "title rule," under which each spouse owns whatever property is titled to him or her, have been greatly mitigated by the overwhelming change in legislative and case law requiring equitable distribution of marital property, defined to include most of the property acquired by either spouse during the course of the marriage.[81] In the 1994 case *Ferguson v. Ferguson*,[82] the Mississippi Supreme Court caused that state to become the last of the title states to move to an equitable-distribution approach, noting that the title-division approach systematically undervalues the contributions of the non-wage-earning spouse. As Alicia Kelly has noted, courts continue to undervalue these contributions even today;[83] to the extent that the law unconsciously creates incentives for couples to hedge their bets on the marital partnership.

Indeed, the logic of expectation does not compel restricting the division to marital assets. Couples married for a long time often come to view all property, however and whenever acquired, as "theirs." Recognition of this common reality has led the American Law Institute (ALI) to recommend that even separate property held by each spouse at the time of marriage be progressively "recharacterized" as marital property in marriages of long duration.[84] While no states have yet adopted this suggestion,[85] a few have gone even further; they simply toss all property, belonging to either spouse (or to both) however and whenever acquired, into a great "hotchpot," where it becomes fair game for equitable distribution.[86]

No less than the division of assets, support payments are also structured with an eye toward protecting the spouses' expectations. New Jersey, for example, allows various, targeted forms of support designed to protect reasonable expectations that have now been defeated. Specifically, one spouse who supported the other's education "anticipating participation in the fruits of the earning capacity generated by that education" can be reimbursed for doing so.[87] More difficult to quantify but no less important is so-called "rehabilitation alimony," designed to enable a spouse who has put a career on hold for the good of the marital unit to attempt to "catch up" by acquiring new skills that might lead to better employment.[88]

The legal rules discussed above can be negated by prenuptial agreements, but perhaps the failure of these contracts to come into widespread use reflects an enduring view – or a fool's hope – that marriages will survive. The law's acceptance of prenuptial agreements also suggests the erosion of the status of marriage; if parties can contract around the default rules, why not simply allow the entire institution to be replaced by such mutual, a la carte understandings?

The undermining of status leads back into a discussion of the relationship between unmarried cohabitants and invites consideration of the extent to which the dissolution of such relationships should trigger default legal protections. First, marriages and cohabitation agreements are, on average, different. With rare exceptions, marrying couples have an expectation of long-term commitment; cohabitating couples, by contrast, fall along a continuum ranging from the extremely short-term to monogamous relationships lasting many decades.

Deciding on what protections, if any, to afford cohabitators after the dissolution of their relationship is related to the question of how strongly the state should attempt to coerce parties into marrying. Certainly there is an argument that the dissolution of marriage closes a cleaner, clearer circuit than the end of a nonmarital relationship, and it is therefore defensible that the law offers correspondingly sturdier protections to those ending marriages. Until recently, that commitment to clarity, combined with a strong societal disapproval of cohabitation without marriage, resulted in little protection for cohabitating couples. But surely that position is too extreme in light of today's realities.

At least since the 1970s, those same contemporary realities have caused courts to modify the rules that formerly enforced a crisp division between marriage and cohabitation. First came judicial recognition of agreements – even implied agreements – between unmarried cohabitants, pioneered by the California Supreme Court in *Marvin v. Marvin*.[89] The court's endorsement of a host of equitable remedies to protect the expectations of cohabitating parties upon dissolution has been in ascendance since then, and culminated at the beginning of the twenty-first century with the American Law Institute's Principles of the Law of Family Dissolution ("Principles").[90] The ALI devotes an entire chapter to suggested rules for first defining, and then allocating property between, domestic partners. First, the ALI calls upon the states to establish their own minimum time period during which a couple must cohabitate in order to be considered "domestic partners" entitled to distribution of the partnership's assets upon dissolution.[91] The Principles also provide, however, that a person seeking to stake a claim to property can establish the domestic partnership even without meeting a time requirement by showing that the couple "share[d] a life together."[92] This determination, in turn, is made by looking at all circumstances, many of the most common of which are set forth in a long list. On that list are the very sorts of facts that suggest the interdependency that marriage assumes: intermingling of finances; "the extent to which [the] relationship fostered the parties' economic interdependence" (or one's party's dependence on the other); the assumption of specific roles and tasks within the relationship; the extent to which the relationship made changes in the parties' lives; the assumption of responsibility for children; and the usually undervalued but often vital "emotional or physical intimacy of the parties' relationship."[93] Once a couple is established as having been in a domestic partnership, the ALI's equitable distribution principles, otherwise applicable to dissolving marriages, operate almost identically.

From the point of view of the broader welfare of society that comes from private sources of support, the ALI's approach seems balanced and likely to lead to good outcomes. On the one hand, it recognizes that many couples in long-term yet unmarried relationships in fact have expectations that make unfair a blanket rule that prohibits property division upon dissolution. On the other hand, for couples in states that do not formally recognize domestic partnership status, it ends up supporting the state's policy in favor of marriage because a party wishing to invoke the dissolution principles' protection risks uncertainty. It seems unclear whether this approach ends up supporting marriage. The ALI argues that it does because "to the extent that some individuals avoid marriage in order to avoid responsibilities to a partner, this [approach] reduces the incentive to avoid marriage because it diminishes the effectiveness of that strategy."[94] That is one side of the argument, from a party who wishes to avoid the responsibilities; the other side, from the person who wishes to gain the responsibilities, is that marriage is less "necessary" in order to do so. Of course, if the goal of state sponsorship of marriage is to encourage people to enter into long-term, committed relationships, then we should be less concerned about whether such a "responsibility seeker" actually marries.

It seems, then, that the law (to the extent that it recognizes something like the ALI approach) is moving toward a position on marriage and cohabitation that could support good public health outcomes. Marriage retains its favored position – one that recognizes the interdependency and long duration that most married couples want and expect – but the expectations of those in other long-term, committed relationships are also protected. As suggested earlier, the dichotomy presented here is too simple, because the state must always consider the signaling functions, both positive and negative, of marriage. Given that marriage is probably here to stay, at least for a good long time, questions of distributional fairness and actual need cannot be ignored by policy makers. Proper attention to sound principles of population health demands continued vigilance, criticism, and reconsideration.

Granting marriage equality to committed same-sex couples is a good, overdue, and necessary start in the project of establishing and supporting structures that support and lead to sound public health and policy outcomes, but an opportunity will have been lost if this national debate does not also lead to a broader consideration of the vast social and legal support that the institution of marriage continues to enjoy.

Notes

1. Strauss v. Horton, 207 P.3d 48 (Cal. 2009). My analysis and summary of the case is at http://wordinedgewise.org/?p=110 (posted May 26, 2009).
2. Varnum v. Brien, 763 N.W.2d 862 (Iowa 2009).
3. Perry v. Schwarzenegger, No. 3:09-cv-02292 (N.D. Cal. Jan. 8, 2010) challenges Proposition 8 on federal constitutional grounds, while the Massachusetts case, Gill v. Office of Pers. & Mgmt., 1:09-cv-10309 (D. Mass. Dec. 4, 2009) challenges only section 3 of the federal Defense of Marriage Act ("DOMA") that defines marriage for federal benefit purposes as the union of a man and a woman, even where a particular state (such as Massachusetts) has recognized same-sex marriages.
4. Vt. Stat. Ann. tit. 15 § 8 (2009).Vermont had already recognized civil unions since 2000.

5. N.H. Rev. Stat. Ann. § 457:1-a (2009).
6. Me. Rev. Stat. Ann. tit. 19 § 650-A (2009) (*repealed by* popular referendum, Question 1: People's Vote Nov. 3, 2009).
7. Religious Freedom and Civil Marriage Equality Amendment Act of 2009, A18–0248. The law took effect after Congress has had thirty legislative days to consider it. That time elapsed on March 2, 2010, and the bill then became law.
8. Kevin Miller & Judy Harrison, *Gay Marriage Repealed in Maine*, Bangor Daily News, Nov. 4, 2009, online at http://www.bangordailynews.com/detail/128048.html
9. In both states, the senates defeated the measures by margins that were unexpectedly lopsided. FoxNews.com, *New Jersey Senate Defeats Gay Marriage Bill*, http://www.foxnews.com/politics/2010/01/07/new-jersey-gay-marriage/ (accessed February 14, 2010) (The New Jersey Senate defeated the measure by a vote of 20 to 14, whereas the New York Senate rejected the gay marriage bill, 38 to 24).
10. Trip Jennings, *Domestic Partnership Bill on Life Support*, New Mexico Independent, Feb. 2, 2010, online at http://newmexicoindependent.com/46247/domestic-partnership-bill-on-life-support. In Hawaii, Governor Linda Lingle's veto of a civil unions bill resulted in the filing of a lawsuit by six gay and lesbian couples, alleging that excluding them from the rights of marriage violates the State Constitution. Card J. Williams, *Same-Sex Couples in Hawaii Look to California*, L.A. Times, Aug. 28, 2010, online at http://www.latimes.com/news/nationworld/nation/la-na-gay-marriage-hawaii-20100829,0,2392642.story
11. Compare, for example, David Brooks, *The Power of Marriage*, N.Y. TIMES, Nov. 22, 2003, online at http://www.nytimes.com/2003/11/22/opinion/the-power-of-marriage.html (supporting same-sex marriages as in line with conservative value of fidelity) with Heather MacDonald, *Reengineering the Family*, National Review Online, http://article.nationalreview.com/423469/reengineering-the-family/heather-mac-donald?page=1 (Feb. 1, 2010) (worrying that recognition of same-sex marriages will further erode the connections between biology, marriage, and parenting).
12. See, for example, Libby Adler, *The Gay Agenda*, 16 Mich. J. Gender & L. 147 (2009). Professor Adler argues that focus on marriage diverts the LGBT community from other, more vital efforts, and causes the mainstreaming of gays and lesbians in order to make gay relationships seem less threatening.
13. 531 U.S. 98 (2000).
14. See, for example, William N. Eskridge, Jr. & Darren R. Spedale, Gay Marriage: For Better or for Worse: What We've Learned from the Evidence (2007).
15. See, for example, Baker v. Nelson, 191 N.W.2d 185 (Min. 1971). Singer v. Hara, 522 P.2d 1187 (Wash. Ct. App. 1974).

16. Baehr v. Lewin, 852 P.2d 44 (Haw. 1993) (court held that excluding same-sex couples from marriage was sex discrimination and sent the case back to trial court for a determination of whether the state had met the high burden of justifying such discrimination).
17. 28 U.S.C. § 1738C (2010).
18. 142 Cong. Rec. S10117 (statement of Sen. Faircloth).
19. 142 Cong. Rec. S10109 (statement of Sen. Byrd).
20. 142 Cong. Rec. H7494 (statement of Rep. Smith).
21. 142 Cong. Rec. H7486 (statement of Rep. Meehan). ("Our society encourages and values a commitment to long-term monogamous relationships – and we honor those commitments by creating the legal institution of marriage. If we then deny the right of marriage to a segment of our population, we devalue their commitment without compelling reasons... We can't have it both ways. Protecting everyone's right to make a legal commitment to another is a defense of marriage.")
22. 744 A.2d 864 (Vt. 1999).
23. Vt. Stat. Ann. tit. 15 § 1201 (2000) (*repealed by* Vt. Stat. Ann. tit. 15 § 8 (2009).
24. Developments are so rapid in this area of the law that one seeking up-to-date information is cautioned to consult any of numerous, reliable web sources. See, for example, http://www.hrc.org/issues/marriage/marriage_laws.asp (providing summaries of all fifty states on marriage and relationship recognition) and http://www.domawatch.org/index.php (summarizing both legislation and litigation relating to both marriage recognition and the Defense of Marriage Act).
25. Andersen v. King County, 138 P.3d 963 (Wash. 2006).
26. Hernandez v. Robles, 855 N.E.2d 1 (N.Y. 2006).
27. Conaway v. Deane, 932 A.2d 571 (Md. 2007).
28. Goodridge v. Department of Public Health, 798 N.E.2d 941 (Mass. 2003).
29. In In Re Marriage Cases, 183 P.3d 384 (Cal. 2008), the court held that denying marriage licenses to same-sex couples was a denial of the equal protection guaranteed by the state's constitution, but in Strauss v. Horton, 207 P.3d 48 (Cal. 2009)., the court ruled that the ballot initiative known as Proposition 8 had validly amended that same constitution to remove the right to marry from same-sex couples (who nonetheless retained the right to enter into domestic partnerships with all of the rights and benefits of marriage).
30. Kerrigan v. Commissioner of Public Health, 957 A.2d 407 (Conn. 2008).
31. Varnum v. Brien, 763 N.W.2d 862 (Iowa 2009).
32. Goodridge v. Dept. of Pub. Health, 798 N.E.2d 941, 954 (Mass. 2003) (citations omitted) (quoting Opinion of the Justices, 168 N.E.2d 858 (1960)).

33. *Id.* (quoting Ludec v. Commonwealth, 657 N.E.2d 755 (1995)).
34. William N. Eskridge, Jr., THE CASE FOR SAME-SEX MARRIAGE: FROM SEXUAL LIBERTY TO CIVILIZED COMMITMENT 106 (1996).
35. *Goodridge*, 798 N.E. at 948.
36. *Id.* at 954 (quoting French v. McAnarney, 195 N.E. 714, 715 (Mass. 1935).
37. *Id.*
38. *Andersen*, 138 P.3d at 985.
39. For example, two journalists investigated the financial cost of being a gay, as opposed to straight, couple, and discovered that, in a "worst case scenario," the gay couple would incur more than $200,000 in costs over their straight counterparts. Tara Siegel Bernard and Ron Lieber, *The High Price of Being a Gay Couple*, N.Y. TIMES, Oct. 2, 2009, online at http://www.nytimes.com/2009/10/03/your-money/03money.html?_r=1&em (accessed Feb. 19, 2010).
40. Linda J. Waite & Maggie Gallagher, THE CASE FOR MARRIAGE, at 200. Gallagher opposes marriage equality whereas Waite favors it, but the two write that a same-sex couple would likely realize at least some of the benefits that they impute to marital status.
41. I have explored these issues, with citations to the emerging social science literature and with a fuller narration in John G. Culhane, *Beyond Rights and Morality: The Overlooked Public Health Argument for Same-Sex Marriage*, 17 LAW & SEXUALITY 7, 27–37 (2008).
42. See, for example, Carolyn Vogler, *Cohabiting Couples: Rethinking Money in the Household at the Beginning of the Twenty First Century*, 53 SOC. REV. 1, 12–13 (2005).
43. Studies have looked at the overall economics of same-sex couples, but not specifically at financial interdependence. See Dan A. Black et al., *The Economics of Lesbian and Gay Families*, 21 J. ECON. PERSPECTIVES 53 (2007). One exception appears to be a study by Marieka Klawitter, summarized in Shoshana Grossbard & Lisa K. Jepsen, *The Economics of Gay and Lesbian Couples: Introduction to a Special Issue on Gay and Lesbian Households*, 6 REV. ECON. HOUSEHOLD 311, 319 (2008) (finding that 54% of gay couples and 63% of lesbian couples, as compared to 83% of married heterosexuals and 24% of unmarried heterosexual couples, had joint accounts).
44. See Vogler, *supra* note 41 at 12 (finding that cohabitators are just as likely as married couples to be financially interdependent when they have a biological child together; Catherine Kenney, *Cohabiting Couple, Filing Jointly? Resource Pooling and U.S. Poverty Policies*, 53 FAM. REL. 237, 244 (2004) (finding only small differences between biological children and stepchildren in this regard).
45. Lawrence v. Texas, 539 U.S. 558, 605 (U.S. 2003) (Scalia, A., dissenting).
46. Hernandez v. Robles, 855 N.E.2d at 15; Andersen, 138 P.3d at 1002.

47. Hernandez, 855 N.E.2d at 32 (Kaye, C.J., dissenting).
48. *Id.* (Kaye, C.J., dissenting).
49. 763 N.W.2d at 904.
50. State v. Green, 99 P.3d 820 (Utah 2004), quoted in Andersen, 138 P.3d at 1008.
51. See Loving v. Virginia, 388 U.S. 1 (U.S. 1967) (ban on interracial marriages violates guarantee of equal protection); Turner v. Safley, 482 U.S. 78 (U.S. 1987) (ban on prisoner marriages is an unconstitutional deprivation of liberty); Zablocki v. Redhail, 434 U.S. 374 (U.S. 1978).
52. In Re Marriage Cases, 183 P.3d at 779–80.
53. *Goodridge*, 798 N.E. at 976–77.
54. See, for example, Martha Albertson Fineman, THE NEUTERED MOTHER, THE SEXUAL FAMILY & OTHER TWENTIETH CENTURY TRAGEDIES 228 (1995).
55. *Goodridge*, 798 N.E. at 964.
56. I discuss the evidence in *Culhane, supra* note 41. Anita Bernstein in particular has been effective in deconstructing the assumptions behind the "marriage is best" school. Anita Bernstein, *For and Against Marriage: A Revision*, 102 MICH. L. REV. 129, 140–41 (2003); Anita Bernstein, *Afterword: Narrowing the Status of Marriage*, in MARRIAGE PROPOSALS: QUESTIONING A LEGAL STATUS 233 (Anita Bernstein ed., 2006).
57. Cynthia Grant Bowman, *Social Science and Legal Policy: The Case of Heterosexual Cohabitation*, 9 J. L. FAM. STUD. 1, 13 (2007).
58. Amy L. Wax, *The Family Law Doctrine of Equivalence*, 107 MICH. L. REV. 999 (2009)(reviewing Nancy D. Polikoff, BEYOND (STRAIGHT AND GAY) MARRIAGE: VALUING ALL FAMILIES UNDER THE LAW (2008)).
59. Baker v. State, 744 A.2d 864, 911–12 (Vt. 1999) (Johnson, J., concurring and dissenting).
60. Bernstein, *supra* note 56, at 196.
61. See Gilbert Herdt & Robert Kertzner, *I Do, but I Can't: The Impact of Marriage Denial on the Mental Health and Sexual Citizenship of Lesbians and Gay Men in the United States*, 3 SEXUALITY RESEARCH & SOC. POL'Y 35, 35–37, 40–41 (2006).
62. Jonathan Rauch, GAY MARRIAGE: WHY IT IS GOOD FOR GAYS, GOOD FOR STRAIGHTS, AND GOOD FOR AMERICA (2004).
63. 26 U.S.C.S. § 1(a) (2010).
64. 42 U.S.C.S. § 402 (2010); 42 U.S.C.S § 416 (a)-(c), (f)-(g) (2010)(defining the terms "wife," "husband," "widow," and "widower.").
65. 8 U.S.C. § 1151(a)(1), (b)(2)(A)(i) (2010).
66. KAN. STAT. ANN. § 79–15, 126(g) (2008); MICH. COMP. LAWS § 207.505(i) (2009).
67. M. Henner, A COMPENDIUM OF STATE STATUTES AND INTERNATIONAL TREATIES IN TRUST AND ESTATE LAW 132 (1985).

68. Wrongful death statutes typically name the class of eligible claimants, either specifically or by reference to the rules of intestacy. As might therefore be expected, spouses are included; cohabitating partners are not. Injuries to intimates are covered by the common law torts of loss of consortium – covering the loss of society, sex, and (less frequently today) "service" – and by negligent infliction of emotional distress. With few exceptions, courts have restricted standing to recover under these torts to "family" members, as defined by marriage or by close blood relation. A few states have begun to make inroads on these strict rules, however. I have written about these matters in depth. See John G. Culhane, *Even More Wrongful Death: Statutes Divorced from Reality*, 32 FORDHAM URBAN L.J. 171 (2005); John G. Culhane, *A "Clanging Silence": Same-Sex Couples and Tort Law*, 89 KY. L. J. 911 (2000–01).
69. 8 U.S.C. § 1227(a)(1)(G) (2010).
70. As of the middle of 2009, for example, well over half of the Fortune 500 companies granted domestic partner benefits to their employees. See http://www.upi.com/Business_News/Business_Daily/2009/06/03/286-of-Fortune-500-companies-offer-domestic-partner-benefits/18316/
71. Nancy D. Polikoff, BEYOND (STRAIGHT AND GAY) MARRIAGE 126 (2008).
72. 391 U.S. 68 (1968).
73. *Id.* at 71–72.
74. Donna St. George, *The Forgotten Families: Grandparents Raising Slain Soldiers' Children are Denied a Government Benefit Intended to Sustain the Bereaved*, WASH POST, Dec. 16, 2007, at A1.
75. 29 U.S.C. § 2611(12) (2008) ("'[S]on or daughter' means a biological, adopted, or foster child, a stepchild, a legal ward, or a child or a person standing in loco parentis ...").
76. 29 C.F.R. § 825.122(c)(3) (2009).
77. *Id.*
78. CAL. FAM. CODE §7540 (2009); MINN. STAT. §257.55 (2009); Jeffrey Blustein, GENETIC TIES & THE FAMILY: THE IMPACT OF PATERNITY TESTING ON PARENTS AND CHILDREN 39 (2005).
79. See, for example, MINN. STAT. §257.55 (2009) (presumption can be rebutted through clear and convincing evidence; MINN. STAT. §257.57 (2009) (describing when and how the claim can be brought.).
80. There are nine community property states: Texas, Arizona, New Mexico, California, Wisconsin, Idaho, Louisiana, Nevada, and Washington. Alaska allows couples to "opt in" to the community property regime. See, for example, Robert L. Mennell, COMMUNITY PROPERTY IN A NUTSHELL (1988); Jeremy T. Ware, *Section 1014(b)(6) and Boundaries of Community Property*, 5 NEV. L. J. 704 (2005)(Discussing Alaska's "opt in" approach to the community property doctrine).
81. For consideration of different approaches to defining and dividing marital property, see Leslie Joan Harris et al., FAMILY LAW 354–86 (2010).

82. 639 So. 2d 921 (Miss. 1994).
83. Alicia Brokars Kelly, *Rehabilitating Partnership Marriage As A Theory of Wealth Distribution at Divorce: In Recognition of A Shared Life*, 19 Wis. Women's L.J. 141 (Fall 2004).
84. Principles of the Law and Family Dissolution: Analysis and Recommendations §4.12(1) (A.L.I. 2002).
85. See Michael R. Clisham & Robin Fretwell Wilson, *American Law Institute's Principles of Family Dissolution, Eight Years After Adoption: Guiding Principles or Obligatory Footnote*, 42 Fam. L.Q. 573, 589, 603 (2008).
86. For a then-current listing of "hotchpot" states, see Elijah L. Milne, *Recharacterizing Separate Property at Divorce*, 84 U. Det. Mercy L. Rev. 307, 312 n.44 (2007).
87. N.J. Stat. Ann. § 2A:34–23(e) (West 2009).
88. *Id.*, § 2A:34–23(d).
89. 557 P.2d 106, 110 (Cal. 1976).
90. Principles, *supra* note 84.
91. *Id.* § 6.03(1), § 6.04(1)-(2).
92. *Id.* § 6.03(7).
93. *Id.* § 6.03(7)(c)-(l).
94. *Id.* § 6.02 cmt. b.

PART III DIMENSIONS OF VIOLENCE

5 USING PUBLIC HEALTH TO REFORM THE LEGAL AND JUSTICE RESPONSE TO DOMESTIC VIOLENCE

Evan Stark

INTRODUCTION

The model of abuse that guides society's understanding and response to domestic violence has failed us. Based on a straightforward analogy between domestic violence and assault, this model identifies the seriousness of a partner's acts according to legal degrees of criminal abuse: according to how much violence is involved and the degree of injury inflicted. No matter how well intended, application of this model to protect women and their children has been disastrous for all concerned. This is because the phenomenon that advocates and policy makers are trying to manage and for which millions of primarily female victims and their children seek help annually has little in common with the types of assault the paradigm describes. For a way out of this morass, I turn to public health.

Society's response to violence against women in families and relationships has been revolutionized since the first battered women shelters opened in the early 1970s. The material foundation of this revolution is women's increasing importance to the economy worldwide and their corresponding attainment of formal legal equality. On the ground, the revolution has been characterized by a vast array of legal reforms and the adoption of public policies designed to support the basic goals of women's advocacy groups worldwide – enhanced safety and support for victims and accountability for offenders. These changes are supported by the development of a vast knowledge base documenting the extent, seriousness, dynamic and, context of violence against women in relationships.

At first glance, the reforms in law and justice seem to have been effective. Whereas there were virtually no services explicitly designed for battered women until the mid-1970s, as of 2010, more than three million women and children were being serviced by shelters and other community-based programs annually in the United States, and police were arresting more than one million offenders. Every state now hosts specialized Batterer Intervention Programs (BIPs) whereas criminal and family courts routinely provide victims with emergency protection and relief. Over the last few decades, partner-inflicted fatality and severe injury have declined significantly, almost certainly because of these and concurrent changes in service and support.

Even though partner violence against women is no longer "just life," there are increasing signs that the domestic violence revolution is stalled, particularly in the areas of law enforcement, protection, and support where most efforts at reform have focused. Arrest in domestic violence cases may be commonplace. Even so, only a small proportion of reported incidents result in arrest and only a tiny proportion of those arrested receive any serious punishment. This is because partner abuse is typically treated as what amounts to a second-class misdemeanor except in those rare cases where abuse causes a fatal or near-fatal injury. As many as 27 percent of abused women using shelters report being sexually assaulted by their partners "often" or "all the time."[1] Yet these incidents are almost never prosecuted as rapes. Despite widespread recognition of the threats posed by abuse to life and liberty, confusion remains about how to best represent battered women who retaliate violently against their abusive partner, commit other crimes in situations where they have been entrapped, or who seek to limit their abusive partner's access to children in disputed custody cases.

Moreover, the treatment of victims and perpetrators of domestic violence varies so greatly among criminal, family, and child welfare cases that the respective proceedings have been described as separate "planets."[2] For instance, family courts often order mothers to provide access to their children for an abusive partner with whom they have been ordered to have no contact by the criminal court or in a child welfare proceeding. Conversely, the same man who is prosecuted for domestic violence may be framed as a "good enough" father in family court.

Close examination also suggests that optimism about the effects of intervention may be premature. For instance, men have benefited far more than women from the decline in partner-caused fatality. Between 1974, when the first shelters opened in the United States, and 2004, the incidence of homicides by female partners declined 72 percent, far higher than the overall drop in homicide, almost certainly because women now have options of retaliation when they feel they or their children are being threatened in an abusive situation. By contrast, the incidence of men killing female partners has dropped only 36 percent, far less than the overall drop in homicide.[3] Since abusive men tend to kill female partners during a separation or when they are threatened with separation, the same options that afford women temporary safety may actually have increased their risk in the long term. Moreover, whereas the most injurious forms of partner assault have declined, so-called minor partner violence against women has risen sharply during this same period. As we shall see, because of their frequency, these acts of "minor" violence comprise the infrastructure of coercive control, the most prevalent form of partner abuse. Coercive control is typically more devastating than the severe assaults that receive most publicity.

This chapter describes the promise held out for reform in domestic violence law and the criminal justice response, and the failure of reforms to live up to this promise. I argue that this failure reflects a disjuncture between the domestic violence paradigm that underlies the reform strategy and the lived experience of abuse victims with perpetrators. I focus my criticism on a specific aspect of the current model: its adaptation of a narrow, incident-based definition of violence that equates abuse with discrete episodes of assault, and on the associated calculus of physical injury and psychological trauma used to assess whether and how to intervene. The analogy in medicine to the violent-incident model is a model of domestic violence as an acute or emergent health problem. For a contrasting picture, I draw core concepts from public health, particularly its holistic focus on well-being, its emphasis on the socio-historical context of population health, and its recognition that inequality is a principal source of health disparities. This approach allows us to recognize domestic violence as coercive control, an ongoing, multifaceted, and patterned course of conduct that elicits a range of harms to personhood and political identity extending far beyond threats to physical security. From this perspective, women's experience of domestic violence is analogous to a chronic illness – one that is rooted in sexual inequality – rather than to an acute disease. Adapting this public health model could put criminal justice and legal intervention in cases of domestic violence on a more productive course.

The Criminal Justice and Legal Response to Domestic Violence: Promise and Disappointment

The Promise

The legal and police response before shelters opened in the early 1970s has been widely criticized. By the mid-1960s, although there were no legal protections specifically designed for abuse victims, "domestics" were a more common source of police calls than all other violent acts combined. To manage these complaints, calls were lumped into a very low-status category with other family trouble calls, and callers were often diverted to other services. Among the impediments to an aggressive police response was the distaste for social work among officers, ambiguity about men's prerogatives in these situations, the mixed response the arrival of law enforcement elicited, and the belief that responding officers faced serious risks.[4] Because most domestic violence incidents were classified as misdemeanor or simple assaults, and police had to actually witness a misdemeanor to make an arrest without a warrant, they understood their role in these situations as peripheral as well as distasteful. They were expected to defuse tension and impose order rather than make an arrest. Studies in Washington, D.C., Boston, and Chicago revealed that police were about four times more likely to arrest strangers for assault than partners.[5]

Between the opening of the first shelters and the passage of the Violence against Women Act in 1994, the legal and criminal justice response to partner violence changed more profoundly than in the preceding three centuries. Among the factors contributing to the changed response were pressure from advocates based on a growing awareness of the harms caused by abuse; litigation brought against police departments in New York City, Los Angeles, Torrington, Connecticut, and other major cities, alleging the denial of equal protection under the law when police failed to respond appropriately; and research showing the relative efficacy of arrest compared to nonarrest in reducing domestic violence.

These developments were then supported by legal reforms. Between 1974 and 1994, most states amended their laws to specifically identify domestic violence as a form of criminal assault, and every state expanded women's access to criminal and civil remedies from battering, including court orders restraining offenders from contacting their victims.[6] These reforms were largely based on recognition that violence by partners was treated less seriously than similar acts by strangers and on the equal protection guarantees of both the U.S. Constitution and state constitutions. Today, in all but two states, the arrest of batterers is mandatory, and a majority of states authorize their courts to order the abuser into treatment. Most jurisdictions also utilize counseling or psycho-education for perpetrators provided by BIPs. Typically, these are nine- to twelve-session programs designed to teach perpetrators how to recognize and manage behaviors that may lead to violence. Many of these programs hold the threat of prison over offenders who fail to attend.

A number of administrative and policy changes have also been widely implemented to facilitate the successful implementation of legal and justice reform, particularly in the face of the increased workload created by a more aggressive state response. These include specialized police domestic violence response teams, dockets, or courts; integrated family violence courts (where the same judge hears civil as well as criminal charges against an offender); prosecutorial units dedicated to domestic violence (so-called vertical prosecution); "no drop," or evidence-based prosecution policies; and justice centers where victims can access a range of services in "one-stop shopping." Domestic violence education is now required to a greater or lesser extent for police, probation and parole, judges, and other court personnel. According to a 1998 study of the nation's largest police departments, almost 99 percent of officers make arrests "the usual response" if domestic violence occurred in the officer's presence, 81 percent if it occurred before police arrived, and 28 percent if violence was threatened but had not occurred.[7] Emphasis in the civil arena has been on relief, primarily through protection orders, and on putting domestic violence at the center of consideration in the award of custody.

The seriousness of battering justifies this response. The men arrested for domestic violence tend to be chronic offenders, averaging almost fourteen prior criminal charges on their record for all crimes, a little less than half of these for assault.[8] Many of the violent acts that prompt domestic violence arrests would be classified as felonies if committed against strangers, and most of the men arrested resemble the worst class of felons: they are repeat offenders, typically unrepentant, and frequently retaliate against, threaten, or otherwise intimidate their victims after an arrest.[9] All of these facets suggest a high-profile crime worthy of an aggressive criminal justice response.

Recognizing the risks posed by domestic violence, most states accept the so-called "battered woman's defense," where a history of domestic violence provides a context for mitigating a criminal charge or a sentence or arguing self-defense in an abuse-related assault or homicide. Based on this approach, governors in Ohio, Massachusetts, and several other states have pardoned abused women previously sentenced to jail for killing violent partners.[10]

More than 100 studies have shown that exposure to domestic violence harms children, with the degree of harm dependent on the duration and type of exposure as well as on the developmental age and resilience of children who are exposed.[11] Most child welfare agencies now recognize the potential harm to children in domestic violence cases, and many have integrated domestic violence expertise into the assessment process. Based largely on the belief that children were not safe if their mothers were unsafe, Congress passed House Concurrent Resolution 172, known widely as the "Morella" resolution after its drafter, Congresswoman Morella (R–Maryland), who introduced it to the Committee on the Judiciary jointly with Congressman Miller (D–California) in 1989. The resolution recommended that state courts give presumptive custody to victims of abuse. All but two states changed their custody laws to favor abuse victims.[12]

THE FAILURE OF REFORM

Change in criminal justice policy has been dramatic. Arrest reduces subsequent violence better than any other intervention. However, only a small proportion of domestic violence incidents overall result in calls to police; most victims of partner violence have called police at least once and often multiple times. Nonetheless, offenders are actually arrested in only a small proportion of these cases, few of these cases are prosecuted, and almost no offenders go to jail.

The problems with the police response are illustrated by evidence from Charlotte, North Carolina, considered a model jurisdiction in terms of domestic violence law enforcement. Researchers found that out of 47,687 calls classified by Charlotte police under the city's domestic violence code, mandatory arrest policies were applied to just 785 (.016 percent) either because the case was misclassified, no "spouse-like" situation was found at the scene, a domestic violence crime could not be verified, or the perpetrator had fled.[13] Moreover, fewer than 1 percent of the men in Charlotte who were arrested, convicted, and sentenced for domestic violence actually served time in jail. Data from other cities confirms these findings. A study of the efficacy of mandatory arrest in Milwaukee indicated that 95 percent of the men arrested for domestic assault were not prosecuted and only 1 percent of them were convicted.[14] In England, the attrition from a police call to imprisonment is 99.5 percent.[15] The result is that men who batter their partners are only slightly more likely to be held accountable for their actions today than when the domestic violence revolution began.

Whatever potential effect arrest and prosecution may have on deterring an offender's subsequent violence is minimized by the small proportion of cases in which sanctions are applied. Returning to Charlotte, we find that almost a third (31 percent) of the offenders arrested for domestic violence committed another assault on their initial victim within two weeks of arrest, and that almost two-thirds (61.5 percent) had done so within six months after their initial contact with police.[16]

Other justice interventions have proved equally ineffective. Restraining or protection orders prohibiting an abusive partner from contacting a victim have been an important front-line legal response to abuse and appear to improve the safety of certain classes of victims. However, it is unclear that women who maintain such orders are any safer than victims who drop them. Klein found no differences in re-abuse among victims who maintained their orders and those who dropped them by the one-year termination date or within a two-year period.[17]

BIPs have fared even worse than protection orders. Of the five best-designed studies of these programs, three show they have no effect on subsequent violence, one shows they may reduce the *rate* of re-offending over time, and one found that men who attended the programs were actually more likely to re-offend than men who were simply sent home after trial.[18]

Domestic violence reforms may have been even less successful on the civil than on the criminal side. In 2001, a federal class action law suit, *Nicholson v. Williams*, was filed by mothers who alleged that their children were being removed to foster care by New York City's child protection agency and they were being charged with neglect solely because they had been abused.[19] The federal court ruled in favor of the plaintiff mothers and children and enjoined the child protection agency from continuing this practice. While New York may have stopped this punitive response to abuse, anecdotal evidence suggests it remains widespread in other jurisdictions.

Administrative directives to favor abused women in disputed custody cases have been greatly weakened by the fact that many of the same states that direct judges to give domestic violence important weight in custodial decisions also have "friendly parent" provisions that constrain judges to favor shared custody or co-parenting. In light of these pressures, and with advocates for so-called Fathers' Rights at their back, many family judges simply dismiss claims of domestic violence as unfounded, embrace the allegations of "parental alienation" that are being widely used by fathers to counter claims of abuse, and find victims who press their claims "uncooperative." Studies in New York, Kentucky, California, and Washington show that cases involving domestic violence are routinely referred for mediation (even where law prohibits such referrals), and that disclosure of abuse leads to worse outcomes for victims than nondisclosure.[20] In Seattle, Kernic studied all couples with minor children petitioning for dissolution of marriage in the target year.[21] She found that of the cases with a documented pre-existing history of abuse (a total of 257) typically involving a prior arrest and/or protection order, almost three-quarters had either no mention of domestic violence in the marital dissolution file (47.6 percent) or only unsubstantiated allegations (28.9 percent). After adjusting for a range of potential confounding factors (such as allegations that the mother had herself been violent), mothers with a history of abuse were no more likely than the nonabused mothers to be granted child custody. Whereas fathers whose abuse was substantiated in both criminal and family court files were more likely to be denied child visitation and assigned to relevant services than comparison fathers, the vast majority of abusive fathers (83 percent) had no such restrictions. Conversely, the outcomes for fathers whose abusive history was not included in the dissolution file or included only as an allegation were no different than the outcomes for nonabusive fathers.

The two major goals of these reforms in law, criminal justice, policy, and intervention by child welfare were to hold offenders accountable and better protect domestic violence victims and their children. As we've seen, these changes have not affected the improvements they intended and, in some cases, may actually have made things worse, as in the child welfare response. From the start of the battered women's movement, victims insisted "violence wasn't the worst part." Our failure to understand what they meant turns out to be a major reason why the domestic violence revolution has stalled.

THE PROBLEM OF THE DEFINITION

Explanations are readily available for why specific interventions may have failed. For instance, the police response to domestic violence is shaped by a lack of funding for domestic violence teams, the social class and marital status of the partners, victim preference, whether the victim or a neighbor initiates the complaint, whether the victim requires medical attention, whether the victim has a protection or restraining order, whether the offender is present when the officer arrives, whether the offender (or the victim) is drunk or abusive to the officer, and whether the officer believes violence is normal for a specific subgroup.[22] The limited effectiveness of protection orders is shaped by similar factors as well as by the presence of stalking, a signal that the offender intends to maintain contact no matter what. Training, normative pressure to support adult victims, and the appointment of domestic violence specialists influence the child welfare response. However, an underlying reason why reforms in the legal and justice response have failed to fulfill their initial promise is the huge gap that separates the working assumptions on which domestic violence interventions are based across a broad spectrum of what I term the "domestic violence paradigm" and the actual context, dynamics, and consequence of partner abuse.

At the heart of the domestic violence paradigm is a definition of abuse taken from the criminal justice understanding of assault. This definition equates partner abuse with an "act carried out with the intention or perceived intention of causing physical pain or injury to another person."[23] In theory, applying this definition should have been a simple matter of determining whether partners or former partners are responsible for assaults and then sanctioning these offenders (and protecting their victims) as we now do in cases of stranger assault. Instead, this definition has failed to facilitate either identification or intervention. More than three decades after researchers started studying the problem in large numbers, for instance, widespread disagreement remains about the prevalence of abuse, who commits it, the principal causes and dynamics involved, and what types of assistance are required or effective. To cite just one example, surveys using the incident-specific definition have generated vastly divergent estimates of the annual prevalence of woman abuse; based on whether respondents were asked about violent acts used to address "conflicts" (136/1,000), violent acts that elicited fear or "safety" concerns (15/1,000), or violent acts they considered a "crime" (7/1,000).[24] Without agreement on which phenomenon should be classified as abuse or how to recognize it, it is unreasonable to expect courts, police, or other law or justice personnel to agree on the nature of the problem or to mount a consistent or effective response.

The definition of partner abuse contains three core assumptions: (1) abuse can be equated with violence; (2) this violence should be disaggregated into discrete episodes of coercion; and (3) the severity of the domestic violence, hence which cases should receive priority and whether and how criminal justice and the legal system should intervene, can be assessed by applying a straightforward calculus of physical or psychological harm to these episodes. Each of these assumptions is contradicted by extensive evidence on the context, dynamic, and consequence of partner violence drawn from studies conducted at points of service, general population surveys, crime surveys, such as the National Crime Victimization Survey (NCVS), and from the National Violence Against Women Survey (NVAWS) conducted in 1995–1996. These data consistently show that the hallmark of women's physical abuse is frequent, but predominantly minor assault extending over a considerable time period, and that abuse typically includes a range of oppressive, degrading, and exploitive tactics among which violence is often not the most salient or consequential. This evidence also shows that abuse has a cumulative impact on victims that is far more devastating than suggested by the results of a particular episode, and that extends far beyond injury. No other class of assault victims experiences anything approaching the effects of male partner abuse on women, including men assaulted or otherwise abused by female partners.

Based on case evidence and data from the several dozen population or point-of-service studies that have asked about abusive tactics other than violence, advocates and some social scientists have attempted to broaden the official definition of domestic violence to include so-called "psychological abuse" and/or "control."[25] Despite these efforts, major intervention strategies and policies continue to focus on violence almost exclusively.

Depending on whether the data are drawn from arrests, shelter populations, or BIPs, in 60 to 80 percent of the cases where women are victimized by male partners, violence is accompanied by a range of tactics designed to isolate, intimidate, exploit, degrade, and control them as well as to hurt them physically. The most widely cited complements to physical abuse are other coercive or threatening behaviors such as stalking and sexual assault. But researchers have also identified a range of structural constraints that accompany violence in a majority of cases and involve material deprivations sufficient to directly induce a condition of subordination and dependence. In one well-designed study, six out of ten men arrested for domestic violence reported they had taken their partner's money as well as assaulted them, and had restricted their partners in three or more additional ways.[26] In a British sample of women who used shelters, 79 percent reported their partners had limited their access to money some or all the time.[27] There is also evidence from both the U.S. and the UK that in a majority of cases for which women seek shelter or perpetrators are referred for batterer intervention, the abusive partner monitors his victim's movement and behavior, keeps her from working or from going to work, harasses her, threatens to take the children or have them placed in foster care, uses tactics such as genital inspection to sexually degrade her, and deploys a range of other tactics to frighten or cut her off from friends, family, helping professionals or other sources of support.[28] In the U.S. study that included interviews with offenders referred to counseling, half of the men admitted that, in addition to threatening them physically, they had used at least six behaviors that controlled female partners, including "monitoring time" (59 percent), "treating like an inferior" (62 percent), and "ordering around" (58 percent), with between 20 and 40 percent acknowledging they kept their partners from seeing friends (37 percent) and/or their family (20 percent), prevented them from leaving the house (26 percent), and restricted their use of the car (21 percent).[29] Men also reported being subjected by female partners to some of these tactics (such as "being treated like an inferior"). The vast majority of structural constraints, however, were imposed by men. For instance, males comprised 82 percent of the perpetrators who kept their partners from getting "self-help," 76 percent who forbade a partner to work, and 70 percent who prevented a partner from leaving the house.[30] Even if men impose structural constraints on their partners more frequently than women do, these tactics are not intrinsically gendered. Importantly, however, in a significant proportion of abuse cases, control includes the micromanagement of activities specific to how women enact their default roles as wives, mothers, and housekeepers, and may include "rules" about everything from how they dress, walk, talk on the phone, clean, or cook to how they toilet or make love. There is growing evidence that the victimization associated with these types of controls can elicit the experience of subordination and entrapment even among women who have never been physically assaulted. In one study, 25 percent of the women who exhibited the classic signs of abuse have never been physically assaulted by a partner.[31]

The second and related assumption is that the assaults targeted by intervention consist of discrete episodes that should be identified, assessed, and/or charged based on the characteristics of the particular incident. While some jurisdictions impose more severe sanctions for offenders who have repeated domestic violence convictions, each incident constitutes a separate offense tried independently of the others. Of course, safety planning, protection orders, counseling for batterers, and other intervention strategies would presumably be unnecessary if domestic violence was limited to a single event. Nevertheless, their underlying presumption is that there is sufficient space 'between' episodes (called "time to violence" in the treatment literature) for perpetrators and victims to exercise the decisional autonomy needed to end the abuse.

In fact, partner assault is limited to isolated incidents in only a tiny proportion of cases. The average victim suffers between 3.5 and 8 assaults annually, with well over a third reporting experiencing "serial" abuse (once a week or more).[32] Meanwhile, the average duration of an abusive relationship is between 5.5 and 7 years.[33] When we combine the frequency of abusive violence with the co-occurrence of other coercive and controlling tactics, it is not surprising to find that victims typically define the experience of abuse as "ongoing" rather than as episodic. In my forensic practice, it is by no means unusual to come across cases that involve hundreds of assaults, even several thousand.

Following logically from the emphasis on discrete episodes of violence is the third set of assumptions key to the paradigm – that injury is the best marker of abuse, that its severity can be roughly assessed by applying a calculus of physical injury and psychological trauma to partner assaults, and therefore, that the need for and intensity of intervention can be gauged to the degree of violence used and injury inflicted. In terms of state statutes, the physical harms required for a probable cause to arrest run the gamut from Wisconsin, where only a complaint of pain is required, to Nebraska, which requires visible injuries. Regardless of statutory differences, police consistently report that injury is their most important consideration in arrests. A similar calculus is applied by criminal and family courts as well as by other institutional providers, including some shelters, either out of the belief that domestic violence could not have been serious if no injury resulted or as a simple matter of rationing resources according to a widely accepted principle. The corollary of this assumption is that low levels of physical violence are less harmful than injurious violence. In the National Family Violence Surveys (NFVS) for instance, acts with a low probability of causing injury were classified as "not abuse" or as a "normal" part of interacting with children or a spouse.[34]

Of course, partner abuse often involves severe and even fatal violence, as the current emphasis on injury suggests. Among a sample of 500 women who had sought shelters in the UK, for instance, 70 percent had been choked or strangled at least once, 60 percent had been forced to have sex against their will, 26 percent had been "beaten unconscious," and 24 percent had been cut or stabbed at least once.[35] However, the vast majority of reported incidents of abusive violence are noninjurious and "minor," at least from a medical or criminal justice standpoint, falling into the category of violent acts population researchers consider "normal." The minor nature of most violence reported to population surveys is reflected in the small proportion of respondents who have sought outside assistance. However, their minor nature also characterizes the overwhelming proportion of incidents presented at sites where we might expect to find the most serious cases of abuse. Thus, abuse is noninjurious or involves only minor injury in 96 percent of the cases where women seek help in the Emergency Room or call police (97 percent) or report abuse to the military (93 percent).[36]

Given the duration of abuse and the array of oppressive tactics deployed, lay observers have reasonably asked "why victims stay" with violent partners. Early explanations highlighted psychological characteristics of victims, particularly an ambivalence about separation rooted in feelings of love or obligation. However, researchers have failed to identify any set of personality traits that distinguish victims from nonvictims prior to the onset of abuse. Moreover, the majority of female (as well as male) victims are physically separated or divorced at the time they are abused; separated or divorced women face the highest risk of abuse-related fatality. If 'intimate' is an inaccurate predicate for a good deal of partner abuse, evidence on the frequency with which stalking and other types of surveillance are part of a pattern of coercive control suggests that abuse typically 'crosses social space.' This means that offenders often harass or otherwise access victimized partners at work, in school, or while they are driving or shopping, for instance, as well as at home. For victims confronting coercive control, a physical separation (or a decision to "leave" or "stay") may only change the dynamic in the abuse and should be considered part of an ongoing process of disengagement rather than the point that demarcates when abuse ends or resumes.

In lieu of a psychological explanation for the duration of abusive relationships, proponents of the dominant paradigm have highlighted the mechanical properties of violent acts, emphasizing how life-threatening violence can either induce dependency directly, a pattern termed "learned helplessness," or indirectly by eliciting a post-traumatic syndrome that may include the range of physical, psychological, and behavioral problems that disables independent judgment.

Seemingly supporting trauma theory is the considerable evidence that battered women present a distinctive problem profile found among no other class of assault victims. In addition to a markedly greater risk of injury than nonbattered women, this profile includes vastly disproportionate rates of alcohol and drug abuse, depression, attempted suicide, homelessness, an elevated risk of HIV and other SDTs, unwanted and high-risk pregnancies, and fear of child abuse.[37] These problems only become disproportionate in the context of ongoing violence, suggesting that abuse is their context if not always their proximate cause. Many of these problems can inhibit the exercise of an independent will to leave. Still, the relative infrequency of severe as opposed to minor assaults in a typical abuse dynamic suggests these problems develop in response to something more than traumatic violence. Among abused women who come to the emergency room with a complaint of injury, for instance, only two in every one hundred have ever been hurt seriously enough to require a hospital stay.[38]

Abuse may be traumatic, but it does not appear that the severity of the violence is what makes it so.

In summary, where the dominant legal and social paradigm defines domestic violence as consisting of discrete violent episodes whose severity can be gauged by the presence or probability of injury, research shows something quite different. The typical case of abuse is "ongoing," involves multiple forms of coercion and control, and is characterized by frequent but generally minor violence. This pattern of "coercive control" entraps women with abusive men both directly through structural controls over their material resources, movement, and access to social support, among other things, and indirectly by inducing a problem profile in response that can inhibit independent action.

Proponents of the current approach have ready answers for the types of evidence summarized here. They point out that while psychological or other nonviolent forms of abuse can be harmful, including such "soft" behaviors in our working definition of violence so muddies the water that comparative research on abuse becomes impossible. Moreover, disagreement about the threshold of physical force considered abusive pales in comparison to the difficulty of separating abusive from nonabusive forms of insult, threats, degradation, or instances of control in relationships. Asking police or courts to make this distinction could invite a level of speculation and inquiry about our personal lives that many would find unacceptable. Meanwhile, the frequency of physical abuse is described as "recidivism," another concept borrowed from criminal justice, and identified with a certain subtype of "chronic" batterer. The final defense for using injury as a marker is practical, that it is the most tangible and most widely accepted indicator of harm we have. Nor does the emphasis on injury exclude the possibility that persons who suffer other forms of harm can be supported, resources permitting. What these explanations fail to acknowledge is that the application of the violent-incident model of abuse has failed all concerned, but particularly the women and children left unprotected.

Applying the Paradigm

Many of the problems we identified in the current approach to domestic violence by law and criminal justice can be directly traced to how superimposing this definition distorts the typical pattern of relationship abuse. When police, courts, or other institutional or community-based providers interpolate male partner abuse through the prism of the violent-incident frame, the coercive control battered women experience is disaggregated, trivialized, normalized, or rendered invisible, with interventions actually becoming more perfunctory as abuse becomes more comprehensive over time.

As we've seen, the effect of frequent minor assaults is cumulative, with the fear prompted by one event building on the fear elicited by all previous events and mounting over time. When the woman's growing subjective sense of dependence and danger finds its objective correlate in the material deprivation, social isolation, and the regulation of everyday activities associated with independent living, the result is an almost hostage-like sense of *entrapment*, an experience expressed by the high levels of anxiety, fearfulness, and physical distress demonstrated in the risk profile that accompanies battering.

What happens when a woman in this predicament calls police, seeks an order of protection, or becomes embroiled in a custody dispute? The law requires police to seek probable cause to make an arrest in the physical valence of each incident. Since considerably more than 95 percent of the abuse incidents the woman is experiencing are non-injurious or involve only minor injuries, when criminal justice bases its response on the severity of these incidents, domestic violence is reduced to a second-class misdemeanor for which few are arrested and almost none sanctioned. Conversely, if medical or criminal justice providers wait for "real" violence to occur before intervening, they will miss considerably more than 95 percent of the abuse for which victims seek help.

An even greater dilemma accompanies abused women to family court. The low level of criminal justice intervention means women with a long history of abuse may nonetheless lack the documentation needed to move an evaluator or a family court judge from their commitment to shared parenting. If abuse is long-standing, the woman will typically be presented with a high level of fear for herself and her children, possibly accompanied by the psychological, physical or behavioral adaptations to chronic stress. To the legal professionals who view this history through the prism of injurious incidents, the level of fear and concern presented can seem grossly disproportionate to the woman's proximate danger. From here, it is a short step to the conclusion that the woman is exaggerating, emotionally unprepared to parent, or even fabricating her history to gain advantage in the proceedings or to alienate her children – all stances for which a punitive response from the bench may seem not merely appropriate but required.

At each point of service to which she turns, the gap between the relatively low level of ostensible or proximate harm the victimized woman has suffered and the level of her physical or psychological distress is closed by identifying the problem "in" her. If the victimized woman has self-medicated her predicament with licit or illicit drugs, this behavior will add to her predicament, and once such a pattern of behavioral adaptation is established, all professionals involved may even come to see why a beleaguered husband or boyfriend might find such a partner intolerable. Since the incident-specific response does little to manage the ongoing problem she faces, she calls police repeatedly, returns to court for additional protective orders, or makes repeat visits to the hospital's ER. At each setting, patience wears thin. Clinicians label the woman who uses services repeatedly with few positive test results as a "crock" or "hypochondriac." As her secondary problems mount, cause and effect may be reversed, with the problems or problem behavior being identified as the cause of her propensity to get into "fights" and be injured. In some instances, the abusive partner may even be enlisted to help manage her behavior, something he is all too willing to do. In the civil arena, judges become frustrated when the protective order proves not to be the magic antidote they'd hoped for. This failure creates a disconnect between the victim's hopefulness that this time intervention will help and the court's increasing sense that her situation is tragic but somehow inevitable given the personalities involved.

The ongoing physical entrapment caused by complementary tactics of coercion and control is rarely picked up by the identification protocols used to detect violence at institutional helping sites. What authorities observe is the effects of these tactics: the victim's psychological, behavioral, and physical deterioration as abuse escalates. A woman who was once independent and apparently untroubled may now have no money of her own, miss days or weeks of work, develop an odd assortment of behavioral problems or medical complaints, or even neglect her children. As she or her abusive partner or her "situation" become "well known," the justice response becomes more perfunctory, assuming there is any response at all. The overall situation created exemplifies "ineffective demand." Police calls, arrests, court appearances, and the like are common enough but lead to none of the outcomes criminal justice is designed to produce. The result is a negative feedback loop, like the failure in the electric grid that darkened the East Coast a few summers ago. As the men they have arrested are immediately returned to the street, law enforcement officers become demoralized.

For female victims, the message now is that *she* is the problem to be managed, not the offender. She is caught in a "battered woman's dilemma": if she fails to call police or otherwise press her claims for help, she may be seriously hurt, even killed. But if she presses these claims, a punitive response from the authorities is likely. She may lose her children, be arrested herself, or be sent for psychiatric care, perhaps even under the studied supervision of her benefactor at home. If she strikes out on her own or retaliates violently to the abuse, her defense attorney faces the same predicament. The woman may claim to have feared for her life, but unless she has an extensive record of physical injury, which is rare, neither judge nor jury is likely to recognize self-defense.

REFRAMING DOMESTIC VIOLENCE FROM THE PERSPECTIVE OF PUBLIC HEALTH

In 1985, the U.S. Surgeon General C. Everett Koop convened an unprecedented workshop designed to frame violence as a "public health issue" rather than solely as a criminal justice concern. Two decades later, we are still debating what this means.

The most basic principle drawn from public health is that population health must be understood in its sociological and historical context. So too must the health problems of individuals be put and understood in relation to their life history and social dimensions. As we've seen, abuse typically involves a combination of frequent, even routine, but generally low-level assaults, sexual assaults, and threats with a range of nonviolent tactics. Even if assaults become less frequent over time or even end for significant periods, oppression continues as long as nonviolent forms of coercion and control continue, making the experience of victimization *ongoing* rather than incident-specific. In a Finnish population survey, for example, the highest levels of fear and other abuse-related symptoms were reported by older abuse victims who had not been physically assaulted for at least ten years.[39]

From a historical standpoint, then, male partner abuse should be depicted as a course of conduct crime that has more in common with kidnapping or harassment than with assault. Several examples illustrate how putting violent acts in a historical context benefits our understanding of abuse and the response.

A major debate in the domestic violence field concerns the claim that there is gender parity in violent acts.[40] This claim is based on survey evidence that women use violent tactics with male or female partners as often or even more often than male partners. For instance, one of the best designed and comprehensive surveys to date, the NVAWS, found that the ratio of male to female partner violence was only 1.4:1, far smaller than most observers would expect. But claims to gender parity were put to rest when attention shifted from reported violent acts during the study year to partner assault over the life course, where the ratio was more than 3:1 (22.1 percent versus 7.4 percent),[41] the same ratio reflected in domestic violence arrests. Gender differences in sexual abuse and stalking over time were many times larger.

The benefit of the historical approach taken by public health is also illustrated by the controversy about the overall incidence of domestic violence identified early in this chapter. In public health, the critical distinction is between *incidence* and *prevalence*. Incidence refers to new cases of a problem that arise in a specific time period, usually a year; prevalence refers to the number of persons who have the problem at any given time and so may require assistance. Knowing incidence allows us to calculate the risk that any given individual will be abused. Because prevention depends on stopping a problem before it emerges, or reducing the number of *new* cases, we can only tell if prevention efforts are working if we already know its incidence. By contrast, if a problem lasts for a nontrivial amount of time, called its *duration*, the number of persons suffering from the problem at a given time will consist of the sum of new cases and cases that have yet to be resolved. Prevalence is the key measure used to determine what resources are needed to manage a problem or whether intervention is reducing the overall burden a problem places on the community.

Since most crimes are over almost as soon as they occur, criminology generally treats incidence and prevalence as interchangeable. In this sense, a robbery is like the flu. When researchers adapted the case definition from criminology, they measured domestic violence in much the same way we would gauge the flu. They looked at the number of violent acts respondents reported for a given year and alternately called this the incidence or prevalence of domestic violence. This approach made it impossible for law or police to distinguish someone who called after a single incident of slapping from a caller who had been victimized for years. Conversely, unless there was severe injury – a rare case – they had no way of distinguishing a high-risk offender from a low-risk one.

In fact, partner abuse is far closer to a chronic illness, like heart disease or HIV infection, than it is to the flu. Between 17 and 25 percent of abusive incidents are isolated events. But "spontaneous remission" is atypical. In the Yale Trauma Studies, we found that if a woman had ever presented a domestic violence–related injury to the hospital, there was a 72-percent chance that her hospital visit during the study year was prompted by abuse and a 92-percent chance that she had presented at least one abusive injury at the hospital in the past five years.[42]

Approaching abuse as an ongoing or chronic problem rather than as episodic changes everything. A doctor who views each complaint of chest pain as separate may become frustrated by multiple visits with identical complaints, just as many police, physicians, mental health practitioners, judges, and advocates are frustrated when abused women return repeatedly for help or "remain" in abusive relationships. The result is that victims are often thought to be exaggerating or misrepresenting their situation. However, when physicians recognize that the particular complaint is a symptom of heart disease, a chronic problem, they become proactive, view repeated use of their services as appropriate and even desirable, and take steps to ensure long-term risk reduction. The same shift to a proactive response would be expected once police and the courts redefined partner abuse as a course of ongoing conduct, applied sanctions appropriate to and designed to curtail the course of conduct, and approached each subsequent call or appearance as evidence that risk had escalated and stepped up sanctions were required.

An analogy comes from early in the AIDS epidemic, when patients stricken with the disease presented a series of opportunistic infections. Until clinicians appreciated that a patient's susceptibility to these infections was a function of an underlying disease process, identified the virus at the root of this process, and shifted to antiviral intervention, they were treated symptomatically and soon died.

Importantly, when we apply this public health model to measuring abuse, we learn that the vast majority of abuse cases in the general population, somewhere between 79 and 86 cases of every 100 are long-standing rather than "new."[43] This means that early and determined intervention could dramatically reduce the burden partner abuse places on our communities, even if it would not eliminate it altogether. By contrast, treating each episode as a "new" crime meriting relatively few sanctions has had little or no effect.

A second core principle adapted from public health is that individual health should be defined holistically and in a way that includes psychological, experiential, social, and even political well-being alongside physical functioning. This broad definition allows us to encompass nonviolent control tactics as part of the abusive pattern along with coercive tactics. Elsewhere,[44] I have categorized the dimensions of *coercive control* under four tactical headings: violence, intimidation, isolation, and control. Intimidation includes the varied forms of sexual degradation noted earlier, whereas control includes constraints over everything from basic material resources (money, food, sleep, etc.) to imposed "rules" about everyday living. As discussed earlier, these control tactics are properly understood as "structural" because they can affect subordination and dependence independently of their psychological effect on victims or a victim's personality or standing in life.

This holistic understanding also helps us appreciate why many battered women describe their experience of abuse as "ongoing" even though violence may be sporadic. As we've seen, applying a calculus of harms to assess the seriousness of partner abuse leads to the mistaken belief that most cases of abuse are trivial. The more holistic approach brings the broader range of harms associated with coercive control to the fore. Violations of a victim's physical integrity remains the key, but a growing literature documents the ways in which coercive control also inhibits women's self-direction and compromises their liberty, harms that suggest the limits of simply providing temporary safety to victims. Each of the broad tactical categories that comprise coercive control can be linked to a corresponding rights violation, though any of the particular tactics can abrogate any or all of these rights. As a practical matter, however, it is helpful to link violence to the right to security and bodily integrity; intimidation to the right to dignity and to live without fear; isolation to the right to autonomy and social connection; and control to liberty rights and the rights of all persons to fulfill their potential as persons and as citizens.

The final concept drawn from public health highlights the importance of justice and equality as health concerns and the role of systemic change in any reform strategy as a necessary complement to therapeutic intervention and behavioral change. This core concept is reflected in the broad emphasis in public health research on the link between socio-economic inequality and health disparities.

There are few more dramatic examples of how inequality shapes health than the incidence of woman battering. Inequality is implicated in the prevalence of coercive control, its substantive focus, and in its major social consequence.

As we've noted, survey evidence shows that female partners frequently assault and injure men. However, there is no comparable evidence suggesting that any substantial proportion of women use coercive control to subordinate male partners. Nor does it appear that the differential socialization of males and females explains this asymmetry in abuse. Indeed, the same population surveys that reveal high rates of female partner assault consistently show that women are only slightly less interested than men in controlling their partners or getting their way. If men and women have similar interests in control, the fact that men are so much more likely than women to actually implement these controls suggests they are in a stronger position to start, almost certainly because of persistent sexual inequalities in the relative share of resources and opportunities men and women bring to relationships. Men cannot be unequal to women in the same way and at the same time as women are unequal to them. This is why the major forms of partner abuse committed by men and women look so different.

We can assume a broad social logic is at work when we encounter a form of categorical dominance among formally equal adults that is as widespread as coercive control. As with other major public health problems, so here too, to identify causes we must look beyond the individual or couple. I have argued[45] that coercive control is both a response to women's attainment of formal equality and made possible by persistent inequalities. Women's improved social, economic, and legal status in the most highly developed societies has made it increasingly difficult for men to establish their dominance over women with violence alone, if for no other reason than that women's access to income, legal remedies, and cultural supports makes them increasingly able to reject "bad bargains" in marriages and relationships. Conversely, to establish dominance in the face of women's formal equality, men must effectively disable women's access to their new rights and resources, rendering "escape" more difficult, if not impossible. This is the logic behind coercive control: To extend the sex-based privileges men once enjoyed by virtue of law, religion and culture into a period where women have formal equality, they must reconstruct these constraints at the level of personal life, the aim of coercive control.

Fearing the implications of real or substantive sexual equality, a subset of men has sought to win through coercive control what they once could secure with violence alone. But their success in this venture reflects a different reality. If women are no longer subordinate by law or social fiat, they have merely moved "up to inequality." There is no space here to detail the dramatic sex-based disadvantages that women continue to face in the economy, culture, and political life. Suffice it to say that a key reflection of these persistent inequalities is women's continued and default consignment to housework, child care, and sexual service. In coercive control, not surprisingly, men exploit and target this remnant of women's subordinate status, making it impossible for them to translate their new independence outside the home into equal status in relationships. Ironically, the fact that the domestic roles targeted by coercive control are already devalued by their default consignment to women has made the micromanagement of daily activities "invisible in plain sight."

If coercive control arises at the interstices of sexual equality/inequality and takes the reinforcement of gender-stereotypic behavior in families and relationships as its means, it also exacerbates sexual inequality by disabling the autonomy, liberty, and self-interested decision-making of somewhere between 8.5 and 12 million women in the United States alone.

The role of inequality as predicate, focus, and consequence of coercive control suggests that male partner abuse poses a unique set of justice concerns that distinguish what Dempsey terms "domestic violence in the strong sense" from other forms of partner abuse, "domestic violence in the weak sense."[46] Neither the dynamic of male partner abuse nor the full scope of the harms it inflicts on women's rights as fully entitled citizens are apparent so long as we approach domestic violence solely as a criminal justice issue. Ironically, it is only by reframing domestic violence from the perspective of core public health values and concepts that we are able to view partner abuse as a violation of the rights to security, dignity, autonomy, and liberty – all widely recognized as meriting state protection – and link it to an affirmative concept of freedom that echoes through our history as a democracy.

Notes

1. Anne Rees, Roxanne Agnew-Davies, and Michael Barkham, "Outcomes for Women Escaping Domestic Violence at Refuge," Paper presented at Society for Psychotherapy Research Annual Conference (Edinburgh) (2006).
2. See Marianne Hester, *The Contradictory Legal Worlds Faced by Domestic Violence Victims*, in Evan Stark & Eva Buzawa, Violence Against Women in Families and Relationships. Vol. Two: The Family Context, at 127–146 (2010).
3. James Allen Fox & Marianne W. Zawitz, United States Dep't of Justice, Bureau of Justice Statistics, *Homicide Trends in the United States* (2004), online at http://bjs.ojp.usdoj.gov/content/homicide/homtrnd.cfm (accessed Feb. 24, 2010).
4. See generally Sara Fenstermaker Berk & Donileen R. Loseke, *"Handling" Family Violence: Situational Determinants of Police Arrests in Domestic Disturbances*. 15 Law & Soc'y Rev., 317, 317–346 (1980).

5. Eva Buzawa & Carl Buzawa, *Domestic Violence: The Criminal Justice Response* (2003).
6. *Id.*
7. Carol Kennedy Chaney & Grace Hall Saltzstein, *Democratic Control and Bureaucratic Responsiveness: The Police and Domestic Violence*, 42 AMERICAN JOURNAL OF POLITICAL SCIENCE 745, 750–751 (1998).
8. Andrew R. Klein, *Re-Abuse in a Population of Court-Restrained Male Batterers: Why Restraining Orders Don't Work*, in EVA BUZAWA & CARL BUZAWA (eds.), DO ARRESTS AND RESTRAINING ORDERS WORK? at 192–213 (1996).
9. *Id.*
10. Linda Ammons, *Discretionary Justice: A Legal and Policy Analysis of a Governor's Use of the Clemency Power in the Cases of Incarcerated Battered Women*, 3 J.L.& POL'Y 1, 30 (1994).
11. See generally Evan Stark, *The Battered Mother in the Child Protective Service Caseload: Developing an Appropriate Response*, 23 WOMEN'S RTS. L. REP. 107, 107–131 (2002).
12. Family Violence Project, National Council of Juvenile and Family Court Judges, *Family Violence in Child Custody Statutes: An Analysis of State Codes and Legal Practice*. 29 FAM. L.Q. 197 (1995).
13. J. David, Hirschel & Ira.W. Hutchison, III, *Realities and Implications of the Charlotte Spouse Abuse Experiment*, in BUZAWA & BUZAWA, *supra* note 8, at 54–82.
14. Joan Zorza, *The Criminal Law of Misdemeanor Domestic Violence, 1970–1990*, 83 J. CRIM. L. AND CRIMINOLOGY 46, 71 (1992).
15. Hester, *supra* note 2, at 81.
16. Hirschel & Hutchinson, *supra* note 13.
17. Andrew R. Klein, *Offenders and the Criminal Justice System*, in EVAN STARK & EVA BUZAWA (eds.), VIOLENCE AGAINST WOMEN IN FAMILIES AND RELATIONSHIPS at 115–133 (2009).
18. Evan Stark, COERCIVE CONTROL: HOW MEN ENTRAP WOMEN IN PERSONAL LIFE (2007).
19. Nicholson v. Williams, 2003 F. Supp.2d 153 (E.D.N.Y. 2002).
20. See generally Evan Stark *Rethinking Custody Evaluation in Cases Involving Domestic Violence*, 6 Journal of Child Custody 287 (2009).
21. See generally Mary A. Kernic et al., *Children in the Crossfire: Child Custody Determinations Among Couples with a History of Intimate Partner Violence*, 11 VIOLENCE AGAINST WOMEN 991, 991–1021 (2005).
22. See generally BUZAWA & BUZAWA, *supra* note 5.
23. Richard J. Gelles, INTIMATE VIOLENCE IN FAMILIES 14 (3d ed. 1997).
24. Murray A. Straus, *Trends in Cultural Norms and Rates of Partner Violence: An Update to 1992*, in Murray A. Straus & Sandra M. Stith (Eds.), UNDERSTANDING CAUSES, CONSEQUENCES AND SOLUTIONS 30–33 (1995);

Patricia Tjaden & Nancy Thoennes, *Prevalence and Consequences of Male-to-Female and Female-to-Male Intimate Partner Violence as Measured by the National Violence Against Women Survey*, 6 VIOLENCE AGAINST WOMEN 142 (2000); John Schafer et al., *Rates of Intimate Partner Violence in the United States*, 88 AMERICAN J. PUBLIC HEALTH 1702, 1702–1704 (1998).

25. Walter S. DeKeseredy, *Current Controversies on Defining Nonlethal Violence Against Women in Intimate Heterosexual Relationships: Empirical Implications*, 6 VIOLENCE AGAINST WOMEN 72 (2000).
26. Eva Buzawa & Gerald Hotaling, NATIONAL INSTITUTE OF JUSTICE, AN EXAMINATION OF ASSAULTS WITHIN THE JURISDICTION OF ORANGE DISTRICT COURT, FINAL REPORT (2000).
27. Rees, *supra* note 1.
28. See generally Richard M. Tolman, *The Development of a Measure of Psychological Maltreatment of Women by their Male Partners*, 4 VIOLENCE & VICTIMS 159, 159–177 (1989); Rees, *supra* note 1.
29. Tolman, *supra* note 28, at 164–65.
30. *Id.*
31. C.W. Lischick, *Divorce in the Context of Coercive Control in* Stark & Buzawa, *supra* note 2 at 191–224.
32. R.H Teske & M.L. Parker, SPOUSE ABUSE IN TEXAS: A STUDY OF WOMEN'S ATTITUDES AND EXPERIENCES, Huntsville, TX: Sam Houston State University, Criminal Justice Center (1983); Evan Stark & Anne Flitcraft, WOMEN AT RISK: DOMESTIC VIOLENCE AND WOMEN'S HEALTH (1996).
33. *Id.*; Jacquelyn Campbell et al., *Voices of Strength and Resistance: A Contextual and Longitudinal Analysis of Women's Responses to Battering*, 13 J. INTERPERSONAL VIOLENCE 743 (1998).
34. Gelles, *supra* note 23, at 14.
35. Reese, *supra* note 1.
36. Stark, *supra* note 18, at 95; CONNECTICUT DEPARTMENT OF PUBLIC SAFETY, FAMILY VIOLENCE ARRESTS 2006 (2007); Caliber Associates, Symposium, *On Domestic Violence Prevention Research*, Department of Defense (2002), online at http://www.militaryhomefront.dod.mil/dav/lsn/LSN/BINARY_RESOURCE/BINARY_CONTENT/1683971.doc (accessed Feb. 24, 2010).
37. See generally Stark, *supra* note 18; IRENE FRIEZE, HURTING THE ONE YOU LOVE: VIOLENCE IN RELATIONSHIPS (2005).
38. Stark, *supra* note 18, at 12.
39. Minna Piispa, *Complexity of Patterns of Violence against Women in Heterosexual Partnerships*, 8 VIOLENCE AGAINST WOMEN 873 (2002).
40. Donald G. Dutton, *Domestic Abuse Assessment in Child Custody Disputes: Beware the Domestic Violence Research Paradigm*, J CHILD CUSTODY, January 2006, at 23.
41. Tjaden &Thoennes, *supra* note.24
42. Stark, *supra* note 18, at p. 11.

43. *Id.*
44. *Id.*
45. *Id.*
46. Michelle Madden Dempsey, PROSECUTING DOMESTIC VIOLENCE: A PHILOSOPHICAL ANALYSIS 170 (2009).

6 LAW AND POLICY APPROACHES TO KEEPING GUNS FROM HIGH-RISK PEOPLE

Jon S. Vernick, Daniel W. Webster and Katherine A. Vittes

INTRODUCTION

Public Health Problem of Gun Violence in the United States

The United States is often described as a nation with a car culture. Many Americans love their cars and find life difficult to imagine without them. There were approximately 250 million registered highway vehicles in the United States in 2006.[1]

If this is evidence for a car culture, then the United States certainly has a gun culture as well. There are an estimated 280 million guns in private hands in the United States, nearly one gun for every man, woman, and child.[2] Approximately two-thirds of these guns are rifles and shotguns, used mostly for hunting and sport. Nearly all of the rest are handguns whose owners cite personal protection as the primary reason for ownership.[3] About 38 percent of U.S. households contain at least one gun, with a higher prevalence of ownership in southern and southwestern states as well as more rural parts of the country.

The social consequences of the ubiquity of guns in the United States are profound. Firearms were associated with about 100,000 fatal and nonfatal shootings in the nation in 2006. Of these shootings, about 65 percent were instances in which one person intended to harm another (approximately 13,000 homicides and another 52,000 nonfatal assaults). The remainder includes 20,000 acts of self-directed violence (suicides and suicide attempts) and more than 15,000 unintentional or accidental shootings, including 600 deaths. In just the ten-year period from 1997 to 2006, more than one million Americans were shot; of these, more than 300,000 died.[4]

Harmful social consequences of firearms are, of course, not limited to deaths and injuries. There were more than 475,000 victims of a violent crime with a firearm in 2005.[5] Firearm-related crime and violence depress property values, cause people to avoid engaging in certain beneficial activities such as walking, and can generate a pervasive fear that affects individuals, families, and communities. The total social cost of firearm violence has been estimated at $100 billion per year.[6]

What people believe should be done about these deaths, injuries, and crimes probably depends, at least in part, on their perspective about the relative risks and benefits of guns. For those who believe that guns are associated with more individual and societal risks than benefits, a wide variety of interventions – including banning some weapons – might be on their legislative and policy agenda. But if one believes, as some gun owners do, that a firearm is an important means of home[7] or personal protection[8] – and possibly even acts as a form of deterrence to tyrannical government[9] – then the scope of policy responses one might support would likely be much narrower.

Despite their policy differences, one category of intervention that most Americans – even a majority of gun owners – support would make it harder for high-risk persons to buy, sell, possess, or carry firearms.[10] This approach is consistent with a public health perspective that develops, implements, and evaluates interventions according to level of risk – and political feasibility – designed to have maximum impact on lives saved.

Many law-abiding people own firearms with no negative consequences. But for persons with a history suggesting a higher risk for future violence or recklessness with a firearm, the social costs of gun ownership clearly outweigh any possible benefits. High-risk persons generally include those with a prior history of violence, misuse of firearms, or other characteristics that suggest they pose a danger to themselves or others with a gun (such as a history of mental illness, drug abuse, or dangerous intoxication). Juveniles also are generally thought to lack the requisite maturity and judgment to safely possess a firearm – especially a handgun – at least without close adult supervision.

No intervention will make it impossible for some very determined criminals with adequate resources to obtain a gun. But there are a range of proven or promising interventions that can reduce gun availability to criminals or other high-risk people and thereby reduce gun violence.

This chapter begins with an overview of law and policy approaches to make it harder for high-risk people to obtain guns. Interventions are then divided into sections focusing on: 1) buyers; 2) sellers; and 3) owners, possessors, or carriers. We also discuss strategies employing technological modifications to firearms. Ultimately, we argue that through public health interventions such as these, our communities and our nation can be a safer, more fulfilling place for all Americans.

Overview of U.S. Gun Laws Affecting Access for High-Risk Persons

Despite the enormous impact of firearm-related deaths and injuries, federal law affecting access to guns for high-risk persons in the United States is relatively limited. Under federal law, certain persons are prohibited from purchasing or possessing firearms. These persons include: 1) felons; 2) fugitives; 3) unlawful users or those addicted to controlled substances; 4) those who have been "adjudicated as a mental defective" or committed to a mental institution; 5) illegal aliens; 6) those dishonorably discharged from the armed forces; 7) persons who have renounced their U.S. citizenship; 8) those subject to certain domestic violence restraining orders; and 9) domestic violence misdemeanants.[11]

Persons who are "engaged in the business" of selling guns must obtain a federal dealer's license from the Bureau of Alcohol, Tobacco, Firearms, and Explosives (ATF).[12] When guns are bought from licensed dealers, a background check must be conducted.[13] In addition, persons under eighteen years of age may not buy a long gun, such as a rifle or shotgun, from a licensed dealer. For handguns, the minimum purchase age from a dealer is twenty-one years.[14] Oddly, the minimum age under federal law to buy a handgun from someone who is *not* a dealer is eighteen years.[15] Handgun buyers must reside in the state in which the gun is purchased.[16] Gun dealers must also maintain sales records[17] and promptly report thefts from their inventory.[18]

Certain guns that may be especially attractive to high-risk persons are more heavily regulated under federal law. Fully automatic weapons (i.e., machine guns) have been tightly controlled since the 1930s.[19] So-called Saturday night specials, or "junk guns" – poorly-made, highly concealable, inaccurate guns often lacking basic safety features – may be manufactured and sold domestically[20] but may not be imported.[21] The sale of certain models of assault weapons – essentially civilian versions of military-style weapons – was outlawed from 1994 to 2004, but that law was allowed to sunset without being reauthorized by Congress.[22]

Federal gun laws contain many important gaps. Perhaps most striking is that gun purchases from non-dealers do not require a background check, including sales occurring at gun shows.[23] An estimated 40 percent of all firearm transactions involve these private sales,[24] and most armed criminals report obtaining their guns in private transactions with non-dealers.[25] In addition, some potentially high-risk buyers – including alcohol abusers and certain violent misdemeanants – are not prohibited from gun purchase or possession under federal law. Federal law also does not prohibit the bulk purchase of firearms. Persons may buy several, even hundreds, of guns at once and need only to complete a multiple-purchase form.[26]

Gun ownership – unlike car ownership – is not registered in the United States. Figures estimating the number of guns in the nation are just that – *estimates*, typically based on telephone surveys. The Firearm Owners Protection Act of 1986 actually prohibits the establishment of a federal registration system for firearms.[27] That same law makes it difficult for the ATF to engage in oversight of gun dealers, limiting routine inspections to a maximum of one per year[28] and making it very hard to revoke a dealer's license.[29] Also unlike every other consumer product in the United States, no federal agency has the authority to mandate standards for the safe design of firearms, or even to recall guns when they are defective (for example, if they are unreasonably prone to accidental discharge). In fact, the U.S. Consumer Product Safety Commission is forbidden to regulate guns or ammunition.[30]

Because federal law acts as a floor rather than a ceiling for gun regulation in the United States, many states have additional laws regulating access to firearms. These laws include: 1) requirements for a police-issued permit to purchase firearms prior to beginning a transaction with a seller; 2) limits on the number of firearms that may be bought; 3) additional categories of persons forbidden to purchase or possess guns; 4) gun registration rules; 5) safety or other design standards for firearms; 6) additional licensing or oversight of gun dealers; and 7) safe storage requirements to prevent child access to guns.[31] New Jersey, for example, includes each of these additional laws.

Local laws regarding firearms – especially laws that might affect access to guns for high-risk persons – are relatively uncommon in the United States. In part, this is because most states have some form of preemption of local firearm laws. Statewide preemption means that some or all gun laws must originate in the state legislature, and that localities are forbidden to enact their own laws.[32] Beginning in the 1980s, the National Rifle Association made preventing the enactment of firearm preemption laws one of its top legislative priorities.[33] Today, more than 40 states preempt some or all local gun laws.[34]

TARGETING HIGH RISK BUYERS

The Brady Law

Prior to 1994, federal law did not even require a criminal history background check for the purchase of firearms. To be sure, the Gun Control Act of 1968 established a list of categories of persons – since updated and amended – forbidden to own guns. But until the Brady Handgun Violence Prevention Act took effect on February 28, 1994, the "honor system" prevailed under federal law and in many states. Amazingly, this meant that a gun buyer – even from a licensed dealer – would complete a purchase form (ATF Form 4473) with a series of "yes/no" questions regarding the prohibited categories of persons. As long as the buyer checked the "no" answer to questions such as "Are you a fugitive from justice?" and related queries, the sale could proceed. No one was required to verify the truth of those statements.

With the enactment of the Brady Act, this system changed. Initially, this meant that in states that did not already have their own background check laws, gun dealers were required to process background checks for handgun buyers through the chief law enforcement officers of those states. A maximum five-day waiting period was also established to allow time for the completion of the check.[35] In 1997, the U.S. Supreme Court declared unconstitutional the portion of the background check provision that required state law enforcement officers to complete the checks.[36] Under the provisions of the original law, however, by 1998 the background check provision had changed to a "national instant check system" (NICS) administered by the FBI and applicable to all firearm purchases, including long guns. Under NICS, a check can generally be completed over the phone, and no waiting period is required by federal law. If the NICS system does not immediately approve or deny an applicant, the dealer must wait a maximum of three business days before the sale can be completed.[37]

From 1994 to 2007, the Brady Act resulted in the denial of more than 1.6 million attempted purchases of firearms from licensed dealers by persons forbidden to own guns.[38] Of those, about half were because the prospective buyer had a felony conviction. More than 200,000 were for some domestic violence-related disqualifier.[39] There are no data, however, to indicate how many denied persons went on to acquire a gun from another source, such as through theft or by enlisting someone without a criminal history to purchase the gun for them (called a "straw purchase").

Even prior to 1994, however, some states did have their own laws requiring a background check. Ludwig and Cook exploited this variation in the effect of the Brady Act – it mandated a new background check in some states but didn't substantially change the status quo in others – in an attempt to evaluate the effects of the Act. They reasoned that if the Brady Act were effective, one would expect larger declines in firearm homicide and suicide rates in states that had no background check prior to Brady than in states that already had such checks.

Ludwig and Cook found that the Brady Act was not associated with a reduction in homicide rates.[40] They did conclude, however, that the Act may have been responsible for a modest decline in firearm-related suicides among older persons, presumably attributable to the waiting period. Ludwig and Cook's study has significant limitations (which they acknowledge). Perhaps most important is a limitation of the Brady Act itself: it did not apply to the 40 percent of all firearm sales that do not involve a licensed dealer.

As with any specific law intended to reduce access to guns for high-risk people, it is very difficult for that law to be successful without complementary laws establishing a more comprehensive scheme of regulation. Many of those laws and policies are discussed in the sections that follow.

Universal Background Check Laws

Most firearms are durable products that can last many decades with proper care. In fact, there is a large "secondary market" in which firearms are sold by private individuals (not licensed gun dealers). An estimated 40 percent of all firearm transactions involve these private sales. Because only 15 states regulate handgun sales by non-dealers,[41] it is not surprising that more than 85 percent of armed criminals report that they acquired their firearms from private sellers.[42]

Given this large loophole in current gun sales laws, enacting universal background check laws is a top priority of some organizations working to reduce gun violence. Under a universal background check law, all gun sales would be subject to a records check to ensure that the prospective buyer was legally permitted to own a gun. In states with universal background check laws, such as Maryland and California, a private seller can conduct the background check with the assistance of a licensed dealer (who simply facilitates the request for the check), or the seller can initiate the check through law enforcement.

Oddly, there has been little research on the effectiveness of state universal background check laws. A recent study found that these laws were associated with significantly lower levels of within-state trafficking of guns,[43] but there has yet to be a rigorous evaluation of the impact of universal background check laws on violent crime.

Permit-to-Purchase Licensing and Registration

Despite the background check system established by the Brady Act, high-risk people remain able to acquire firearms in the United States. One important way that this occurs is through a so-called "straw purchase," in which a person without a disqualifying criminal history buys a gun from a dealer for someone who is prohibited from buying one themselves. This type of illegal gun trafficking can occur on a small scale – one gun at a time – or can involve organized (sometimes interstate) trafficking rings buying and selling hundreds of guns at once. In addition, guns also move from the licit to the illicit market when a lawful owner simply chooses to sell his or her used gun – perhaps some time after its initial purchase – to another person without conducting a background check.

Licensing and registration laws – on the books in just a few states – are designed to make these kinds of transactions more difficult or risky for the buyer and seller. Licensing laws require a prospective buyer to first obtain a permit to purchase the gun, usually issued by state or local law enforcement. The licensing process may include fingerprinting the buyer to confirm his or her identity and an extensive background check that goes beyond a simple check of criminal records. Some states have a discretionary licensing system allowing law enforcement to deny permits if the background check suggests the applicant would pose a danger to himself or others. By forcing buyers to have direct contact with the police, licensing laws may also discourage straw buyers.

Registration systems record, in a manner accessible to law enforcement, the guns purchased or owned by residents of the state. Registration systems, especially in conjunction with a universal background check and/or licensing law, foster accountability among gun owners. If a lawful owner transfers his or her gun to an unlawful purchaser – without conducting a background check – and the buyer then commits a crime with that gun, the police can use the gun's serial number and the registration system to easily identify its last lawful owner. The police can then prosecute the seller for making an illegal sale. The mere existence of licensing and registration systems may deter persons from unlawfully transferring their guns. Registration systems also allow law enforcement officials to identify persons who subsequently become disqualified from gun ownership and whose firearms must then be surrendered or confiscated.

Research suggests that licensing and registration systems make it harder for criminals to acquire guns. Daniel Webster and colleagues found that cities in states with both licensing and registration laws had a much smaller share of their crime guns originating from within the state, after controlling for other factors. Out-of-state gun acquisition by criminals is, other things being equal, an indication that in-state guns are more difficult to obtain. Among cities with licensing laws, those that afforded police some discretion to deny permits to potentially dangerous persons had an even smaller share of their guns coming from in-state. For example, Jersey City, New Jersey, with licensing and registration laws, had just 13 percent of its crime guns originating from in-state sources, compared with 86 percent for Atlanta with neither of these laws. Interestingly, proximity to a state with weaker laws reduced (but did not eliminate) the benefit of licensing and registration laws, further underscoring the problem of interstate gun trafficking.[44]

Expanded Categories of Persons Who May Not Own Guns

It is a common misconception that criminals cannot legally purchase or possess firearms in the United States. Federal law does prohibit felons and persons convicted of misdemeanor domestic assaults from owning guns. Yet under federal law and in many states, individuals with multiple convictions for other misdemeanors (some resulting from felony charges plead down to lesser charges) involving violence, firearms violations, drug offenses, drunk driving, and even felony crimes committed as a juvenile may legally purchase and possess firearms.

State laws vary greatly in the breadth of criminal convictions that result in firearm prohibitions. Some state gun laws are even less restrictive than federal law. On the other end of the continuum, New Jersey has the broadest criminal prohibitions, banning gun possession by anyone convicted of a criminal offense for which the penalty could be six months imprisonment or longer.

Individuals with non-felony offense histories have much higher rates of subsequent violent offending than do law-abiding citizens. Garen Wintemute and colleagues studied a cohort of young purchasers of firearms in California and found that those with prior misdemeanor convictions had subsequent rates of arrests for violent crime many times higher than truly law-abiding handgun purchasers. Elevated risks were greatest for those with misdemeanors involving violence and/or firearms.[45] Commission of serious crimes at a very young age is one of the most robust predictors of serious adult offending, including murder.[46] Multiple drug offenses are also associated with significantly increased risk for committing acts of violence.[47] Individuals with multiple convictions for drunk driving commonly have very high rates of substance abuse or other psychiatric disorders.[48] Such offenders often have less self-control[49] and have higher rates of repeated arrests.[50] National surveys show that neither gun owners nor those who do not own guns want individuals convicted of even nonviolent misdemeanors, or drug and alcohol abusers, to have guns.[51]

There are currently scant data to estimate the likely impact on public safety of expanding current prohibitions for who may own guns. Philip Cook and colleagues found that just 43 percent of homicide offenders in Illinois had a prior felony conviction. That study, however, did not examine misdemeanor convictions. A survey of inmates convicted of violent felonies in large urban areas in the U.S. found that 38 percent had been convicted of a prior felony and an additional 18 percent had convictions for misdemeanors.[52] Similarly, a 1997 Bureau of Justice Statistics (BJS) survey of inmates found that half of the prisoners who had been convicted of firearm-related crimes had previously been incarcerated for a "serious offense" likely to have been a felony. Inmates who had *not* used a firearm in the commission of the crime for which they were incarcerated were more likely than inmates incarcerated for gun crimes to have previously committed a serious offense that would have likely prohibited them from purchasing firearms.[53] This suggests that the inmates' prior prohibited status may have reduced their likelihood of subsequent offending with a firearm.

Prohibiting misdemeanants from owning guns can reduce violence. California tightened its requirements for legal handgun purchase in

1991 to exclude individuals convicted of misdemeanors involving violence or firearms offenses. Wintemute and colleagues found that those whose handgun purchase applications were denied in 1991 due to misdemeanor convictions had significantly lower rates of committing crimes of violence in the years following the denial than did a demographically similar group with misdemeanor convictions that had been permitted to purchase handguns in the late 1980s.[54]

TARGETING HIGH-RISK SELLERS AND ILLEGAL TRAFFICKING

Enhanced Dealer Regulation and Oversight

Like any illegal market, the market for illicit guns is difficult to study. Yet several analyses, using different types of data, provide evidence that a relatively small proportion of federally licensed gun dealers play an important role in the diversion of guns to criminals. It appears that a very small number of dealers (about 1 percent) sell the majority of guns later traced to crime.[55] The disproportionate involvement of these gun dealers cannot be explained solely by their overall sales volume, the location of their stores, or the demographic characteristics of their customers.[56] Data from a national study of gun trafficking investigations by the ATF found that scofflaw retail gun dealers accounted for more guns diverted into the illegal market than any other channel of trafficking.[57]

Licensed gun dealers played a role in arming criminals in three main ways: 1) selling guns to criminals "off the books" by falsifying gun sales records; 2) conspiring with gun traffickers who buy large numbers of guns for later resale to criminals; and 3) facilitating illegal straw sales when it is clear that the purchaser of record is buying guns directly on behalf of a prohibited person. Susan Sorenson and Katherine Vittes conducted a telephone survey of a national sample of retail gun dealers to gauge their willingness to sell guns to straw purchasers. A member of the research team phoned gun dealers and asked whether the dealer would sell the caller a gun intended for a "boyfriend/girlfriend who needed me to buy him/her a gun." Just over half of the dealers surveyed indicated a willingness to make the sale under these circumstances of (at best) questionable legality.[58] This suggests that, although a relatively small number of dealers are responsible for the bulk of guns traced to crime, many other (perhaps smaller scale) dealers are at risk for unlawful transactions as well.

Federal laws regulating gun dealers are relatively weak, and only a few states have their own comprehensive gun dealer laws. In fact, just eighteen states even require a state license – compare that with all fifty states requiring licenses for cosmetologists. Comprehensive laws include: 1) state licensing of dealers; 2) improved record-keeping rules; 3) permitting and conducting regular inspections; 4) store and merchandise security requirements; 5) provisions for readily revoking a license if sales rules are violated; 6) mandatory theft reporting; and 7) requirements for background checks of sales staff. Very few states, however, have each of these components of comprehensive dealer regulation – for example, just six even require reporting of stolen firearms.[59]

Findings from several studies demonstrate that the diversion of new guns to criminals can be significantly reduced by enhanced regulation and oversight of retail gun sellers. States with strong gun dealer regulations, and which regularly conduct inspections of dealers, have much lower rates of within-state gun trafficking.[60] Law enforcement in Chicago and Detroit conducted undercover stings of gun dealers connected with significant numbers of crime guns. Lawsuits followed against gun dealers who were caught facilitating illegal straw sales. These crackdowns on gun dealers were associated with citywide reductions in new guns diverted to criminals.[61]

More recently, New York City undertook a similar initiative, but one that targeted *out-of-state* dealers, because the vast majority of New York's crime guns originate out of state. Nearly all of the dealers who were caught making illegal sales entered legal agreements with New York City to adopt reforms to their business practices to reduce the likelihood that guns would be diverted to criminals. These measures include videotaping the point-of-sale area, employee background checks, training staff on responsible sales practices, ID verification, regular inventory audits, and keeping all guns locked. These reforms were followed by significant reductions in the probability that guns sold by these dealers were recovered by New York City Police within one to two years following retail sale.[62] Later, though not involved in the stings themselves, Wal-Mart, the largest retail seller of firearms in the United States, voluntarily adopted a "code of conduct" with a similar set of gun sales rules.

In Milwaukee, publicity about a local gun dealer having sold more guns subsequently recovered from criminals than any other gun dealer in the nation prompted the dealer to alter its sales practices. Following this voluntary change, the flow of new guns to criminals that had been sold by this dealer dropped by 73 percent, and new crime guns that had been sold by *any* gun dealer fell by 44 percent in that city.[63]

Regulating Sales at Gun Shows

A gun show is an organized event at which guns (and other items) are sold by both licensed dealers and private sellers. Gun shows can range from small events with perhaps only a dozen gun sellers to much larger gatherings with thousands of attendees. Between 2,000 and 5,200 gun shows are held each year in the United States.[64]

Under federal law, both licensed dealers and unlicensed private sellers are permitted to sell firearms at gun shows. As in other retail venues, federally licensed firearm dealers must conduct a background check on all potential purchasers and keep record of all sales. Unlicensed sellers – who typically comprise 25–50 percent of gun show vendors[65] – are exempt from these regulations. Often referred to as the "gun show loophole," prohibited purchasers can nonetheless buy firearms from unlicensed sellers at gun shows – in most states – without showing identification and without a background check. Firearms acquired in this manner are extremely difficult for law enforcement to trace, because unlicensed sellers are not required to keep sales records.

As a result, gun shows are a popular source of firearms for felons and other prohibited firearm purchasers. According to a report by the ATF, gun shows and flea markets were associated with 31 percent of all firearms recovered in illegal trafficking investigations in the United States during a two-and-a-half-year period.[66] Many of these diverted guns are subsequently recovered in crimes such as homicide, assaults, and robberies.[67] A 1999 review of 314 ATF gun trafficking investigations involving gun shows revealed that more than half of the investigations identified illegal activity by unlicensed private sellers.[68]

Two recent undercover investigations confirm that both licensed dealers and unlicensed sellers were willing to engage in unlawful transactions. Garen Wintemute attended seventy-eight gun shows in nineteen states from 2005 to 2008. He observed numerous straw purchases and other violations of sales laws.[69] In 2009, investigators hired by New York City recorded simulated illegal transactions at seven gun shows in three states. Licensed gun dealers were frequently willing to engage in blatant straw purchases, and unlicensed vendors often agreed to sell to those who admitted that they "probably couldn't pass a background check."[70]

Laws governing firearm sales at gun shows vary from state to state. States with laws that require all gun show vendors to conduct background checks on all handgun sales appear to have lower rates of crime gun exports than states without such laws.[71] One study compared gun shows in California, a state requiring background checks for all gun sales, with gun shows in several states without this law. The researchers found that undocumented sales and illegal straw purchases at gun shows were much more common in the less regulated states than in California.[72]

From a public health perspective, it is also important to determine whether gun shows and laws governing them have an effect on firearm fatalities. To our knowledge, the only study to directly consider these questions compared the relationship between gun shows and firearm-related homicide and suicide in California and Texas between 1994 and 2004.[73] The study found that gun shows and laws governing gun shows were not associated with gun-related homicide and suicide. However, that study is subject to very substantial limitations and has been criticized by criminologists and public health researchers.[74] For example, the authors acknowledge that they included only the geographic areas immediately surrounding gun shows and only firearm-related homicides and suicides that occurred during the three weeks following a gun show. Thus, they did not capture any effects of guns that were transported more than twenty-five miles or those that were used more than three weeks after being purchased. Their method of identifying gun shows was also limited and is likely to have missed a significant share of shows.

One-Handgun-Per-Month Laws

Federal law places no limit on the number of guns that may be purchased at one time. Licensed dealers must complete a multiple purchase form when two or more handguns are transferred within five days to any one person who is not also a dealer, but no further investigation is mandated.[75] However, in an ATF analysis of more than 1,500 trafficking investigations, more than 200 (13.4 percent) were begun following a review of the multiple sales forms.[76]

One-handgun-per-month laws limit the number of handguns that can be purchased to one per thirty-day period. These laws generally include exceptions for licensed dealers, collectors, and certain emergency situations. For high-volume traffickers, bulk purchase may be more efficient than buying one gun at a time. One-handgun-per-month laws are intended to make it harder for gun traffickers to purchase guns in bulk for later resale to criminals or other high-risk persons. Among guns sold in 2000 and traced to crime that same year, approximately 20 percent were originally part of a multiple transaction.[77]

Four states currently have one-handgun-per-month laws: Virginia, California, Maryland, and New Jersey. Virginia enacted its one-handgun-per-month law in 1993 following adverse publicity indicating that the state had become a prominent source of guns used in crime in many other jurisdictions, notably states with stronger laws such as New York. An evaluation of Virginia's law concluded that crime guns recovered in other states were less likely to have originated in Virginia after the enactment of its one-handgun-per-month law.[78]

TARGETING HIGH-RISK POSSESSORS AND CARRIERS

Removing Guns from Domestic Abusers

Guns pose a substantial danger to victims of intimate partner violence (IPV). When such assaults involve a firearm, death is twelve times more likely than when guns are not used.[79] Women, who comprise 80 percent of the victims of intimate partner homicides, are at highest risk.[80] According to a multisite study of abused women, a batterer's ownership of a gun is the strongest factor in determining whether an assault will be fatal.[81]

Guns also play a role in nonfatal IPV. In a study of patient records from U.S. hospital emergency departments, victims of IPV sought emergency medical care for nonfatal gunshot wounds and blunt trauma injuries such as bruises, lacerations, and fractures that result from being beaten with a firearm.[82] In another study, more than one-third of a sample of 417 residents of battered women's shelters across California reported that an intimate partner had ever used a gun against them, and two-thirds of shelter residents who lived in a home with a gun during their most recent relationship reported that their abusers had used the gun to scare, threaten, or harm them.[83] A firearm does not have to be used to coerce behaviors and cause terror, however. Men in batterer intervention programs have reported purposely cleaning, loading, or holding a gun during an argument to intimidate their intimate partners.[84]

Two federal laws were enacted in the mid-1990s to limit batterers' access to firearms. In 1994, a component of the Violence Against Women Act made it illegal for individuals subject to certain domestic violence restraining orders to purchase or possess a firearm.[85] Restraining orders issued at *ex-parte* hearings (where one party is absent) do not carry the firearm restrictions. The 1996 Lautenberg Amendment to the federal Gun Control Act extended these firearm prohibitions to persons who have been convicted of certain domestic violence misdemeanors.[86] Both laws define "intimate partner" to include current and former spouses, cohabitants, and persons who have a child in common.[87]

Many states have enacted IPV gun laws that exceed federal law. For example, some states make it illegal for persons under any type of domestic violence restraining order – including restraining orders issued at *ex-parte* hearings – to purchase or possess a firearm. In addition, laws that permit or require law enforcement to remove some or all firearms at the scene of a domestic violence incident have been enacted by some states.[88]

Researchers have exploited differences in state laws to examine their effect on intimate partner homicide rates. Laws that restrict firearm purchase from batterers subject to restraining orders are associated with an 8-percent reduction in rates of intimate homicide of women and a 10-percent reduction in rates of intimate homicide of women by firearms. However, these laws are only effective in reducing intimate partner homicides in states that have the ability to screen and identify potential firearm purchasers who are subject to a restraining order. Laws that allow law enforcement officers to confiscate firearms at the scene of a domestic violence incident and those that restrict firearm access from domestic violence misdemeanants did not have an effect on intimate partner homicide rates. As noted by the authors, because many states lack the ability to identify domestic violence misdemeanants during background checks, it may be the implementation of these laws rather than the laws themselves that are inadequate.[89]

Child Access Prevention (CAP) Laws

Children and adolescents often lack the self-restraint and maturity to be trusted with unsupervised access to firearms.[90] Yet a 2000 national survey found that 55 percent of gun owners with a child or adolescent under eighteen years old kept at least one unlocked firearm in the home.[91] In addition to increasing the risk for accidental shootings, adolescents' access to firearms has been linked in several studies to increased risk of adolescent suicide.[92] Unsupervised access to firearms can also play a role in youth-perpetrated homicides, as was the case in several high-profile school shootings.[93]

In response to this problem, eighteen states and the District of Columbia have passed some form of child access prevention (CAP) law that requires gun owners to store their guns so that underage youth cannot easily gain access.[94] Interestingly, some of these states otherwise have relatively lax laws on gun sales and large numbers of gun owners (e.g., Nevada, Texas, and Virginia), suggesting that the desire to protect children sometimes trumps advocacy for "gun owners' rights." CAP laws vary with respect to the age limits of protected youth (under age fourteen to under age eighteen), which storage practices are considered acceptable, which types of incidents lead to violation of the law (e.g., any access by a child or only that which results in a child injuring someone with the gun), and allowable penalties.

Research evaluating CAP laws provides evidence that the laws are effective in reducing accidental shootings[95] and adolescent suicides.[96] Some of this research has indicated these laws are most effective when penalties are strongest.[97]

Juvenile Ownership Laws

Young people are at high risk for firearm-related death. Persons between the ages of fifteen and nineteen are about three times more likely to be the victim of a firearm-related homicide than those aged thirty or older; for persons between the ages of twenty and twenty-four, the risk increases more than fourfold. There were also more than 2,000 firearm-related suicides among persons under the age of twenty-four in 2006.[98]

Under federal law since 1968, persons under the age of twenty-one may not buy handguns from licensed dealers (the minimum age for rifle and shotgun purchase from a dealer is eighteen). A different federal law, enacted in 1994, forbids handgun possession and purchase from *non-dealers* by persons less than eighteen years old. This means that under federal law, those between the ages of eighteen and twenty can legally purchase handguns from private persons – where no background check is required – but not from licensed dealers where the Brady Law does mandate background checks.

A number of states have their own laws establishing a minimum age for the purchase and/or possession of handguns – some as high as twenty-one years. To date, efforts to evaluate the effects of these laws on deaths among young people have not suggested beneficial effects. Thomas Marvell examined state laws banning juvenile gun possession, with minimum ages ranging from sixteen to twenty-one. He found no significant effects for these laws on firearm homicide or suicide among juveniles or young adults.[99] Webster and colleagues similarly detected no significant effects of youth purchase or possession laws on suicides of youth ages fourteen to twenty.[100] Rosengart and colleagues examined state laws setting the minimum age for purchase or possession at twenty-one years. They also found no significant associations between these laws and homicide or suicide rates.[101] To date, however, convincing research on the effects of these laws on homicide *perpetration* – arguably the most relevant outcome – is lacking. In addition, it is difficult to disentangle the effects of these state laws from the 1968 federal law.

Targeted Police Efforts to Prevent High-Risk Carrying

Although it is obviously preferable to prevent high-risk persons from obtaining firearms in the first place, some have argued that preventing high-risk *carrying* of firearms in public – by high-risk persons in high-risk places – should be an important law enforcement goal.[102] In fact, police in at least three major U.S. cities – Kansas City, Indianapolis, and Pittsburgh – have conducted targeted enforcement efforts to identify and deter illegal gun carrying, which have been the subject of careful evaluation and research.

Efforts in Kansas City largely became the model for other cities that followed. In what was dubbed the "Kansas City Gun Experiment," police conducted extra patrols in one high-crime area of the city from July 1992 to January 1993. Those patrols were devoted exclusively to identifying people carrying concealed weapons in their cars or on the streets. Traffic stops were conducted and searches were performed based on reasonable suspicion that a weapon might be present or incident of arrest for some other crime. Searches of pedestrians – based on consent or on telltale signs of weapon carrying – were also conducted.

During the twenty-nine weeks that the Kansas City Gun Experiment patrols were operational, the number of guns seized by law enforcement increased by 65 percent and gun crime declined 49 percent compared with the prior twenty-nine weeks. A comparison area that did not receive the intervention had no statistically significant change in gun crime during the same period. Importantly, neighboring areas of Kansas City also experienced no change in gun crime – suggesting that gun crime had not been simply "displaced" to these areas from the intervention neighborhood.[103]

In Indianapolis, two neighborhood target areas were selected for a gun-carrying intervention for a ninety-day period in 1997. In one neighborhood, the focus of the intervention was on increasing the number of traffic stops; in the other, a more selective approach to vehicle stops was used with the primary goal of maximizing the seizure of illegal weapons. Only with the latter approach were there significant reductions in overall gun crime comparable to the success of the Kansas City experiment.[104]

In Pittsburgh, a 1998 gun-carrying suppression intervention by special police units was associated with a 71-percent reduction in assault-related gunshot wounds treated in hospitals. Using hospital data eliminates a potential source of bias if residents are less likely to report crimes in intervention neighborhoods. As in Kansas City, there was no spill-over effect to other areas.[105]

Taken together, these three evaluations suggest a powerful – though underutilized – intervention to deter high-risk gun carrying. Since 1998, other cities have adopted some form of the Kansas City approach. However, these interventions have rarely been sustained for long periods, and no well-designed, published evaluations are available.

TECHNOLOGICAL APPROACHES

Personalized Guns

Several new or developing technologies have the potential to make it harder for high-risk persons to acquire, carry, or keep firearms. One such technology, "personalized" guns, would allow only an authorized user to operate the firearm. This might be accomplished through built-in systems that would recognize the authorized user – perhaps by reading a fingerprint – and deactivate the gun for anyone else.[106] The idea of modifying the firearm itself derives, in part, from the public health tradition of successful approaches to reducing injuries associated with other products, such as cars. Seat belts and passive restraint systems such as air bags are two life-saving examples.

Although several prototypes have been developed, personalized guns are not yet readily available for sale. But once on the market, personalized guns have the potential to keep guns out of the hands of dangerous people and save lives.[107] If a firearm were not operable by a young child, some accidental gun deaths might be prevented. In addition, the majority of gun-related suicides of juveniles involve a firearm kept in the home of a relative.[108] A personalized gun might prevent some of these deaths as well. Personalized guns could also make straw purchases more difficult by limiting the gun's use to its legally authorized buyer rather than the felon or juvenile for whom the gun is actually intended. If a firearm were not immediately operable following its theft, some homicides and assaults also could be averted.[109] An estimated 500,000 firearms are stolen each year.[110]

State legislatures are just beginning to enact laws regarding personalized guns. New Jersey has a law mandating that, beginning two years after personalized handguns are available for sale, all new handgun models sold in the state must incorporate that technology.[111] Maryland, which currently requires childproofing technology for guns (built-in locking devices but not full personalization), compels an annual report on the feasibility of personalization technology to permit legislators to consider future legislation.[112]

Despite their promise and the theoretical basis for their life-saving potential, there is little research attempting to quantify the potential benefits of personalized guns. In a review of gun-related deaths in two states, Vernick and colleagues determined that personalized guns might have prevented 37 percent of the accidental deaths examined.[113] Based on several assumptions about personalized guns, Cook and Leitzel estimate that if all U.S. handguns were personalized, more than 4,000 lives might be saved annually.[114]

Microstamping

About 38 percent of homicide cases in the United States go unsolved.[115] At many shooting scenes, a crime gun is never recovered. However, expended cartridge casings are often found by the police. A new technology – microstamping – has the potential to exploit these recovered casings to solve crimes and thereby reduce the incentive for high-risk persons to carry and use guns.

As a byproduct of the manufacturing process of a firearm, machine tools create unintentional markings on the interior surfaces of the gun. When a firearm is discharged, these unintentional tool marks come in contact with the cartridge case and transfer impressions from the firearm. For over 100 years, trained firearm examiners have compared marks on casings found at a crime scene with a test-fired casing from a recovered firearm to establish that the firearm actually discharged the casing. These comparisons are based on the assumption that each firearm creates a unique "ballistic fingerprint." A 2009 study by the National Academy of Sciences, however, questions this assumption, suggesting that the scientific basis for traditional ballistic matching may be flawed.[116]

Microstamping represents an evolution in ballistic identification because it can identify the serial number of a firearm directly from an expended cartridge case found at a crime scene. Originally created in the 1990s, microstamping uses precise laser technology to engrave intentional microscopic markings on the internal mechanisms of a semiautomatic pistol. When the pistol is fired, these engravings are stamped onto the cartridge – identifying essential information including the make, model, and serial number of the weapon in the form of alphanumeric and geometric codes. Information extracted from these codes can be used to trace a firearm used in a violent crime, even if the crime gun itself is never recovered.[117]

As with any new, innovative technology, there are questions concerning the effectiveness and durability of microstamping. One line of criticism has focused on whether the technology can withstand wear and tear under the extreme conditions that exist within the chamber of a firearm.[118] In response to these questions, microstamping's inventors have conducted a series of tests that demonstrate that firearms equipped with the latest version of the technology can consistently produce identifiable codes even after thousands of rounds of firing. For example, in 2007, Lizotte and Ohar fired over 2,500 rounds from a microstamped Smith and Wesson .40 caliber semiautomatic handgun using five different brands of ammunition. The results were impressive, with all eight digits of the alphanumeric code legible 97 percent of the time.[119] Lizotte and Ohar also tested a used .45 Colt semiautomatic pistol with over 1,500 rounds and produced extractable marks over 95 percent of the time using optical microscopy.[120] Other firearms also yielded positive test results.[121] Microstamping technology also includes several redundant marks intended to defeat efforts to tamper with the gun.

Microstamping can serve as a deterrent to criminal use and illegal trafficking of firearms. Because the technology allows police to link a cartridge casing found at a crime scene to the original purchaser of the firearm, gun buyers may be less likely to commit crimes with microstamped guns. Similarly, straw purchasers might be less likely to purchase firearms for convicted felons and other prohibited buyers if they believe those guns could be easily traced back to them after being used in crimes. Microstamping can also help identify gun traffickers by providing more data (i.e., successfully traced crime guns) for law enforcement to analyze.

Microstamping is available for a wide variety of firearms, although recent policy proposals have focused on implementing the technology on semiautomatic pistols because they are the most common type of gun used in crime and because they discharge spent casings through an ejection port. Revolvers, in contrast, store spent casings in their revolving cylinder and may not leave any cartridge evidence at a crime scene.

On October 13, 2007, California Governor Arnold Schwarzenegger signed first-of-its-kind legislation mandating the microstamping of all new models of semiautomatic handguns sold in the state beginning in 2010.[122] The District of Columbia followed suit in 2009 with a law scheduled to take effect in 2011.[123] Evaluations of the effectiveness of the California and D.C. laws must await their implementation.

CONCLUSION

There are many policy options to make it more difficult for dangerous people to purchase, possess, and use firearms. But there are also a variety of ways that high-risk people use to acquire guns. No single intervention will address the problem of gun violence in the United States. In fact, it is becoming increasingly clear that enacting policies in isolation is often not effective – comprehensive systems are needed. Systems for keeping guns from being diverted from the legal to the illegal market can be thought of as a dam that protects the community. If the dam has a dozen holes, plugging just one or two will not solve the problem. But plugging all or nearly all of the holes can greatly enhance public safety.

Of course, enacting gun laws in the United States can be politically challenging. Powerful interest groups oppose most laws. In fact, sometimes frustrated by the pace of legislative progress, cities and states have brought lawsuits against firearm manufacturers and dealers arguing, in part, that the industry's distribution practices make it too easy for high-risk persons to acquire guns.[124] However, a 2005 federal law – the Protection of Lawful Commerce in Arms Act – provides the firearm industry with broad immunity from liability. As a result, most of the municipal lawsuits have been dismissed by the courts.[125] It may be politically easier, however, to enact laws focusing on especially dangerous people, scofflaw gun dealers, children, or carrying in high-risk places by high-risk persons than to pass more broadly applicable laws.

Such laws may also be less likely to pose constitutional problems than more all-inclusive weapons bans. The Supreme Court's 2008 decision in *District of Columbia v. Heller* struck down Washington, D.C.'s handgun ban as a violation of the Second Amendment. But the Court, at least for now, closely tied that right to having a handgun in the home for protection. Writing for the Court, Justice Scalia instructed that "… nothing in our opinion should be taken to cast doubt on longstanding prohibitions on the possession of firearms by felons and the mentally ill, or laws forbidding the carrying of firearms in sensitive places such as schools or government buildings, or laws imposing conditions and qualifications on the commercial sale of arms."[126] In June 2010, the Court decided another case involving a broad handgun ban, *McDonald v. City of Chicago*.[127] In *McDonald*, the Court concluded that the Second Amendment applies to state and local governments, not just to the federal government, an issue left undecided in *Heller*. In *McDonald*, the Court also reaffirmed the language from *Heller* about presumptively valid gun laws. But the constitutionality of specific firearm laws (other than handguns bans) has yet to be decided by the Supreme Court.

Returning to the comparison between guns and cars with which we opened this chapter, there is still more reason for hope. By instituting a broad range of strategies – including making cars safer, targeting high-risk driving and drivers (such as intoxicated persons), and improving roadway design – the rate of fatal car crashes per mile driven in the United States has declined by more than 70 percent since the 1960s. No single strategy could achieve this success; a comprehensive approach was needed for focusing on higher-risk cars, drivers, and roadways. If the United States can take the problem of gun violence as seriously as it has motor vehicle deaths, we have an opportunity to save thousands of lives and reshape our communities for everyone's benefit.

ACKNOWLEDGMENTS

The authors thank Joshua Horwitz for the material devoted to micro-stamping technology and gratefully acknowledge a gift from an anonymous donor to support the writing of this chapter.

Notes

1. U.S. Dept. of Transp., Bureau of Transp. Statistics, online at http://www.bts.gov/publications/national_transportation_statistics/html/table_01_11.html (accessed July 13, 2009).
2. Lisa Hepburn et al., *The U.S. Gun Stock: Results From the 2004 National Firearms Survey*, 13 Inj. Prevention 15 (2007).
3. Philip J. Cook & Jens Ludwig, Guns in America: Results of a Comprehensive National Survey on Firearms Ownership and Use (1996).
4. Centers for Disease Control and Prevention, Web-based Injury Statistics and Query System (WISQARS), online at http://www.cdc.gov/injury/wisqars/index.html (accessed July 13, 2009).
5. U.S. Dept. of Justice, Bureau of Justice Statistics, Firearms and Crime Statistics, online at http://www.ojp.usdoj.gov/bjs/guns.htm (accessed July 13, 2009).
6. Philip J. Cook & Jens Ludwig, Gun Violence: The Real Costs (2000).

7. Jon S. Vernick et al., *Regulating Firearm Advertisements that Promise Home Protection*, 277 JAMA 1391 (1997).
8. Kim A. Howard et al., *Beliefs about the Risks of Guns in the Home: Analysis of a National Survey*, 5 INJ. PREVENTION 284 (1999).
9. Joshua Horwitz & Casey Anderson, GUNS, DEMOCRACY, AND THE INSURRECTIONIST IDEA (2009).
10. Stephen P. Teret et al., *Support for New Policies to Regulate Firearms: Results of Two National Surveys*, 339 NEW ENG. J. MED. 813 (1998). See also Greenberg Rosner Research & The Terrance Group, *Americans Support Common Sense Measures to Cut Down on Illegal Guns*, online at http://www.mayorsagainstillegalguns.org/downloads/pdf/polling_memo.pdf (accessed September 2, 2009).
11. 18 U.S.C. § 922 (g) (2009).
12. 18 U.S.C. § 923 (a) (2009).
13. 18 U.S.C. § 922 (s) (2009).
14. 18 U.S.C. § 922 (b) (1) (2009).
15. 18 U.S.C. § 922 (x) (2009).
16. 18 U.S.C. § 922 (b) (3) (2009).
17. 18 U.S.C. § 922 (g) (1) (A) (2009).
18. 18 U.S.C. § 923 (g) (6) (2009).
19. NATIONAL FIREARMS ACT, 26 U.S.C. §5801 et seq. (2009).
20. Garen J. Wintemute, RING OF FIRE: THE HANDGUN MAKERS OF SOUTHERN CALIFORNIA (1994).
21. 18 U.S.C. § 925 (d) (3) (2009).
22. U.S. DEPT. OF JUSTICE, BUREAU OF ALCOHOL, TOBACCO, FIREARMS, AND EXPLOSIVE, SEMIAUTOMATIC ASSAULT WEAPONS BAN: QUESTIONS AND ANSWERS, online at http://www.atf.gov/firearms/saw-faqs.htm (accessed July 13, 2009).
23. Jon S. Vernick & Daniel W. Webster, *Policies to Prevent Firearm Trafficking*, 13 INJ. PREVENTION 78 (2007).
24. Philip J. Cook & Jens Ludwig, GUNS IN AMERICA: RESULTS OF A COMPREHENSIVE NATIONAL SURVEY ON FIREARMS OWNERSHIP AND USE (1996).
25. Caroline W. Harlow, FIREARM USE BY OFFENDERS: SURVEY OF INMATES IN STATE AND FEDERAL CORRECTIONAL FACILITIES (2001).
26. 18 U.S.C. § 923 (g) (3) (A) (2009).
27. 18 U.S.C. § 926 (a) (2009).
28. 18 U.S.C. § 923 (g) (1) (B) (2009).
29. 18 U.S.C. § 923 (e) (f) (2009).
30. Jon S. Vernick & Stephen P. Teret, *A Public Health Approach to Regulating Firearms as Consumer Products*, 148 U. PA. L. REV. 1193, 1196 (2000).
31. Jon S. Vernick & Lisa M. Hepburn, STATE AND FEDERAL GUN LAWS: TRENDS FOR 1970–99, in Jens Ludwig & Philip J. Cook eds., EVALUATING GUN POLICY 345 (2003).

32. Eric Gorovitz et al., *Preemption or Prevention? Lessons from Efforts to Control Firearms, Alcohol, and Tobacco*, 19 J. PUB. HEALTH POL'Y 36 (1998).
33. Stephen P. Teret et al., *Gun Deaths and Home Rule: A Case for Local Regulation of a Local Public Health Problem*, 9 (Supp. 1) AM. J. PREVENTIVE MED.44 (1993).
34. Legal Cmty. Against Violence, *Preemption and Local Authority to Regulate Firearms and Ammunition*, online at http://www.lcav.org/content/preemption_local_authority.pdf (accessed July 13, 2009).
35. 18 U.S.C. § 922 (s) (2009).
36. Printz v. United States, 521 U.S. 898 (1997).
37. 18 U.S.C. § 922 (t) (1) (2009).
38. U.S. DEPT. OF JUSTICE, BUREAU OF JUSTICE STATISTICS, BACKGROUND CHECKS FOR FIREARM TRANSFERS, 2007, online at http://ojp.usdoj.gov/bjs/pub/html/bcft/2007/table/bcft07st01.htm (accessed July 15, 2009).
39. BRADY CTR. TO PREVENT GUN VIOLENCE, BRADY BACKGROUND CHECKS: 15 YEARS OF SAVING LIVES 7 (2008).
40. Jens Ludwig & Philip J. Cook, *Homicide and Suicide Rates Associated with Implementation of the Brady Handgun Violence Prevention Act*, 284 JAMA 585 (2000).
41. BUREAU OF JUSTICE STATISTICS, SURVEY OF STATE PROCEDURES RELATED TO FIREARMS SALES (2006).
42. Caroline W. Harlow, FIREARMS USE BY OFFENDERS: SURVEY RESULTS FROM INMATES IN STATE AND FEDERAL CORRECTIONAL FACILITIES (2001).
43. Daniel W. Webster et al., *Effects of State-level Firearm Seller Accountability Policies on Firearms Trafficking*, 86 J. URB. HEALTH 525 (2009).
44. Daniel W. Webster et al., *Relationship Between Licensing, Registration, and Other Gun Sales Laws and the Source State of Crime Guns*, 7 INJ. PREVENTION 184 (2001).
45. Garen J. Wintemute et al., *Prior Misdemeanor Convictions as a Risk Factor for Later Violent and Firearm-related Criminal Activity Among Authorized Purchasers of Handguns*, 280 JAMA 2083 (1998).
46. Richard R. Berk et al., *Forecasting Murder in a Population of Probationers and Parolees: A High-stakes Application of Statistical Learning*, 172 J. ROYAL STAT. SOC'Y 191 (2009).
47. Beth M. Huebner et al., *Gangs, Guns, and Drugs: Recidivism among Serious, Young Offenders*, 6 CRIMINOLOGY & PUB. POL'Y 187 (2007).
48. Howard J. Shaffer et al., *The Epidemiology of Psychiatric Disorders Among Repeat DUI Offenders Accepting a Treatment-sentencing Option*, 75 J. CONSULTING & CLINICAL PSYCHOL. 795 (2007); Sandra C. Lapham et al., *Prevalence of Psychiatric Disorders among Persons Convicted of Driving While Impaired*, 58 ARCHIVES GEN. PSYCHIATRY 943 (2001).
49. Carl Keane et al., *Drinking and Driving, Self-control, and Gender – Testing a General Theory of Crime*, 30 J. RESEARCH IN CRIME & DELINQUENCY 30 (1993).

50. G. William Lucker et al., *The Prevalence of Antisocial Behavior Among U.S. Army DWI Offenders*, 52 J. Studies on Alcohol 318 (1991).
51. Stephen P. Teret et al., *Public Support for Innovative Gun Policies: The Results of Two National Surveys*, 339 N. Eng. J. Med. 813 (1998).
52. Brian A. Reaves, *Violent Felons in Large Urban Counties: State Court Processing Data 1990–2002*, Bureau of Justice Statistics Special Report (2006).
53. Caroline W. Harlow, Firearm Use by Offenders: Survey of Inmates in State and Federal Correctional Facilities (2001).
54. Garen J. Wintemute et al., *Subsequent Criminal Activity Among Violent Misdemeanants Who Seek to Purchase Handguns: Risk Factors and Effectiveness of Denying Handgun Purchase*, 285 JAMA 1019 (2001).
55. Bureau of Alcohol, Tobacco and Firearms (ATF), Crime Gun Trace Reports (2000): The Youth Gun Interdiction Initiative (2002).
56. Garen J. Wintemute et al., *Risk Factors Among Handgun Retailers for Frequent and Disproportionate Sales of Guns Used in Violent and Firearm Related Crimes*, 11 Inj. Prevention 357 (2005).
57. Bureau of Alcohol, Tobacco and Firearms, Commerce in Firearms in the United States (2000).
58. Susan B. Sorenson & Katherine A. Vittes, *Buying a Handgun for Someone Else: Firearm Dealers' Willingness to Sell*, 9 Inj. Prevention 147 (2003).
59. Jon S. Vernick et al., *Regulating Firearms Dealers in the United States: An Analysis of State Law and Opportunities for Improvement*, 34 J.L. Med. & Ethics 765 (2006).
60. Daniel W. Webster et al, *Effects of State-level Firearm Seller Accountability Policies on Firearms Trafficking*, 86 J. Urb. Health 525 (2009).
61. Daniel W. Webster et al., *Effects of Undercover Police Stings of Gun Dealers on the Supply of New Guns to Criminals*, 12 Inj. Prevention 225 (2006).
62. Daniel W. Webster, Supplemental Expert Report Submitted for City of New York v. A-1 Jewerly & Pawn, Inc. et al., 06 CV 2233, City of New York V. Bob Moates' Sport Shop, Inc., et al., 06 CV 6504, May 27, 2008.
63. Daniel W. Webster et al., *Effects of a Gun Dealer's Change in Sales Practices on the Supply of Guns to Criminals*, 83 J. Urb. Health 778 (2006).
64. U.S. Dept. of Justice, Bureau of Alcohol, Tobacco, Firearms, and Explosives, The Bureau of Alcohol, Tobacco, Firearms, and Explosives' Investigative Operations at Gun Shows, online at http://www.usdoj.gov/oig/reports/ATF/e0707/final.pdf (accessed August 2, 2009).
65. U.S. Dept. of the Treasury, Bureau of Alcohol, Tobacco, and Firearms, Gun Shows: Brady Checks and Crime Gun Traces (1999).
66. U.S. Dept. of Justice, Bureau of Alcohol, Tobacco and Firearms, Following the Gun: Enforcing Federal Laws Against Firearms Traffickers (2000).
67. U.S. Dept. of the Treasury, Bureau of Alcohol, Tobacco, and Firearms, Gun Shows: Brady Checks and Crime Gun Traces (1999).

68. U.S. Dept. of the Treasury, Bureau of Alcohol, Tobacco, and Firearms, Gun Shows: Brady Checks and Crime Gun Traces (1999).
69. Garen J. Wintemute, *Inside Gun Shows: What Goes On When Everybody Thinks Nobody's Looking*, online at http://www.ucdmc.ucdavis.edu/newsroom/releases/wintemute9–2009/index.html (accessed November 5, 2009).
70. The City of New York, Gun Show Undercover: Report on Illegal Sales at Gun Shows, online at http://www.gunshowundercover.org/main.cfm?actionId=globalShowStaticContent&screenKey=cmpContent&htmlKey=about&s=gunshow (accessed November 5, 2009).
71. Mayors Against Illegal Guns, The Movement of Illegal Guns in America, online at http://www.mayorsagainstillegalguns.org/downloads/pdf/trace_report_final.pdf (accessed August 5, 2008).
72. Garen J. Wintemute, *Gun Shows Across a Multistate American Gun Market: Observational Evidence of the Effects of Regulatory Policies*, 13 Inj. Prevention 150 (2007).
73. Mark G. Duggan et al., *The Effect of Gun Shows on Gun-Related Deaths: Evidence from California and Texas*, online at http://www.nber.org/papers/w14371 accessed August 5, 2009).
74. Letter from Garen J. Wintemute et al. to Mark Duggan et al., online at http://www.jhsph.edu/gunpolicy/Critique_of_recent_gun_show_study.pdf (accessed August 18, 2009).
75. 18 U.S.C. § 923 (g) (3) (2009).
76. U.S. Dept. of Justice, Bureau of Alcohol, Tobacco and Firearms, Following the Gun: Enforcing Federal Laws Against Firearms Traffickers 9 (2000).
77. U.S. Dept. of Justice, Bureau of Alcohol, Tobacco and Firearms, Crime Gun Trace Reports 2000 51 (2000).
78. Douglas S. Weil & Rebecca C. Knox, *Effects of Limiting Handgun Purchases on Interstate Transfer of Firearms*, 275 JAMA 1759 (1996).
79. Linda E. Saltzman et al., *Weapon Involvement and Injury Outcomes in Family and Intimate Assaults*, 267 JAMA 3043 (1992).
80. James A. Fox & Marianne W. Zawitz, Homicide Trends in the United States (2007).
81. Jacqueline C. Campbell, et al., *Risk Factors for Femicide in Abusive Relationships: Results from a Multisite Case Control Study*, 93 Am. J. Pub. Health 1089 (2003).
82. Douglas J. Wiebe, *Sex Differences in the Perpetrator-victim Relationship Among Emergency Department Patients Presenting with Nonfatal Firearm-related Injuries*, 42 Annals Emergency Med. 405 (2003).
83. Susan B. Sorenson & Douglas J. Wiebe, *Weapons in the Lives of Battered Women*, 94 Am. J. Pub. Health 1412 (2004).
84. Emily F. Rothman et al., *Batterers' Use of Guns to Threaten Intimate Partners*, 60 J. Am. Med. Women's Ass'n 62 (2004).
85. 18 U.S.C. § 922 (g) (8) (2009).

86. 18 U.S.C. § 922 (g) (9) (2009).
87. 18 U.S.C. § 922 (a) (32) (2009). See Legal Community Against Violence, Regulating Guns in America: An Evaluation and Comparative Analysis of Federal, State and Selected Local Laws, online at http://www.lcav.org/library/reports_analyses/regulating_guns.asp (accessed August 2, 2009).
88. Shannon Frattaroli & Jon S. Vernick, *Separating Batterers and Guns: A Review and Analysis of Gun Removal Laws in 50 States*, 30 Evaluation Rev. 296 (2006).
89. Elizabeth R. Vigdor & James A. Mercy, *Do Laws Restricting Access to Firearms by Domestic Violence Offenders Prevent Intimate Partner Homicide?*, 30 Evaluation Rev. 313 (2006).
90. Marjory S. Hardy, *The Effects of Gun Admonitions on the Behaviors and Attitudes of School-Aged Boys*, 24 J. Dev. & Behav. Pediatrics 1 (2003).
91. Mark A. Schuster et al., *Firearm Storage Patterns in U.S. Homes with Children*, 90 Am. J. Pub. Health 588 (2000).
92. David A. Brent et al., *Firearms and Adolescent Suicide: A Community Case-control study*, 147 Am. J. Diseases of Child. 1066 (1993). See also: Arthur L. Kellermann et al., *Suicide in the Home in Relation to Gun Ownership*, 327 New Eng. J. Med. 467 (1992); David A. Brent et al., *The Presence and Accessibility of Firearms in the Homes of Adolescent Suicides: A Case-Control Study*, 266 JAMA 2989 (1991); Matthew Miller and David Hemenway, Guns and Suicide in the United States, 359 New Eng. J. Med. 989 (2008).
93. United States Secret Service and Dept. of Educ., Final Report and Findings of the Safe Schools Initiative: Implications for Prevention of School Attacks in the United States (2002).
94. Legal Community Against Violence, Regulating Guns in America: An Evaluation and Comparative Analysis of Federal, State and Selected Local Laws (2008).
95. Lisa Hepburn et al., *The Effect of Child Access Prevention Laws on Unintentional Child Firearm Fatalities, 1979–2000*, 61 J. Trauma 423 (2006). See also: Daniel W. Webster & Marc Starnes, *Reexamining the Association Between Child Access Prevention Gun Laws and Unintentional Firearm Deaths Among Children*, 106 Pediatrics 1466 (2000); Peter Cummings et al., *State Gun Safe Storage Laws and Child Mortality Due to Firearms*, 278 JAMA 1084 (1997).
96. Daniel W. Webster et al., *Effects of Youth-focused Firearm Laws on Youth Suicides*, 292 JAMA 594 (2004).
97. Daniel W. Webster & Marc Starnes, *Reexamining the Association Between Child Access Prevention Gun Laws and Unintentional Firearm Deaths Among Children*, 106 Pediatrics 1466 (2000); Peter Cummings et al., *State Gun*

Safe Storage Laws and Child Mortality Due to Firearms, 278 JAMA 1084 (1997).

98. Centers for Disease Control and Prevention, Web-based Injury Statistics and Query System (WISQARS), online at http://www.cdc.gov/injury/wisqars/index.html (accessed July 13, 2009).
99. Thomas B. Marvell, *The Impact of Banning Juvenile Gun Possession*, 44 J.L. & Econ. 691 (2001).
100. Daniel W. Webster et al., *Association Between Youth-Focused Firearm Laws and Youth Suicides*, 292 JAMA 594 (2004).
101. Matthew R. Rosengart et al., *An Evaluation of State Firearm Regulations and Homicide and Suicide Death Rates*, 11 Inj. Prevention 77 (2005).
102. James Q. Wilson, *Just Take Away Their Guns: Forget Gun Control*, New York Times Magazine 46, March 20,1994.
103. Lawrence W. Sherman et al., The Kansas City Gun Experiment: National Institute of Justice Research in Brief (1995).
104. Edmund F. McGarrell et al., 1 Criminology and Public Policy 119 (2001).
105. Jacqueline Cohen & Jens Ludwig, Policing Crime Guns, in Jens Ludwig & Philip J. Cook eds., Evaluating Gun Policy 217 (2003).
106. Stephen P. Teret & Nancy L. Lewin, *Policy and Technology for Safer Guns: An Update*, 41 Annals of Emergency Medicine 32 (2003).
107. Stephen P. Teret & Patricia Culross, *Product Oriented Approaches to Reducing Youth Gun Violence*, 12 Future of Child. 119 (2002).
108. David C. Grossman et al., *Self-inflicted and Unintentional Firearm Injuries Among Children and Adolescents: The Source of the Firearm*, 153 Archives of Pediatric & Adolescent Med. 875 (1999)
109. Philip J. Cook & James A. Leitzel, *"Smart" Guns: A Technological Fix for Regulating the Secondary Market*, 20 Contemp. Econ. Pol'y 38 (2002).
110. Philip J. Cook & Jens Ludwig, Guns In America: Results of a Comprehensive Survey of Gun Ownership and Use (1996).
111. N.J. Stat. Ann. § 2C:58–2.4 (2009).
112. Md. Pub. Safety Code Ann. § 5–132 (2009).
113. Jon S. Vernick et al., *Unintentional and Undetermined Firearm-related Deaths: A Preventable Death Analysis for Three Safety Devices*, 9 Inj. Prevention 307 (2003).
114. Philip J. Cook & James A. Leitzel, *"Smart" Guns: A Technological Fix for Regulating the Secondary Market*, 20 Contemp. Econ. Pol'y 38 (2002).
115. Uniform Crime Report, Fed. Bureau of Investigation, "Crime in the United States," Table 25, online at http://www.fbi.gov/ucr/05cius/data/table_25.html (accessed September 8, 2009).
116. Strengthening Forensic Science in the United States: A Path Forward, National Research Council of the National Academies (2009)

117. Orest Ohar & Todd Lizotte, *Extracting Ballistic Forensic Intelligence: Microstamped Firearms Deliver Data for Illegal Firearm Traffic Mapping-Technology*," Proceedings of SPIE, Vol. 7434, 743416, p. 2 (2009)
118. David Howitt et al., *What Laser Machining Technology Adds to Firearm Forensics: How Viable are Micro-Marked Firing Pins as Evidence?* California Policy Research Center, Univ. of Cal. at Davis, (Undated), online at http://forensicscience.ucdavis.edu/pdf/microserial.pdf (accessed August 18, 2009).
119. Press Release, NanoMark Technologies, New Test Affirms Validity of Microstamping Technology (May 24, 2007), online at http://www.csgv.org/atf/cf/%7B79FD0842–518D-42AC-8228-AE59B7990689%7D/LIZOTTE%20TEST%20RELEASE%205–25–07.PDF (accessed August 18, 2009)
120. Orest Ohar & Todd Lizotte, Paper Presented at the 2008 SPIE Annual Optics and Technology Conference: Forensic Firearm Identification of Semiautomatic Handguns Using Laser Formed Microstamping Elements, (September 3, 2008), online at http://www.csgv.org/atf/cf/%7B79FD0842–518D-42AC-8228-AE59B7990689%7D/Forensic%20Firearm%20 Identification%20of%20Semiautomatic%20Handguns%20-% 20Lizotte.pdf (accessed August 18, 2009), at 13.
121. Orest Ohar & Todd Lizotte, Paper Presented at the 2008 SPIE Annual Optics and Technology Conference: Forensic Firearm Identification of Semiautomatic Handguns Using Laser Formed Microstamping Elements, (September 3, 2008), online at http://www.csgv.org/atf/cf/%7B79FD0842–518D-42AC-8228-AE59B7990689%7D/Forensic%20Firearm%20 Identification%20of%20Semiautomatic%20Handguns%20-% 20Lizotte.pdf (accessed August 18, 2009), at 13.
122. California Governor Arnold Schwarzenegger, AB 1471 Signing Statement (October 13, 2007).
123. D.C. Code § 7–2505.03 (2009).
124. Jon S. Vernick & Stephen P. Teret, *New Courtroom Strategies Regarding Firearms: Tort Litigation against Firearm Manufacturers and Constitutional Challenges to Gun Laws*, 36 Hous. L. Rev. 1713 (1999). See also John G. Culhane & Jean M. Eggen, *Defining a Proper Role for Public Nuisance Law in Municipal Suits Against Gun Sellers: Beyond Rhetoric and Expedience*, 52 S.C. L. Rev. 287 (2001).
125. Jon S. Vernick et al., *Availability of Litigation as a Tool for Firearm Injury Prevention: Comparison of Guns, Vaccines, and Motor Vehicles*, 97 Am. J. Pub. Health 1991 (2007).
126. District of Columbia v. Heller, 128 S. Ct. 2783, 2816–7 (2008).
127. McDonald v. City of Chicago, 2009 WL 1631802 (U.S.).

PART IV BEYOND COMPENSATION: PUBLIC FEATURES OF PRIVATE LITIGATION

7 TORT LITIGATION FOR THE PUBLIC'S HEALTH

Elizabeth Weeks Leonard[*]

INTRODUCTION

The principal objective of public health is to promote and protect the health of populations. The focus is on the common good of society rather than individual health or welfare. Public health law is the infrastructure by which government can compel, prohibit, track, regulate, incentivize, or otherwise seek to ensure that the health of the population as a whole is optimized. There is an inevitable tension in public health law between the common good and the rights and desires of individuals. Quarantine laws, for example, prevent the spread of infectious diseases and protect the health of society by severely restricting an infected individual's freedom of movement. That "victim" whose rights are infringed generally does not receive individual compensation for the intrusion in his rights. He, in effect, "takes a hit for the team."

The focus of tort law, by contrast, is resolving private disputes between one or more individuals in society by awarding compensatory damages. A tort begins with an injury, or harm, and the question in every case is whether the injured victim should bear the loss oneself, or whether another person, typically the person who brought about the harm, should bear the loss. Tort law offers a set of rules, approaches, and rationales by which government – specifically courts – can require one person to pay a sum of money to another person, with the award representing the value of the injury. From a population-based perspective, simply reassigning loss from one person to another person does not seem to offer any benefit to the larger society beyond those parties.

Beginning with that fundamental understanding of the two fields, the objectives of public health law and tort law seem largely incompatible. The operating principles are utterly at odds: public law versus private disputes; communal benefit versus individual rights; harm prevention versus injury compensation. Public health law seeks to improve the good of society collectively, whereas tort law seeks to make up for the loss that one person suffered by exacting recovery from another person. The aim of this chapter is to demonstrate a number of ways that the seemingly individualistic field of tort law can, in fact, promote the population-based objectives of public health law.

The obvious examples of tort litigation for the public's health involve high-profile lawsuits against products or conduct that resulted in serious, detrimental health effects on large numbers of people in society.[1] Ralph Nader's exposé of the Chevrolet Corvair, and General Motors' attempts to silence him, are almost synonymous with public interest litigation challenging manufacturers' reluctance to invest in product safety.[2] Other examples include asbestos,[3] lead paint,[4] silicone breast implants,[5] the Dalkon Shield,[6] diethylstilbestrol (DES),[7] automobiles,[8] tobacco,[9] firearms,[10] and newer pharmaceutical products, including Phen-Fen,[11] Oxy-Contin,[12] and Vioxx.[13] Litigants also attempted to address the obesity epidemic through litigation, suing fast food vendors for misrepresenting their products as part of a healthy lifestyle.[14] Environmental, toxic torts, and other mass exposure cases similarly seek to address broad, public harms through private litigation.[15] The objective of those lawsuits often is only secondarily about securing compensation for members of a large, disparate class of plaintiffs, each of whom will likely receive a relatively small monetary award. More importantly, those cases send a message about safety and fine the injurers, operating as informal regulation of certain industries and products.[16] Products liability and mass torts cases are exceptional in many respects, relying on special procedural rules for class actions[17] and special rules of fault, causation, and proof to achieve their results.[18] This chapter demonstrates that the less obvious, traditional principles of tort law, beginning with early common law cases intended simply to resolve private disputes between two parties, also promote and protect the public's health.

To demonstrate the perhaps counterintuitive fit between tort law and public health law, the chapter begins by briefly outlining core policies and objectives underlying public health law and tort law. The chapter then describes the evolution and operation of core tort principles, highlighting their alignment with the population-based perspective of public health law. A number of specific doctrines and case examples highlight the actual and potential compatibility of the two fields.

PUBLIC HEALTH AND THE COMMON GOOD

The Institute of Medicine provides a widely accepted definition of public health: "Public health is what we, as a society, do collectively to assure the conditions for people to be healthy."[19] That standard definition emphasizes the "we," the collective, society as a whole. The "we," in most cases, is the government, whose powers are marshaled to control and prevent disease.[20] Some accounts suggest that public health, welfare, and security were the very reasons for establishing government in the origin of society.[21] Traditional public health objectives, including sanitation, infectious disease control, disease prevention, nuisance abatement, public safety, and pure food and drinking water standards, cannot be secured through individual action and call for coordinated responses. Centralized government, with its command-and-control law enforcement powers, is well positioned to coordinate those efforts.[22] The public health field considers health a matter of social concern, not merely the responsibility of individuals to secure their own health care though private transactions with providers and insurers.[23] Collective action and public benefit are hallmarks of public health.[24]

Public health cannot adequately protect the population's health without, sooner or later, intruding on private beliefs, private property, economic freedom, freedom of movement, and personal autonomy.[25] Having clean streets means that citizens cannot dump trash wherever they wish.[26] Clean air may require minimizing vehicle and industrial pollution by altering driving habits or installing emission-control devices. Preventing spread of contagious disease may call for compelling individuals to undergo painful and risky inoculations. Safe workplace standards, minimum age, minimum wage, and maximum hours laws protect workers but cost employers money and limit freedom of contract by limiting the range of permissible employment arrangements. By contrast to torts, in which the disputes are between one individual versus another, in public health, often the conflict is one individual versus society.

Public health faces significant challenges pursuing population-based objectives in a society that gives great deference to individual wants, needs, and rights.[27] Garrett Hardin's classic essay, *The Tragedy of the Commons*, provides a useful illustration of the public health challenge.[28] In a ranch community with a common pasture, the interest of each cattle owner is to add cattle to the commons and thereby increase individual productivity. As the commons become more crowded, the yield of each animal decreases, which requires each rancher to increase the number of grazing cattle to produce the same level of revenue. And so the cycle continues. Eventually the commons is depleted and can be protected only through external (usually, government) controls. The government, for example, may cap the number of cattle that each rancher may graze, or limit the hours of grazing. In any case, the rights of each rancher are restricted to preserve the common resource for all.

This tension between individual interests and societal goals underlies many public health interventions. For example, an individual may prefer not to be vaccinated for a variety of reasons.[29] But the disease-prevention goal of public health requires vaccination, even though an individual may be physically harmed, emotionally hurt, or personally offended. Allowing individuals voluntarily to opt out of vaccination would steadily deplete the "commons" of a disease-free society by increasing the number of unprotected people in the population.[30] Consistent with the tragedy of the commons theory, many infectious diseases, such as polio, measles, mumps, and whopping cough, which were largely eradicated with widespread compliance with vaccination mandates, have begun to reemerge recently as many parents have again begun refusing to vaccinate their children based on health, religious, or other objections.[31]

One response to the individual rights versus common good conflict in public health is to invoke social contract theory.[32] The idea of the social contract is that individuals, by leaving the state of nature and joining society, choose to give up certain individual rights. In exchange, individuals gain protection of social order and laws, considered superior to the state of nature and better for society as a whole. For example, potential polluters or vaccine avoiders may instead consider the loss of some degree of personal autonomy worth the gain of living in a clean, sanitary, and disease-free society. The seminal U.S. Supreme Court public health case of *Jacobson v. Massachusetts*[33] upheld a Massachusetts mandatory vaccination law as a permissible intrusion on individual liberty, invoking the state constitution's "social compact" provision.[34] As the Court noted:

> The possession and enjoyment of all rights are subject to such reasonable conditions as may be deemed by the governing authority of the country essential to the safety, health, peace, good order and morals of the community. Even liberty itself, the greatest of all rights, is not unrestricted license to act according to one's own will.[35]

Social contract theory does not resolve the tension between public health objectives and individual rights but suggests a way of rationalizing the inevitable trade-offs.

Whatever the theoretical rationale, most people have come to recognize and accept a wide range of restrictions on individual rights in the name of the common good of society. For example, states have long-established mandatory vaccination laws to prevent spread of infectious diseases,[36] despite the intrusion on personal autonomy and bodily integrity. Quarantine laws, although rarely invoked in recent history, allow government to isolate infected individuals, even if no treatment is available for the affliction, in order to protect others from the disease. Newer public health laws may be more controversial but derive from the same justifications. For example, many states and localities prohibit smoking in public places because of the perceived health risks of second-hand smoke, despite smokers' desires to enjoy a cigar or cigarette while drinking or eating.[37] States also mandate seatbelts and motorcycle helmets, even though individuals may prefer to travel in their personal vehicles unencumbered by straps and buckles.[38] Other laws restrict the sale of certain food ingredients considered likely to lead to long-term individual health problems, such as obesity, heart disease, and cancer.[39] Such laws have been repeatedly justified and upheld in the interest of public health.[40]

The trade-offs between individual rights and public health, safety, and welfare were cast in a new, especially salient, light after the 9/11 terrorist attacks, SARS threats, London subway bombings, and other recent catastrophes. Those events, as well as unprecedented natural disasters such as Hurricane Katrina, the Greensburg tornado, and the Asian tsunami, highlighted the need for coordinated government interventions to respond to the exigent public health emergencies and take steps to prevent similar catastrophes in the future. In that context, even avowed civil libertarians acknowledged the necessity of individual rights yielding to public health concerns.[41] Post-9/11, the public is all too familiar with major and minor intrusions on civil liberties in the name of public safety. The grossest infractions of bodily integrity and liberty were horrifically depicted to the world in the Guantanamo Bay torture reports. On a much more mundane level, air travelers now accept the inconvenience of removing shoes and a three-ounce limit on liquids taken on-board, as well as the indignity of having their luggage randomly searched and bodies patted-down in the middle of busy, public airport terminals. Most individuals accept those intrusions on privacy, autonomy, and liberty as necessary for national security. They recognize that they cannot individually protect themselves from terrorist attacks.

Public health, by definition, focuses on the health of populations. Individual interests are subordinated to the common good. In many cases, individuals willingly submit to government intrusions on individual rights because they appreciate the public health, safety, and welfare benefits that they receive in exchange. The focus of tort law may be individual compensation for harm, but tort rules and policies also strike a balance between individual rights and societal wants and needs, very much like public health law.

TORT LAW'S INDIVIDUALISTIC ORIENTATION

Tort law provides a centralized, government-run system for resolving private disputes. In that sense, tort law derives from the same social contract as public health law. In the state of nature, neighbors would resolve disputes over land or personal injuries through private redress or negotiation. By moving into society, individuals agree to submit disputes to courts for resolution, under the applicable procedural rules, burdens of proof, standards of fault, and other rules, rather than simply sacking their neighbors' property or person to collect the damages or justice that they think they are due. Despite the similar origin, it may be hard to recognize that the torts system provides any beneficial impact on society beyond resolution of private disputes and judicial awards of compensation to injured persons.

An essential task of tort law is assigning liability for accidental injuries.[42] Tort law also provides compensation for some intentional conduct that involves intrusions on personal autonomy, bodily integrity, or property rights, such as battery and trespass. In addition, some injuries resulting from activities that are not, strictly speaking, accidental, such as defectively designed products or abnormally dangerous activities, are compensable in torts. Accepting that living in society involves a certain level of unavoidable injury, the task of tort law is to distinguish between injuries that the victim should simply bear himself and those for which compensation is proper.[43] This essential loss-allocation task seems a far cry from public health goals of preventing harm and promoting the common good.

The narrow view of tort law suggests that the principal objective is individual compensation: to make the victim whole; to return him, as closely as possible, to the position that he would have occupied but for the injury.[44] That objective is accomplished through civil litigation and the return of a verdict ordering the defendant-tortfeasor to pay a sum of money to the plaintiff-victim as damages. The substantive, procedural, and evidentiary rules of tort litigation often seem tilted in favor of victims' recovery.[45] For example, common law courts have developed special rules, such as the *res ipsa loquitur* inference,[46] alternative liability theory,[47] and other "softer" approaches to strict but-for causation,[48] which allow plaintiffs to recover when under the standard rule they would not have been able to carry their burden of proof. The collateral source rule allows plaintiffs to recover the full value of their injuries, even if they already received compensation from another source, such as pension, health, or life insurance.[49] The pro-compensation goal of torts comports with the general public's pejorative view of shyster personal injury, or "ambulance-chasing," lawyers motivated to seek enormous damages awards for even the most trivial affronts.[50] That common perception of tort law does not suggest much benefit for the health or well-being of the rest of society.[51]

Admittedly, many torts principles do seem more focused on the individual than on broader issues of public health and welfare. Plaintiffs' personal autonomy is protected in many doctrines, including battery,[52] self-defense,[53] and informed consent.[54] Intentional, or "dignitary," torts compensate personal affronts even in the absence of appreciable harm.[55] Battery requires merely intent to touch in a way that a reasonable person would regard as offensive, not intent to harm or injure.[56] Assault does not require any touching at all, or even fear of touching, but merely "apprehension" that an unwanted touching could occur.[57] Trespass may be committed even when the defendant honestly but mistakenly believed that he had permission to be at a particular place,[58] or imperceptible particles unavoidably migrated onto the plaintiff's land.[59] Tort law's protection of individual autonomy, dignity, and bodily integrity seems to conflict directly with public health objectives. For example, tort law would allow an individual to refuse vaccination for even foolish reasons or slight probabilities. An unwanted touching with a sharp needle clearly meets the elements of common-law battery.[60] Yet public health law may mandate the inoculation despite individual objections.[61]

Tort law's protection of individual autonomy is not limited to victims, but also extends to injurers. Various rules protect defendants' freedom of action, allowing a sphere of activity that will not give rise to liability. Most significantly, United States courts rejected the British common law's strict liability standard in favor of a negligence, or fault-based, standard for accidents.[62] Under strict liability, intentional conduct that caused harm established a tort; a person acted at his or her own peril.[63] The negligence standard, by contrast, requires more than an act: carelessness and foreseeability of harm are also requisite to recovery. Actors who cause injuries will not be liable as long as their conduct was "reasonable" in the view of the fact finder.[64] Even defendants who are adjudged negligent may avoid liability if the victim was also negligent,[65] or voluntarily and knowingly assumed the risk of the defendant's careless conduct.[66] On public policy grounds, courts sometimes will not allow individuals to assume certain risks deemed to endanger public health or expose individuals to unacceptable personal safety trade-offs.[67] Despite those exceptions, public health law's objective of promoting and protecting health, safety, and welfare of populations seems hard to square with a tort liability system that tolerates some level of accidental harm without liability.

As further indication of the apparent preference for individual autonomy over population health and safety, tort law generally does not recognize a cause of action for failure to aid, warn, protect, or rescue, no matter how easy or reasonable the rescue may seem.[68] The "no-duty rule" protects privacy and autonomy by not imposing liability if individuals choose not to inconvenience themselves or risk their own safety in attempting to aid another.[69] The contrast is apparent: Tort law imposes no duty to protect other members of society whereas public health law focuses on what we as a society can do to promote the health of the population. Yet the seemingly draconian no-duty rule has been substantially eroded by various exceptions that permit plaintiffs to maintain causes of action against defendants who failed to come to their aid.[70] In particular, landowners,[71] custodial caregivers,[72] certain health care professionals,[73] and those who non-negligently create risks[74] may have affirmative duties to help those in peril. In addition, many states, by statute, have enacted Good Samaritan laws.[75] Those exceptions are consistent with tort law's goal of compensating victims but also promote safety by requiring or encouraging certain actors to take steps to help those in danger.

Even accepting tort law's primarily individualistic orientation does not necessarily mean undermining public health goals. Many public health interventions, such as health promotion campaigns, public service announcements, and health education, seek to empower individuals and foster their self-determination. Those approaches provide individuals with information to assist them in making better choices about their own health without intruding on individual autonomy. Some public health ethicists suggest that health promotion activities are highly preferred over those that mandate or penalize certain activities.[76] For example, providing nutrition education about the health effects of trans-fats and alternative choices, or food ingredients labeling, would be preferred to laws banning trans-fat from restaurant foods, thereby depriving individuals of choice. Tort laws that compensate affronts to personal dignity or uphold plaintiffs' choices to encounter certain risks are consistent with that view of public health ethics.

BEYOND COMPENSATION

Providing individual compensation is one goal of tort law. But compensation cannot be the only goal, or we could envision a system that includes a common pool of funds, payable to injured victims, irrespective of the source of the harm or the wrongful nature of the conduct. For example, workers compensation programs award damages from a common fund without any proof of fault, so long as the injury occurred at the workplace.[77] Similarly, the 9/11 Victim Compensation Fund provided government compensation to victims, irrespective of their ability to identify specific terrorists or others responsible for the tragedy.[78] Instead, the tort system requires plaintiffs to identify the specific injurer, prove the wrongfulness of his conduct, establish a causal link between the defendant's conduct and the plaintiff's injury, and seek recovery from that particular actor. Tort law's necessary connection between the plaintiff-victim and defendant-injurer suggests objectives beyond compensation. Requiring injurers to pay damages to victims deters future dangerous conduct and punishes wrongful actors.

A court order requiring the defendant to pay an award of damages ensures that the injurer internalizes, or "feels," the loss that the victim endured, thereby signaling him to behave differently in order to avoid liability in the future. The tort judgment also sends a message to other would-be injurers about the costs of engaging in dangerous conduct. Tort judgments, accordingly, operate as incentives for safer conduct in society, thereby protecting the public's health. To better achieve those objectives, tort damage awards include not only actual, out-of-pocket economic loss, such as medical bills, property damage, and lost wages, but also noneconomic damages, such as mental suffering, physical pain, interference with personal and professional relationships, fear, fright, and embarrassment.[79] Although not without controversy,[80] tort law recognizes noneconomic harms as real, compensable injuries, essential to make-whole compensation for victims. Moreover, requiring defendants to pay for all of the harm caused, including intangible losses, ensures that they and other potential injurers appreciate the full impact of their actions and adjust their behavior accordingly.[81] The collateral-source rule, although sometimes allowing double recovery to victims, ensures that defendants receive the correct incentive for safety.[82]

Tort damages also punish wrongdoers and sanction socially unacceptable behavior. Requiring a negligent tortfeasor to pay a sum of money to the victim operates as a "private fine," punishing the wrongful actor. In certain cases, additional, punitive damages, above what is necessary to compensate the victim, may be awarded expressly to punish the tortfeasor and deter the particular misconduct at issue in the case.[83] Those punitive, or exemplary, damages are available in exceptional cases if the defendant's conduct is particularly egregious or reprehensible.[84] Even without punitive damages, tort judgments serve an expressive function, communicating society's disapproval of certain conduct.[85] The communicative purpose of torts is particularly salient in cases such as professional malpractice and defamation, in which defendants' reputations are at stake. Medical malpractice actions are recorded in a national database.[86] In defamation cases, nominal compensatory damages, such as one dollar, may be awarded to show that the publication was false even if there was no actual harm to the plaintiff.[87]

Torts damages, accordingly, operate simultaneously on both sides of the dispute, compensating victims while also deterring and punishing wrongdoers. A judgment awarding damages does more than merely compensate injured victims or shift the loss from the injured to the injurer. Tort judgments enhance public safety by discouraging members of society from acting in ways that cause harm to others and punishing actors who acted unreasonably with respect to the safety of others.

EVOLUTION OF THE REASONABLE CARE STANDARD

Negligence is the defining standard of liability for accidental injuries under American tort law. The standard seems to undermine public health and safety by tolerating some injurious conduct in favor of individual freedom of action. But the negligence standard is, in fact, very much in keeping with public health traditions, including the social contract and communitarian goals. It is helpful to consider the historical context for the rise of the seemingly divergent fields of public health and torts. The Industrial Revolution, in particular, necessitated both fields' orientation toward a population-based perspective.

In the late 1800s, the United States shifted from mostly agricultural, local markets to more centralized, industrial production, attracting large immigrant and rural populations to new urban centers.[88] The influx of people to cities brought a myriad of social problems, including crowded housing, inadequate water and sewage systems, rapidly spreading epidemic diseases, and violence. Health, disease, and poverty could no longer be considered the result of individual failings or challenges; population-based public health responses were needed.[89] The Industrial Revolution also brought great advances in transportation, such as trains, trolleys, and automobiles, manufacturing and textile machinery, assembly lines, steam engines, and ironworks. For all the benefits and conveniences of mechanization, the industrial age also brought greater risk of injury and accidents from the new devices, calling for a new approach to tort law.[90]

Traditional English common law recognized a tort, or writ, of trespass for unintentional injuries resulting from intentional acts. Landowners were held strictly liable – that is, liable without fault – for things escaping from their land. For example, in *The Case of the Thorns*, a landowner was held strictly liable in trespass for shrub cuttings that fell onto his neighbor's property, despite the exercise of due care.[91] Similarly, in *Rylands v. Fletcher*, a property owner who constructed a water reservoir to operate a mill was liable when the reservoir broke and flooded his neighbor's property, even though the reservoir was competently constructed with no apparent flaws or defects.[92] The strict liability approach to accidental injury made sense in feudal society where harm resulted from wandering animals, flowing water, and falling boughs and branches. Landowners made roughly comparable use of their property, and harm-causing agents were easily traceable to their sources. As between the one who caused the harm and one who innocently suffered loss, it seemed fair that the injurer should pay, irrespective of fault.[93]

But strict liability was incompatible with the machine age and the Industrial Revolution, with harm resulting not only from animals, water, and naturally occurring conditions but also from newfangled machines and complex instrumentalities. Machines carried both greater potential and less clear attribution for accidental harm. Serious personal injury and property damage could result from explosions, collisions, and moving parts. In addition, it was difficult to determine whether the injury-causing instrumentality was poorly designed, incorrectly assembled, carelessly maintained, or otherwise defective; each scenario suggested a different potential defendant and cause. Moreover, the new machines could malfunction or cause injury despite any want of due care. But holding industrial landowners, machine operators, railroads, mining operations, and automobile drivers strictly liable for harm caused by their activities would have substantially impaired industrial progress.[94] Accordingly, courts compromised safety in favor of other societal wants and needs.

In *Losee v. Buchanan*, the landmark U.S. opinion rejecting strict liability in favor of negligence, the New York court noted: "We must have factories, machinery, dams, and canals, and railroads. They are demanded by the manifold wants of mankind, and lay at the base of all our civilization."[95] The *Losee* court's holding derived from the social contract, the same rationale underlying the *Jacobson* mandatory vaccination decision:

> By becoming a member of civilized society, I am compelled to give up many of my natural rights, but I receive more than a compensation from the surrender by every other man of the same

> rights and the security, advantage, and protection which the laws give me.[96]

In tort law, individuals give up their natural and absolute rights to enjoyment of land, personal autonomy, and bodily integrity, and thereby tolerate some inevitable, accidental harm without compensation. At the same time, they gain the freedom to engage in potentially injurious conduct, shielded by the law of negligence from having to make amends to their neighbors as long as they act with reasonable care. Similarly, in public health, individuals give up the freedom to refuse vaccinations, tolerate restrictions on land use, abide restrictions on employment arrangements, and other limits in order to gain the public health benefits of living in a safer, healthier society.

SOCIAL WELFARE IN TORTS

The adoption of the reasonable-care standard for accidental injuries moved tort law toward a population-based perspective by taking into account the impact of tort judgments on not just the parties before the court but on society as a whole.[97] Under the negligence standard, individuals who are injured by the conduct of others sometimes will not receive compensation for their harm. Correlatively, those who caused the harm sometimes will not be punished or deterred, at least through the torts system, from engaging in the same conduct in the future. Allowing some injuries to go uncompensated and compromising human life and safety seems utterly contrary to public health goals. But the negligence standard realistically acknowledges that society has priorities and desires beyond perfect safety and optimal health for individuals. As a society, we also want the convenience of car and airplane travel, the efficiency of automated assembly lines, and the healing potential of pharmaceutical and medical device product. With each of those wants, there is great potential for injury, some of which we tolerate. Tort law offers a methodology for deciding when the health and safety trade-offs are too great.

Public health law also must contend with scarce resources and necessarily make similar trade-offs. Any number of public health concerns – disease pandemic, obesity, tobacco, natural disasters, automobile safety, environmental pollution, to name just a few – demand priority attention. Yet lawmakers must make choices, funding some initiatives at the expense of others, saving some lives or improving the health of some at the expense of others. The challenge of prioritizing public health concerns is exacerbated by the lack of coordination among governmental actors, agencies, and constituents. Environmental regulators, for example, may urge new laws without regard for the health and safety impact of their program on others.[98] Public health law has not developed a workable approach to balancing those "health-health" trade-offs, as several commentators, advocating a novel cost-benefit approach for environmental, health, and safety regulation, have noted:

> Because society has limited resources to spend on regulation, benefit-cost analysis can help illuminate the trade-offs involved in making different kinds of social investments. In this regard, it seems almost irresponsible to not conduct such analyses, because they can inform decisions about how scarce resources can be put to the greater social good.[99]

Even among competing public health goals, lawmakers struggle to prioritize problems and interventions to achieve optimal public health benefits.[100] Moreover, public health regulators cannot realistically and effectively operate in a complex society by myopically advocating public health priorities above all others.[101] As during the Industrial Revolution, society at times may benefit from resources being directed toward objectives other than public health and safety.

If perfect safety were the goal of tort law, we could not have railroads, firearms, or dynamite because we could never justify the inherent risks to human safety. In a world of scarcity, human life is not priceless; we make trade-offs all the time, favoring other interests over the protection of human life and safety.[102] If we did not care about fuel-efficiency, comfort, aesthetics, speed, hauling capacity, and other features, we could build perfectly safe cars, with "spongy" bumpers,[103] three-point restraints, helmets, and ten-mile-per-hour top speeds. Many tort law doctrines operate from a "utilitarian," or economic efficiency, approach to balance individual and societal interests. From the utilitarian perspective on tort law, health is just one aspect of overall societal welfare to be considered, whereas public health law places human health and safety above all other concerns. Tort law's broader perspective does not mean that it cannot be used as an effective tool for protecting the public's health, at least in some cases. Moreover, tort law at least offers some workable approaches to balancing priorities, a task at which public health law has been less effective.

For purposes of tort law, utilitarianism seeks to maximize societal welfare by improving the happiness or well-being of as many as individuals as possible.[104] Drawing on philosophical notion of utility, economic analysis of the law evaluates the efficiency of legal rules and principles.[105] The objective is to allocate resources in a manner that maximizes their value in society as a whole.[106] In this view, the goal of tort law is to create optimal, but not excessive, levels of safety.[107] Accordingly, some dangerous, even harmful, conduct is tolerated because the benefits to society outweigh the harm inflicted on the individual plaintiff.[108]

The most famous expression of social welfare cost-benefit analysis in tort law is the "Hand formula." Judge Learned Hand offered a rubric for conceptualizing the otherwise nebulous "reasonable person" negligence standard of care in algebraic terms: The defendant is deemed negligent if $B < PL$, where "B" is the burden, or cost, of a given safety precaution that could have prevented the injury; "L" is the magnitude of the plaintiff's loss, or injury, and all other losses that could be avoided with the same precaution; and "P" is the probability of the harm occurring, used as a discounting factor against the L.[109] Under the Hand formula, defendants are liable in negligence for failing to take the cheaper precautions.[110] There is no liability, though, if the cost of the safety precaution, even if feasible, is greater than the total "utils" of safety gained.[111] The Hand formula recognizes the reality of scare resources and necessity of allocating them in the interest of society as a whole, not just the individual seeking compensation for an injury.[112] If resources were unlimited, there would be no reason, arguably, not to take every possible safety precaution, aspire for perfect safety, and compensate every injury. But every amount spent on safety reduces resources to spend on other goods or services. Even seemingly free precautions carry lost opportunity costs, which must be considered.[113]

The Hand formula implicitly rebuts the notion that any societal values, including human health, safety, and life, are priceless.[114] Indeed, the fact that human life and all other elements of compensatory damages are included in the Hand formula leads to moral, practical, and philosophical objections. It may be morally objectionable, for example, to suggest that a defendant is negligent for failing to take precautions that would have prevented fire to a high-rise executive office building but not liable for failing to take similar precautions with respect to a coal mine when the B and P of each accident is the same but the L includes lost earnings of the victims, which would be much higher for the workers in the office building than the coal mine.[115] Practical objections to the Hand formula include the difficulty estimating the monetary value of various elements of damages, pricing the precautions, and estimating risks and probabilities.[116] The formula is also philosophically questionable in that it assumes that people operate as rational cost-benefit analysts, calculating the relative worth of each step they take.[117] Despite those objections, the Hand formula, like policies underlying public health, recognizes that individual interests at times must yield to the greater good of society.

An intriguing example of a court's application of the Hand formula to promote public health is *Helling v. Carey*.[118] A thirty-two-year-old woman sued her ophthalmologist, alleging negligent failure to diagnosis open-angle glaucoma, resulting in severe and permanent vision loss. Glaucoma can be detected by a simple, painless, relatively inexpensive pressure test.[119] Nevertheless, both parties' expert witnesses agreed that the professional standard of care for ophthalmologists did not require routine glaucoma testing for patients under age forty.[120] The incidence of glaucoma in persons younger than forty was one in 25,000. Applying BPL analysis, the B of the relatively cheap, painless pressure test, balanced against the serious, high-magnitude L of permanent vision lost, even discounted by the relatively low P of 1 in 25,000, suggested that the doctor was negligent for failing to administer the test.

The *Helling* court's reliance on the Hand formula to find liability is notable because it overrode the controlling professional standard of care. As a rule, in medical malpractice or other professional negligence cases, liability is judged not by the "reasonableness" standard but the customary, or professional, standard.[121] Once established through expert testimony, the professional standard of care is conclusive; it is not merely "some evidence," which the jury may consider or ignore.[122] Had the court followed the professional standard of care rule, the ophthalmologist would have been absolved of liability because his practice of not testing people under age forty was consistent with the professional standard. Instead, the court applied the BPL formulation of negligence, achieving a better outcome for the plaintiff-patient and the public's health. The court noted that the customary standard failed to protect public safety because an "entire calling may be lagging."[123] If a simple test could prevent serious harm in people over the age of forty, there was no reason to deny the same protection to younger patients.[124]

Helling is one of the few cases to apply cost-benefit analysis to decide a medical liability claim.[125] As a rule, courts defer to professional autonomy and expert judgment in medical malpractice cases, even when that approach denies compensation to injured plaintiffs and seems to undermine public health and safety. The primary criticism of the economic efficiency or utilitarian conception of tort law, from a public health perspective, is that the balance of interests may not always favor safety and health above all other goals.[126] Although exceptional in terms of torts doctrine, *Helling* demonstrates the potential for public health considerations to inform courts' judgments in certain cases. In any event, the fact that courts do not always place human health and safety concerns above other societal interests and objectives does not mean that tort law is antithetical to public health. Evolving from tort law's private dispute resolution origins, the utilitarian conception that considers the broader social effects of decisions in individual cases represents a significant development toward a population-based perspective.

Tort law's utilitarian approach is evident in other doctrines, including products liability, the law applied in many of the "obvious" cases of tort litigation for the public's health involving drugs, devices, vehicles, building supplies, and other consumer products. Products liability was once conceived of as "strict" in the sense that a manufacturer would be absolutely liable simply for placing a dangerous product in the stream of commerce, without regard to privity of contract, warranty, or reasonable care.[127] That approach ensures compensation to injured consumers. From a social welfare perspective, strict products liability efficiently places the loss on the party best able to prevent future harm and bear or spread the loss. As compared to consumers, product manufacturers have more information about their dangerous products and better means to correct the problems through redesign or added safety features. In addition, manufacturers and sellers receive income from the sale of their products. They can spread the cost of tort liability and product modification across society by increasing prices for products or passing the costs on to others in the distribution chain.[128] Consumers each pay slightly more, putting in our "two cents" for the inevitable, occasional injury while still enjoying the benefits of the otherwise desirable product.[129] Society expresses its preference for dangerous products over safety by continuing to purchase the product despite the risks.

For similar reasons, the *Rylands* strict liability standard was retained in the United States for certain types of conduct deemed "abnormally dangerous activities."[130] While victims deserve compensation for the inevitable injuries, society continues to value those activities, despite their inherent danger.[131] Classic examples of abnormally dangerous activities include blasting operations, dynamite storage, atomic energy plants, oil wells, water reservoirs, and insecticide spraying.[132] The conduct may continue as long as the defendant "pays his way" in the form of torts damage awards.[133] As with defective products, the abnormally dangerous activity will continue as long as society continues to tolerate the safety trade-offs.

Over time, products liability law came to incorporate elements of negligence and allocated risk-bearing responsibilities among members of society for much the same reason that negligence replaced strict liability as the standard of care in non-products cases. As a society, we have wants other than safety, which could not be satisfied by imposing liability too readily on dangerous but desirable products. The current standards for determining liability in the largest category of products cases, design defects, come very close to negligence, or fault-based, approaches.[134] A product design may be found defective either because the risks of the challenged design outweigh the benefits, or the product falls below ordinary consumers' expectations of safety.[135] The former test, by definition, turns on a utilitarian, cost-benefit calculus, much like the Hand formula. The latter test favors safety, but from the perspective of a reasonable person. Injuries resulting from unexpected uses or exceptionally rigorous expectations are not compensable. Modern products liability law, like negligence and the doctrine of abnormally dangerous products, operates from a utilitarian calculus. Even the most stringent, no-fault formulations do not aim to produce perfect safety.[136] If that were the goal, consumers would be denied a whole range of useful yet dangerous products.

CONCLUSION

Tort law's core focus on ensuring individual compensation and protecting freedom of action seems antagonistic to public health's core focus on population health and the common good. This chapter does not suggest that the primary objective of tort law is, or even should be, promoting and protecting the public's health. But the discussion highlights a number of areas of historical, theoretical, and doctrinal consistency between the two fields, even in tort law's traditional, foundational principles. Both tort law and public health law offer approaches to addressing inevitable conflicts in organized society between individual interests and community needs. Both fields also acknowledge the reality of scarce resources and strive for the most efficient allocation in terms of overall benefit to society. The fundamental difference is that public health places a premium on human life and safety whereas tort law does not, sometimes tolerating debilitating, serious injuries in favor of other societal interests. Tort law's pragmatic acceptance of the reality that human life, no matter the platitudes, is not priceless does not negate the field's value as a tool for public health promotion.

Notes

* Associate Professor, University of Kansas School of Law.

1. See Lawrence O. Gostin, PUBLIC HEALTH LAW AND ETHICS: A READER 265–67 (2002) (chapter on "Tort Litigation for the Public's Health"); WENDY E. PARMET, POPULATIONS, PUBLIC HEALTH, AND THE LAW 219 (2009) (listing examples of recent tort litigation that "has captured the

headlines, occupied courtrooms, and provoked a heated debate about the role of tort law in protecting public health"); Jon S. Vernick et al., *Role of Litigation in Preventing Product-Related Injuries*, 25 EPIDEMIOLOGIC REVIEWS: INJURY PREVENTION AND CONTROL 90, 92–96 (Stephen B. Thacker & Ellen J. MacKenzie eds. 2003).

2. Ralph Nader, UNSAFE AT ANY SPEED: THE DESIGNED-IN DANGER OF THE AMERICAN AUTOMOBILE (1965).
3. See Anne Bloom, *From Justice to Global Peace: A (Brief) Genealogy of the Class Action Crisis*, 39 LOY. L.A. L. REV. 719 (2006) (Agent Orange, asbestos, and other examples).
4. Thomas ex rel. Gramling v. Mallett, 701 N.W.2d 523 (Wis. 2005) (lead paint).
5. See Wendy Wagner, *When All Else Fails: Regulating Risky Products Through Tort Litigation*, 95 GEO. L.J. 693, 714–20 (2007) (breast implant litigation).
6. See Kenneth R. Feinberg, *Reporting From the Front Line – One Mediator's Experience With Mass Torts*, 31 LOY. L.A. L. REV. 359 (1998) (Dalkon Shield, silicone breast implants, tobacco, and other examples).
7. Hymowitz v. Eli Lilly & Co., 539 N.E.2d 1069, 1075 (N.Y. 1989) (holding manufacturers of DES liable for harm to daughters of women who took the drug while pregnant).
8. See, for example, Richardson v. Volkswagenwerk, A.G., 552 F. Supp. 73 (W.D. Mo. 1982); Henningsen v. Bloomfield Motors, 161 A.2d 69 (N.J. 1960).
9. See Lawrence O. Gostin, PUBLIC HEALTH LAW: POWER, DUTY, RESTRAINT 204–16 (2d. ed. 2008) (case study on tobacco litigation).
10. See, for example, Hamilton v. Beretta U.S.A. Corp., 750 N.E.2d 1055, 1068 (N.Y. 2001) (overturning jury verdict against multiple firearms manufacturers); Deborah R. Hensler & Mark. A. Peterson, *Understanding Mass Personal Injury Litigation: A Socio-Legal Analysis*, 59 BROOK. L. REV. 961 (1993) (discussing same); Vernick et al., *supra* note 1, at 92–95 (describing examples, including Firestone tires, swine flu vaccine, seatbelts, pacemakers, and handguns).
11. For example, HPF, L.L.C. v. Gen. Star Indem. Co., 788 N.E.2d 753 (Ill. App. Ct. 2003); In re Diet Drug Litig., 895 A.2d 493 (N.J. Super. Ct. Law Div. 2005).
12. For example, Price v. Purdue Pharma Co., 920 So. 2d 479 (Miss. 2006); Howland v. Purdue Pharma L.P., 821 N.E.2d 141 (Ohio 2004).
13. For example, Rutherford v. Merck & Co., Inc., 428 F. Supp. 2d 842 (S.D. Ill. 2006); Int'l Union of Operating Engr's Local #68 Welfare Fund v. Merck & Co., Inc., 894 A.2d 1136 (N.J. Super. Ct. App. Div. 2006).
14. For example, Pelman ex rel. Pelman v. McDonald's Corp., 396 F. Supp. 2d 439 (S.D.N.Y. 2005).

15. See Gostin, *supra* note 9, at 197.
16. See generally, Gostin, *supra* note 1, at 265–66 (describing advantages and disadvantages of litigation as informal regulation of public health); Wagner, *supra* note 5, at 695–69 (listing advantages to tort system in consumer and health protection); see also Richard A. Posner, *A Theory of Negligence*, 1 J. LEGAL STUD. 29, 31 (1972) (describing negligence system as form of indirect regulation).
17. John C. Coffee, Jr., *Class Wars: The Dilemma of the Mass Tort Class Action*, 95 COLUM. L. REV. 1343, 1358–67 (1995); Laura J. Hines, *Obstacles to Determining Punitive Damages in Class Actions*, 36 WAKE FOREST L. REV. 889, 902–12 (2001).
18. See Richard A. Epstein, MODERN PRODUCTS LIABILITY LAW 5–6 (1980) (noting that "rigorous requirements of proof everywhere blocked the plaintiff" in earlier products liability law and that "many of the barriers to recovery could not be justified either as a matter of substantive principle or administrative necessity"); Coffee, *supra* note 17, at 1356–57 (describing judicial skepticism to mass tort class actions because of the presence of individual issues of causation, harm, and defenses).
19. COMM. FOR THE STUDY OF THE FUTURE OF PUB. HEALTH, INST. OF MED., THE FUTURE OF PUBLIC HEALTH 19 (1988).
20. See Nan D. Hunter, *"Public-Private" Health Law: Multiple Directions in Public Health*, 10 J. HEALTH CARE L. & POL'Y 89, 89 (2007).
21. See PARMET, *supra* note 1, at 15 (quoting maxim, *salus populi supreme lex*, "The well being of the public is the supreme law," as meaning that attainment of public safety "was the rationale for civil society"); Richard A. Epstein, *In Defense of the "Old" Public Health*, 69 BROOK. L. REV. 1421, 1428 (2004) (quoting same maxim as having "powerful roots in the American political tradition"); James A. Tobey, *Public Health and the Police Power*, 4 N.Y.U. L. REV. 126 (1927) (suggesting that government is "organized for the express purpose, among others, of conserving the public health");); Dan E. Beauchamp, *Community: The Neglected Tradition of Public Health*, THE HASTINGS CENTER REPORT (Dec. 1985), at 30 ("Our root ideas about health and safety policy can be traced to these early state [police power] policies.").
22. See Paul Starr, THE SOCIAL TRANSFORMATION OF AMERICAN MEDICINE 189–90 (1982); Elizabeth Fee, *The Origins and Development of Public Health in the United States, reprinted in* GOSTIN, *supra* note 1, at 27, 28 (from *Oxford Textbook of Public Health*, vol. 1 (3d ed. 1997)); Wendy E. Parmet, *Health Care and the Constitution: Public Health and the Role of the State in the Framing Era*, 20 HASTINGS CONST. L.Q. 267, 290 (1993).
23. Scott Burris, *The Indivisibility of Public Health: Population-Level Measures in Politics of Market Individualism*, 87 AM. J. OF PUB. HEALTH 1607, 1608 (1997) ("to accept the rhetorical structure of market individualism is to

accept a political language that has no words for public health"); Kapp, *supra* note 3, at 586 (noting Gostin's "basic antagonism, shared by most of the public health leadership, to private enterprise and free market solutions to social problems"); *cf.* Joseph M. Boyle, Jr., *The Concept of Health and the Right to Health Care*, 3 SOC. THOUGHT 5, 5 (Summer 1977) (noting common perception that "being healthy is primarily a matter of individual responsibility"); Ynonne Denier, *On Personal Responsibility and the Human Right to Health Care*, 14 CAMBRIDGE Q. OF HEALTHCARE ETHICS, 224, 224 (2005) (discussing "role of personal responsibility in healthcare" and noting that "it is reasonable to hold people responsible for the consequences of their actions").

24. Gostin, *supra* note 9, at 9 (urging that "no single individual or group of individuals can ensure his or her health. Meaningful protection and assurance of the population's health require communal effort."); Michael Walzer, *Security and Welfare*, reprinted in Gostin, *supra* note 1, at 69, 75 (from *SPHERES OF JUSTICE: A DEFENSE OF PLURALISM AND EQUALITY* (1983)) ("Dealing with tuberculosis, cancer, or heart failure, however, requires a common effort. Medical research is expensive, and the treatment of many particular diseases lies far beyond the resources of any individual citizens. So the community steps in ....").
25. See Jacobson v. Massachusetts, 197 U.S. 11, 29 ("[I]n every well-ordered society charged with the duty of conserving the safety of its members the rights of the individual in respect of his liberty may at times, under the pressure of great dangers, be subject to such restraint, to be enforced by reasonable regulations, as the safety of the general public may demand"); see Starr, *supra* note 22, at 180–81 (listing business, religious, and other sources of opposition to public health efforts); Beauchamp, *supra* note 21, at 30 ("It is the private sphere that is problematic for public health. Public health sometimes intrudes into this private sphere in the interest of the health and safety of the community.").
26. See Lemuel Shattuck, *Introduction and Private Rights and Liberties, from Report of the Sanitary Commission of Massachusetts* (1850), at 25 ("It might be said, '[Sanitary measures] will interfere with private matters. If a child is born, if a marriage takes place, or if a person dies, what business is it to the public? ... Men who object and reason in this manner have very inadequate conceptions of the obligations they owe to themselves or to others.").
27. Jonathan Oberlander, *Who Pays? Who Benefits? Distributional Issues in Health Care*, 60 LAW & CONTEMP. PROBS. 245, 252 (2006) (noting that "American political culture values liberty over equality, cherishes markets and individual responsibility over government and social solidarity").
28. Garrett Hardin, *The Tragedy of the Commons*, 162 SCIENCE 1243–8 (1968); *see* Kevin M. Malone & Alan R. Hinman, *Vaccination Mandates: The Public Health Imperative and Individual Rights*, *in* LAW IN PUBLIC HEALTH

PRACTICE 262–63 (Richard A. Goodman et al. eds., 2003) (describing Hardin's essay).

29. See Jacobson, 197 U.S. at 39 (affirming prosecution for refusing vaccination). *Cf.* Malone & Hinman, *supra* note 28, at 273–74 (listing state law exemptions for health, religious, and philosophical objections).
30. See Malone & Hinman, *supra* note 38, at 263.
31. See Donald G. McNeil, Jr., *When Parents Say No to Child Vaccinations*, N.Y. TIMES, Nov. 30, 2002; Saad B. Omer et al., *Nonmedical Exemptions to School Immunization Requirements: Secular Trends and Association with Pertussis Incidence*, JAMA, Aug. 10, 2008, at 1757; Jennifer Steinhauer, *Public Health Risk Seen as Parents Reject Vaccines*, N.Y. TIMES, March 21, 2008.
32. John Locke, THE SECOND TREATISE OF GOVERNMENT 8–10 (J.W. Gough ed., 3d ed. reprint, Basil Blackwell, 1976) (1690); Thomas Hobbes, MAN AND CITIZEN 112 (Bernard Gert ed., Charles T. Wood et al. trans., Hackett Publishing Co. 1991) (1651); see Parmet, *supra* note 1, at 11 (noting public health interventions "justifiable under the prevailing social contract theory, which insisted that governments were legitimated because they were necessary to secure the common good"); Beauchamp, *supra* note 21, at 29–31 (discussing the common good and communitarian traditions of public health).
33. 197 U.S. 11 (1905).
34. *Id.* at 27.
35. *Id.* at 26–27 (quoting Commonwealth v. Alger, 61 Mass. (7 Cush.) 53, 84 (1851)).
36. See, for example, *id.* at 31–32 ("And the principle of vaccination as a means to prevent the spread of smallpox has been enforced in many states by statutes making the vaccination of children a condition of their right to enter or remain in public schools." (citing cases)); Zucht v. King, 260 U.S. 174 (1922) (excluding children or other persons not having a certificate of vaccination from public schools and other places of education); Gostin, supra note 1, at 379–82 & Table 6 ("All states, as a condition of school entry, require proof of vaccination against a number of diseases on the immunization schedule," and cataloguing state laws); Malone & Hinman, *supra* note 28, at 269–70 (noting that as of 1999 all but four states had school vaccination laws).
37. See, for example, James R. Davis & Ross C. Brownson, *A Policy for Clean Indoor Air in Missouri: History and Lessons Learned*, 13 ST. LOUIS U. PUB. L. REV. 749 (1994); Jean C. O'Connor et al., *Preemption of Local Smoke-Free Air Ordinances: The Implications of Judicial Opinions for Meeting National Health Objectives*, 36 J.L. MED. & ETHICS 403, 403 (2008).
38. See, for example, ARK. CODE ANN. § 27–37-702(a); D.C. CODE ANN. § 40–1602(a); HAW. REV. STAT. ANN. § 291–11.6(a)(1); N.C. GEN. STAT. § 20–135.2A(a); OKLA. STAT. ANN. tit. 47, § 12–417A; S.C. CODE ANN. §

56–5–6520; see also Linda Geller Dubinsky, *The Minnesota Mandatory Seat Belt Law: No Right to be Reckless?* 10 HAMLINE L. REV. 229, 229 (1987); Anthony P. Polito, *Constitutional Law: Seatbelt Laws and the Right to Privacy*, 10 HARV. J.L. & PUB. POL'Y 752, 757 (1987); Kenneth M. Royalty, *Motorcycle Helmets and the Constitutionality of Self-Protective Legislation*, 30 OHIO ST. L.J. 355 (1969); Jeffery Thomas, *Freedom to be Foolish? L.B. 496: The Mandatory Seatbelt Law*, 19 CREIGHTON L. REV. 743, 743 (1986).

39. *See* New York City Dep't of Health & Mental Hygiene, Cardiovascular Disease Prevention; Healthy Heart – Avoid Trans Fat (announcing final trans fat regulation and providing links to Health Code amendments) online at http://www.nyc.gov/html/doh/html/cardio/cardio-transfat.shtml; Charisse Jones & Nanci Hellmich, *NYC Bans Trans Fats in Restaurants*, USA TODAY, Dec. 6, 2006; *For Your Own Good*, N.Y. TIMES, Aug. 3, 2008, at WK2 (noting California's new law, among others); Jennifer Steinhauer, *California Bars Restaurant Use of Trans Fats*, N.Y. TIMES, July 26, 2008.
40. See, for example, Jacobson v. Massachusetts, 197 U.S. 11 (1905) (recognizing community's "right to protect itself against an epidemic of disease which threatens the safety of its members"); Picou v. Gillum, 874 F.2d 1519 (11th Cir. 1989) (upholding challenge to Florida's motorcycle helmet law); Benning v. State, 641 A.2d 757 (Vt. 1994) (noting that most states rejected challenges to helmet laws and listing cases).
41. GOSTIN, *supra* note 9, at xxv ("My devotion to civil liberties was particularly strained by events surrounding September 11 and the anthrax attacks, only a year after the first edition of this book was published."); Richard A. Posner, NOT A SUICIDE PACT: THE CONSTITUTION IN A TIME OF NATIONAL EMERGENCY (2006).
42. See, generally, Guido Calabresi, THE COST OF ACCIDENTS: A LEGAL AND ECONOMIC ANALYSIS (1960); Posner, *supra* note 16, at 29.
43. See Marc A. Franklin et al., TORT LAW AND ALTERNATIVES: CASES AND MATERIALS 1 (8th ed. 2006); Robert E. Keeton et al., TORT AND ACCIDENT LAW: CASES AND MATERIALS 1 (4th ed. 2004).
44. See Parmet, *supra* note 1, at 220 ("All tort scholars concede that tort law seeks to compensate injured parties").
45. See Marc Galanter, *Real World Torts: An Antidote to Anecdote*, 55 MD. L. REV. 1093, 1114 (1996).
46. See Byrne v. Boadle, Court of Exchequer, 2 H.C. 722, 159 Eng. Rep. 299 (1863) (shifting the burden of proof to the defendant to prove that he was not responsible when the plaintiff could not explain what, if any, conduct by the defendant caused his injury).
47. See Summers v. Tice, 199 P.2d 1 (Cal. 1948) (shifting burden of proving non-negligence to the defendants when plaintiff was unable to prove but-for causation against either one of two possible defendants).

48. See, for example, Zuchowicz v. United States, 140 F.3d 381 (1998) (adopting "substantial factor" test for actual causation); Hymowitz v. Eli Lilly & Co., 539 N.E.2d 1069 (1989) (adopting "market share" theory to allow plaintiffs to recover against all manufacturers of DES, even though they could not establish which manufacturers' drugs they took); Stubbs v. City of Rochester, 124 N.E. 137, 140 (N.Y. 1919) (allowing plaintiff to proceed upon compliance with "the spirit of the rule" despite lack of proof of direct causation that contaminated city water caused typhoid).
49. See, for example, Helfend v. Southern Cal. Rapid Transit Dist., 465 P.2d 61, 66 (Cal. 1970); Arambula v. Wells, 85 Cal. Rptr.2d 584, 586 (Cal. App. 1999).
50. See, for example, Marc Galanter, *Real World Torts: An Antidote to Anecdote*, 55 Md. L. Rev. 1093, 1095–97 (1996) (describing public's "widespread discontent with the tort system" and perception that the system is "demented, with freakish punitive damage bonanzas for persons who pour coffee on themselves or ricochet golf balls into their own foreheads"); David A. Hyman & Charles Silver, *Medical Malpractice Litigation and Tort Reform: It's the Incentives, Stupid*, 59 Vand. L. Rev. 1085, 1086 (2006); Stuart Taylor, Jr. & Evan Thomas, *Doctors. Teachers. Coaches. Ministers. They All Share a Common Fear: Being Sued on the Job. Our Litigation Nation – and a Plan to Fix It*, Newsweek, Dec. 15, 2003.
51. See Parmet, *supra* note 1, at 220 (suggesting that victim compensation, individual rights view of torts is "highly problematic" from a population-based perspective of the law).
52. See, for example, Vosburg v. Putney, 50 N.W. 403 (Wis. 1891).
53. See, for example, Courvoisier v. Raymond, 47 P. 284 (Colo. 1896).
54. See, for example, Schloendorff v. Society of N.Y. Hosp., 105 N.E. 92 (N.Y. 1914) (Cardozo, J.).
55. See Restatement (Second) of Torts § 19 ("A bodily contact is offensive if it offends a reasonable sense of personal dignity.")
56. See, for example, Vitale v. Henchy, 24 S.W.3d 651 (Ky. 2000) (patient who consented to surgery to be performed by one of two doctors but was operated on by a third could recover even though the procedure was performed without injury, consistent with standard of care); Fisher v. Carrousel Motor Hotel, Inc., 424 S.W.2d 627 (Tex. 1967) (finding battery when a black mathematician speaking at all-white country club had plate snatched from his hand by white waiter); Garrett v. Dailey, 279 P.2d 1091 (Wash. 1955) (finding battery when child pulled lawn chair out from under woman).
57. See, for example, Beach v. Hancock, 27 N.H. 223 (1853) (recognizing assault where defendant threateningly waved a gun, which, unbeknownst to plaintiff, was unloaded); Restatement (Second) of Torts § 21(1)(a) (defining assault as "intending to cause harmful or offensive contact ... or an imminent apprehension of such a contact").

58. See, for example, Southern Countries Ice Co. v. RKO Radio Pictures, Inc., 39 F. Supp. 157 (S.D. Cal. 1941) (studio employees committed trespass while mistakenly believing they had a right to enter movie set); Longenecker v. Zimmerman, 267 P.2d 543 (Kan. 1954) (landowner liable in trespass for trimming neighbor's trees that she mistakenly believed were on her property).
59. See, for example, Martin v. Reynolds Metals Co., 342 P.2d 790 (Or. 1959) (recognizing trespass as interference with possessor's "proprietary or dignitary interest" in land, which may "be violated by a ray of light, by an atomic particle, or by a particulate of fluoride").
60. See O'Brien v. Cunard Steamship Co., 28 N.E. 266 (Mass. 1891) (recognizing mandatory vaccination as potential battery).
61. Jacobson v. Massachusetts, 197 U.S. 11 (1905).
62. Compare Losee v. Buchanan, 51 N.Y. 476 (1873) (finding no liability when non-negligently maintained steam boiler exploded, sending projectile metal shards onto neighbor's property) with Rylands v. Fletcher, L.R. 3 H.L. 330 (1868) (finding liability when non-negligently constructed water reservoir broke through and flooded neighbor's property).
63. See Posner, *supra* note 16, at 29.
64. See Brown v. Kendall, 60 Mass. 292, 293 (1850) (defining "ordinary care" as "that kind and degree of care, which prudent and cautious men would use to guard against probable danger"); Richard A. Posner, Economic Analysis of Law 183 (5th ed. 1998) (noting that many accident cases are won by plaintiffs because cases are judged not by individual capacities for accident-avoidance but rather in terms of "the average (in legal parlance 'reasonable') person in each party's situation").
65. See, for example, Brown v. Kendall, 6 Cush. (60 Mass.) 292 (1850) (discussing contributory negligence rule); see also Williams v. Delta International Machinery Corp., 619 So.2d 1330 (Ala. 1993) (affirming rule of contributory negligence as absolute bar to recovery).
66. See, for example, Krazek v. Mountain River Tours, Inc., 884 F.2d 163 (4th Cir. 1989) (upholding broadly worded, contractual release of liability); see, generally, Stephen D. Sugarman, *Assumption of the Risk*, 31 Val. U. L. Rev. 833 (1997).
67. See, for example, Dalury v. S-K-I, Ltd., 670 A.2d 795 (Vt. 1995) (refusing to enforce express release of liability from injuries at ski resort); Tunkl v. Regents of Univ. of Cal., 383 P.2d 441 (Cal. 1963) (voiding charity hospital's express exculpatory agreement).
68. See Union Pacific Railway v. Cappier, 72 P. 281 (Kan. 1903) ("The moral law would obliterate an attempt to rescue a person in a perilous position – as a drowning child – but the law of the land does not require it, no matter how little personal risk it might involve, provided that the person who declines to act is not responsible for the peril."); Wendy E. Parmet &

Richard A. Daynard, *The New Public Health Litigation*, 21 ANNUAL REV. PUBLIC HEALTH 437, 449 (2000) (noting "strong preference in legal doctrine" for negative rights and noting that "[t]ort law, for example, will generally not hold an individual responsible for failing to come to the aid of another").

69. See Parmet, *supra* note 1, at 226 ("the no-duty-to-rescue rule undoubtedly offers the clearest example of tort law's failure to protect population health").
70. See, generally, Dan B. Dobbs, THE LAW OF TORTS §§ 316–321, at 856–69; *id.* §§ 232–238, at 591–24 (2000) (duties of owners and occupiers of land); RESTATEMENT (SECOND) OF TORTS §§ 314–323.
71. See, for example, Mt. Zion State Bank & Trust v. Consolidated Communications, 660 N.E.2d 863, 868–71 (Ill. 1995) (affirmative duty on landowner to repair latent dangerous condition that the owner knows or should know exists); Wallingford v. Kroger Co., 761 S.W.2d 621, 625 (Ky. Ct. App. 1988) (exception to the no-duty rule when a landowner or occupier creates an inherent danger); see, generally, Dobbs, *supra* note 70, at §§ 232–238, at 591–24 (duties of owners and occupiers of land).
72. See, for example, Clemets v. Heston, 485 N.E.2d 287, 291 (Ohio Ct. App. 1985) (affirmative duty on law officer to protect those arrested and in custody); People v. Wong, 588 N.Y.S.2d 119, 124 (N.Y. App. Div. 1992) (duties on babysitter by "voluntary assumption of complete and exclusive care of a helpless child"); Mirand v. City of New York, 84 N.Y.2d 44 (N.Y. App. Div. 1994) (School Board liable for harm inflicted on a student by two others, recognizing "The duty owed derives from the simple fact that a school, in assuming physical custody and control over its students, effectively takes the place of parents and guardians").
73. See Tarasoff v. Regents of Univ. of California, 551 P.2d 334 (Cal. 1976) (therapist has a duty to warn or protect identified victim of patient's threats); see also Tenuto v. Lederle Labs., 687 N.E.2d 1300 (N.Y. 1997) (physician had a duty to warn father about the risks of contracting polio from infected child); Pate v. Threlkel, 661 So.2d 278 (Fl. 1995) (physician has a duty to warn patient's children about genetic condition).
74. See, for example, Simonson v. Thorin, 234 N.W. 628 (Neb. 1931) (defendant motorist who knocked over a utility pole had a duty to remove the pole or warn others of the hazard); Tresemer v. Barke, 150 Cal. Rptr. 384 (App. 1978) (defendant physician had a duty to warn patient about newly discovered risks of Dalkon Shield intrauterine device).
75. See, generally, Marc A. Franklin, *Vermont Requires Rescue: A Comment*, 25 STAN. L. REV. 51 (1972); Nancy Levit, *The Kindness of Strangers: Interdisciplinary Foundations of a Duty to Act*, 40 WASHBURN L.J. 463, 466–67 (2001).

76. Philip Cole, *The Moral Bases for Public Health Interventions*, EPIDEMIOLOGY, vol. 6, no. 1, Jan. 1995, at 78, 80 ("Educating is highly moral when it is intended to enhance the will of the individual and no penalty is imposed on persons who do not accept the educational message.")
77. See Franklin et al., *supra* note 43, at 816–29 (describing workers' compensation).
78. Air Transportation Safety and System Stabilization Act of 2001, Pub. L. No 107–42, 115 Stat. 230, tit. IV (2001) (Victims' Compensation).
79. See Franklin et al., *supra* note 43, at 698; Dobbs, *supra* note 70, at §§ 377–79, at 1047–56 (2000).
80. See, for example, Seffert v. Los Angeles Transit Lines, 364 P.2d 337, 511 (Cal. 1961) (Traynor, J., dissenting) (noting "forceful criticism of the rationale for awarding damages for pain and suffering in negligence cases").
81. See Marshall S. Shapo, *Responsibility for Injuries: Some Sketches*, 100 NW. U. L. REV. 481, 481–82 (2006); Hyman & Silver, *supra* note 50, at 1129 ("People usually avoid activities that cost them money and engage in activities that make them money.").
82. See Posner, *supra* note 64, at 219.
83. Cooper Indus., Inc. v. Leatherman Tool Group, Inc., 532 U.S. 424, 432 (2001) (punitive damages are "quasi-criminal" in nature and "operate as 'private fines' intended to punish the defendant and to deter future wrongdoing"); Dan Markel, *How Should Punitive Damages Work?* 157 U. PA. L. REV. 1383, 1390–92 (2009) ("the Supreme Court has emphasized that punitive damages should be principally understood as "quasi-criminal" "private fines" designed to punish the defendant and deter the misconduct at issue); Richard A. Nagareda, *Punitive Damage Class Action and the Baseline of Torts*, 36 WAKE FOREST L. REV. 943, 949 (2001) (noting that "punitive damages routinely violate the allocation principle 'to each, her own'" and that "an individual plaintiff enjoys no entitlement to punitive damages, in contrast to compensatory relief").
84. See RESTATEMENT (SECOND) OF TORTS § 908(2); Dobbs, *supra* note 70, § 380.
85. See Mark Galanter & David Luban, *Poetic Justice: Punitive Damages and Legal Pluralism*, 42 AM. U. L. REV. 1393, 1437–38 (1993); Edward L. Rubin, *Reconceptualizing the Runcible Remedies of Common Law*, 1998 WISC. L. REV. 131, 138.
86. National Practitioner Data Bank, 42 U.S.C. §§ 11131 (required reports on medical malpractice payments).
87. See, for example, Reynolds v. Pegler, 223 F.2d 429 (2d Cir. 1955) (upholding verdict of one dollar compensatory damages and $175,000 punitive damages against the defendants).
88. See Fee, *supra* note 22, at 29; see also Starr, *supra* note 22, at 185–87.
89. See Fee, *supra* note 22, at 30.

90. See Gostin, *supra* note 9, at 183; Posner, *supra* note 16, at 29–30.
91. Y.B. 6 Edw. 4, fol 7a, Mich. pl. 18 (1466), reprinted in C. H. S. Fifoot, History and Sources of the Common Law: Tort and Contract 195–97 (1949) ("As if a Man lop a Tree, and the [Boughs] fall upon another *ipso invitio*, yet an Action lies.")
92. 3 L.R.E. & I. App. 330, 331 (H.L. 1868). The plaintiff prevailed at trial, was reversed by the intermediate appellate court (the Court of Exchequer), and won a reversal at highest court, the House of Lords.
93. See Posner, *supra* note 16, at 29–30 (noting that "we have outgrown a morality that would condition the right to compensation upon a showing that the plaintiff was blameless and the defendant blameworthy").
94. *Id.* at 29.
95. 51 N.Y. 476 (NY 1873).
96. *Id.* at 484.
97. See George P. Fletcher, *Fairness and Utility in Tort Theory*, 85 Harv. L. Rev. 537, 542 (1972) (describing "paradigm of reasonableness" as "a commitment to the community's welfare as the criterion for determining both who is entitled to receive and who ought to pay compensation").
98. See Stephen Breyer, *Breaking the Vicious Circle: Toward Effective Risk Regulation* 22 (1993).
99. Kenneth J Arrow et al., *Is there a Role for Benefit-Cost Analysis in Environmental, Health, and Safety Regulation?*, Science, vol. 272, April 12, 1996, at 221, 221; see also Breyer, *supra* note 98, at 60 (urging a coordinated, interagency approach with the "mission of building an improved, coherent, risk-regulating system"); *see generally* Cass Sunstein, *Health-Health Tradeoffs*, 63 U. Chi. L. Rev. 1533 (1996) (discussing difficulty assessing risks and challenges of comparing lives saved by various, uncoordinated regulatory interventions).
100. See Whitman v. American Trucking Ass'ns, 531 U.S. 457 (2001) (noting Trucking Associations' argument that "the economic cost of implementing a very stringent standard might produce health losses sufficient to offset the health gains achieved in cleaning the air-for example, by closing down whole industries and thereby impoverishing the workers and consumers dependent upon those industries"); United States v. Ottati & Goss, 900 F.2d 429 (1st Cir. 1990) (litigation regarding $9.3 million costs to achieve compliance with extremely stringent Environmental Protection Agency standards, despite the very minimal risk to human health).
101. See Breyer, *supra* note 98, at 11 (describing "tunnel vision" as "a classic administrative disease").
102. See Guido Calabresi & Philip Bobbit, Tragic Choices (1978) (describing society's attempts "to obscure the fact of tragic scarcity" and suggesting, "Thus we comfort ourselves in the belief that our society does not establish an acceptable number of auto deaths, but that this figure results from

thousands of independent, atomistic actions."); Victor R. Fuchs, WHO SHALL LIVE? HEALTH, ECONOMICS, AND SOCIAL CHOICE (Expanded ed. 1999) ("The oft-heard statement, 'Health is the most important goal,' does not accurately describe human behavior. Everyday in manifold ways (such as overeating and smoking) we make choices that affect our health, and it is clear that we frequently place a higher value on satisfying other wants.").

103. Calabresi, *supra* note 42, at 136–37.
104. See, generally, William M. Landes & Richard A. Posner, THE ECONOMIC STRUCTURE OF TORT LAW (1987); Saul Levmore, *Probabilistic Recoveries, Restitution, and Recurring Wrongs*, 19 J. LEGAL STUD. 691 (1990).
105. John Stuart Mill, UTILITARIANISM (1863); POSNER, *supra* note 64, at 13–14 (defining "utility in the sense used by philosophers of utilitarianism, meaning (roughly) happiness," and citing Mill).
106. Posner, *supra* note 64, at 12–17.
107. Marshall S. Shapo, Towards a Jurisprudence of Injury: The Continuing Creation of a Substantive Justice in American Tort Law: Report to the American Bar Association, 1984 A.B.A. Sec. Tort Liability Sys. 4–13 (noting that "it would be uneconomic if too few accidents occurred" and near-perfect safety rule "would represent a choice by courts that goes beyond the level of safety that consumers prefer").
108. See, for example, Dreisonstok v. Volkswagenwerk, A.G., 489 F.2d 1066, 1072 (4th Cir. 1974) ("The purposes and intended use of the article is an even more important factor [than safety] to be considered. After all, it is a commonplace that utility of design and attractiveness of the style of the car are elements which car manufacturers seek after and by which buyers are influenced in their selections."); Posner, *supra* note 16, at 32–33 ("If the cost of safety measures … exceeds the benefit in accident avoidance to be gained in incurring that cost, society would be better off, in economic terms, to forego accident prevention").
109. See United States v. Carroll Towing, 159 F.2d 169 (2d Cir. 1947) (Hand, J.); see also Posner, *supra* note 14, at 180–81; Gostin, note 9, at 187; Parmet, note 1, at 221.
110. See, for example, Chicago, Burlington & Quincy R. Co. v. Krayenbuhl, 91 N.W. 880 (Neb. 1902) (railroad negligent for failing to install lock on turntable when child's foot was caught and severed; The T.J. Hooper, 60 F.2d 737 (2d Cir. 1932) (barge company negligent for failing to have weather radio).
111. See Posner, *supra* note 64, at 180; Uwe Reinhardt, *Can Efficiency in Health Care Be Left to the Market?* 26 J. HEALTH POL., POLICY & LAW 967, 970 (2001).
112. See, generally, Calabresi & Bobbitt, *supra* note 100 (suggesting various methods of allotting tragically scarce goods).

113. See, for example, Kimbar v. Estis, 135 N.E.2d 708 (N.Y. 1956) (rejecting claim that summer camp operator was negligent for failing to light path in woods, noting that holding camp liable would deny "youth ... the adventure of living closer to nature").
114. See, similarly, Eric A. Posner & Cass R. Sunstein, *Dollars and Death*, 72 U. CHI. L. REV. 537, 554–57 (2005) (offering alternative algebraic formula for wrongful death damages).
115. See Posner, *supra* note 64, at 209–14 (discussing damages and earnings disparities); William E. Nelson, *Teaching Torts: The Moral Perversity of the Hand Calculus*, 45 ST. LOUIS L.J. 759, 7690–61 (2001).
116. See, for example, Moisan v. Loftus, 178 F.2d 148, 149 (2d Cir. 1949) (describing how Hand himself recognized difficulties in applying the formula).
117. See Posner, *supra* note 64, at 179–83; Calabresi & Bobbitt, *supra* note 62, at 198–225; see also Cass R. Sunstein, *Introduction to* BEHAVIORAL LAW & ECONOMICS 1 (Cass R. Sunstein ed., 2000) ("People are not always 'rational' in the sense that economists suppose").
118. 519 P.2d 981 (Wash. 1974).
119. *Id.* at 983.
120. *Id.* at 982.
121. *Id.*; see Posner, *supra* note 64, at 185 (medical malpractice cases are one area of negligence in which courts "have traditionally allowed a defense of custom").
122. See, for example, Robbins v. Footer, 553 F.2d 123 (D.C. Cir. 1977) ("the technical complexity of the facts and issues usually prevents the jury itself from determining both the appropriate standard of care and whether the defendant's conduct conformed to that standard"); Shapo, *supra* note 81, at 489 (regarding medical malpractice standard of care).
123. *Helling*, 519 P.2d at 983 (citing *The TJ Hooper*).
124. *Id.* at 982–83 ("reasonable prudence required the timely giving of the pressure test ... irrespective of its disregard by the standards of the ophthalmology profession").
125. *See* Rand Rosenblatt et al., LAW AND THE AMERICAN HEALTH CARE SYSTEM 862–63 (1997) (describing *Helling* as "[t]he most famous (and largely unique) recent health law case purporting to overrule a professional standard" by relying on *The T.J. Hooper*, 60 F.2d 737, (2d Cir. 1932)); Peter D. Jacobson & Matthew L. Kanna, *Cost-Effectiveness Analysis in the Courts: Recent Trends and Future Prospects*, 26 J. HEALTH POL. POL'Y & L. 291, 303 (2001) (describing *Helling* as "One of the very few medical liability cases to consider [cost-effectiveness analysis] in setting the standard of care").
126. See Parmet, *supra* note 1, at 221–22 (suggesting that law and economic view of tort law subordinates population health to economic efficiency).

127. See Henningsen v. Bloomfield Motors, 161 A.2d 69 (N.J. 1960); Escola v. Coca-Cola Bottling Co., 150 P.2d 436, 440 (Cal. 1944) (Traynor, J., concurring); Greenman v. Yuba Power Prods., Inc., 377 P.2d 897 (Cal. 1963) (manufacturer of defective lathe strictly liable, without showing of warranty or negligence); RESTATEMENT (SECOND) OF TORTS § 402A(1) ("[o]ne who sells any product in a defective condition unreasonably dangerous to the user or consumer … is subject to liability … although … the seller has exercised all possible care in the preparation and sale of his product").
128. See Calabresi, supra note 42, at 39–67.
129. See Escola v. Coca Cola Bottling Co. of Fresno, 150 P.2d 436, 462 (Cal. 1944) (Traynor, J., concurring) ("The cost of an injury and the loss of time or health may be an overwhelming misfortune to the person injured, and a needless one, for the risk of injury can be insured by the manufacturer and distributed among the public as a cost of doing business."); Jerry J. Phillips, *The Unreasonably Unsafe Product and Strict Liability*, 72 TENN. L. REV. 833, 838 (2005) ("many believe that consumers who benefit from products without suffering harm should share, though increases in prices charged for those products, the burden of unavoidable injury costs that result from manufacturing defects").
130. See RESTATEMENT (SECOND) OF TORTS §§ 519, 520; Gostin, *supra* note 9, at 190 (discussing *Rylands* as precursor to doctrine of "abnormally dangerous activities")
131. See RESTATEMENT § 520 cmt. b (§ 519 "is applicable to an activity that is carried on with all reasonable care, and that is of such utility that the risk which is involved in it cannot be regarded as so great or so unreasonable as to make it negligence merely to carry on the activity at all"); Shapo, *supra* note 81, at 486–87 ("Very simply, strict liability is liability without fault, in the sense that the activity at issue is appraised as one that was permissible, rather than (like speeding on the highway) as conduct that should not have occurred.")
132. See, for example, Indiana Harbor Belt R.R. v. American Cyanamid Co., 916 F.2d 1174 (7th Cir. 1990) (chemical shipping); Exner v. Sherman Power Construction Co., 54 F.2d 510 (2d Cir. 1931) (dynamite storage); In re Hanford Nuclear Reservation Litig., 350 F. Supp. 2d 871 (E.D. Wash. 2004) (nuclear weapons plant); Old Island Fumigation, Inc. v. Barbee, 604 So.2d 1246 (Fla. Dist. Ct. App. 1992) (pest control); *Rylands*, L.R. 3.H.L. 330 (water reservoir).
133. See RESTATEMENT § 519 cmt. d; DOBBS, *supra* note 70, at 950; GOSTIN, *supra* note 9, at 189.
134. RESTATEMENT § 402A(2)(b) (defining design defect as "when the foreseeable risks of harm posed by the product could have been reduced or avoided by the adoption of a reasonable alternative design"); see Mark A. Geistfeld, PRINCIPLES OF PRODUCTS LIABILITY 92–98 (2006) (describing

"negligence-based evolutionary path"); Phillips, *supra* note 127, at 834 (suggesting that Restatement (Third) reporters would "place the standard of liability [for design defects] squarely in negligence").

135. See, for example, Barker v. Lull Engineering Co., Inc., 573 P.2d 443, 457–58 (Cal. 1978) (defining design defect alternatively as "product failed to perform as safely as an ordinary consumer would expect" or "risk of danger inherent in the challenged design outweighs the benefits"); see Shapo, *supra* note 81, at 492 (describing both tests and dispute over Restatement's adoption of exclusive risk-utility test).
136. See, for example, Shetterly v. Crown Controls Corp., 719 F. Supp. 385, 403 (W.D. Pa. 1989), aff'd 898 F.2d 139 (3d Cir. 1990) (holding no liability on manufacturer of pallet truck, despite the absence of a reasonable alternative design, because the benefits of the product in terms of increased productivity and decreased costs outweighed risks, even when eight workers suffered sprained, twisted, and broken ankles).

8 PUNITIVE DAMAGES AND THE PUBLIC HEALTH AGENDA

Jean Macchiaroli Eggen

INTRODUCTION

Punitive damages have been a feature of civil litigation for centuries.[1] Although they are available in only a small number of cases, the media has given disproportionate attention to punitive damages awards. This high profile has led to much criticism. Indeed, few doctrines in legal history have been more vilified than the doctrine allowing the award of punitive damages in civil actions. In 1873, the Supreme Court of New Hampshire characterized the doctrine as "a monstrous heresy" and "an unsightly and unhealthy excrescence, deforming the symmetry of the body of law."[2] More recently, a former Solicitor General of the United States, in a 1994 article, compared punitive damages to a "giant underground fungus."[3] Some observers fear that the amount of punitive damages awards has grown beyond acceptable bounds and, "as if feeding upon itself, has escalated to astronomical figures that boggle the mind" and represents a "destructive force that erodes the economic stability of society."[4]

Notwithstanding such graphic expressions of outrage, the United States Supreme Court has consistently stated that punitive damages may be awarded in civil actions for the purposes of punishing and deterring defendants under appropriate circumstances.[5] Many, but by no means all, of these cases have been tort actions that have involved personal injuries, or insurance bad faith or fraud claims related to personal injuries. Most of them have involved conduct harmful to the general public either because the defendant created a generalized danger to the community (e.g., defective products) or because the overall welfare of the public was compromised (e.g., fraudulent insurance practices). Thus, punitive damages are closely related to the goal of the public health system: to advance the well-being of the members of the community.

The doctrine of punitive damages recognizes that to achieve the goals of the civil justice system, it may be necessary to impose damages greater than the amount sufficient to compensate the plaintiff, because the defendant may have acted in a particularly egregious manner, been unjustly enriched, or conducted a vast nefarious scheme that injured, or had the potential to injure, many persons.[6] Commentators have suggested that punitive damages additionally may serve an array of purposes beyond punishment and deterrence, including serving as a means to finance the litigation or providing compensation for injuries that are either unprovable or unrecognizable under the law.[7] In general, however, the goals of punishment and deterrence have remained the gold standards for the award of punitive damages.

Over the past two decades, the Supreme Court, in a string of cases, has addressed the relationship between punitive damages and the United States Constitution, focusing primarily on the Due Process Clause embodied in the Fifth and Fourteenth Amendments.[8] The Court's concerns have focused both on setting substantive standards for determining when an award of punitive damages is excessive and on fashioning the procedural means by which courts make that determination. But this effort has been incremental and difficult, as the Court has endeavored to establish standards suitable to all cases. If anything, these decisions have demonstrated that circumstances vary considerably among cases, defendants, and desirable policy goals, making the due process standards difficult to apply consistently without removing the teeth from the punitive damages doctrine.

Because punitive damages routinely involve conduct that impacts the public health and welfare, it is beneficial to society as a whole to explore ways in which punitive damages may be used for public health purposes. This chapter examines the legal rules governing and legal obstacles confronting the process of directing punitive damages to these uses.

THE PUBLIC HEALTH GOALS OF PUNITIVE DAMAGES

General Policy Goals

The civil justice system in general, and tort liability in particular, has always served a public purpose in addition to compensation for the individual plaintiff. General deterrence of behaviors detrimental to the general public is a recognized goal of the tort system.[9] By holding up the defendant's actions as an example of conduct that society deems to warrant damages, the hope is that others engaged in, or considering engaging in, similar behaviors will modify their conduct for the benefit of society. This goal focuses on the public by extending the impact of the judgment in the particular case to all of society.

When a case has a specific public health component – toxic torts, products liability, auto and health insurance, for example – the deterrence goals address the public health and welfare. Damages awards have an indirect effect on defendants' conduct, encouraging them to make products safer,[10] comply with environmental regulations, and maintain a close eye on the state of the art in their areas of operation. In the absence of punitive damages, deterrence can often be excruciatingly slow. For example, one reason large punitive damages awards were imposed against the asbestos industry was that the manufacturers ignored the many years of studies and concerns that showed the danger of their insulation products to the employees of contractors who were installing them. In general, the companies did not conduct their own studies of the health effects of exposure in this context and discounted – not to mention failed to warn of – the dangers that had become generally known.[11] Although change came about through the disclosures of litigation, as well as the independent studies of epidemiologists on the hazards of asbestos, one cannot help but think that more resources channeled to public health efforts would have resulted in earlier and more extensive attention to the long-term health issues of exposed workers.

Accordingly, in civil litigation, the most direct mechanism to bring about deterrence for the benefit of the general public is an award of punitive damages. The frequently articulated purposes of punitive damages are to both punish the defendant for past egregious behavior and deter the defendant and others from engaging in the same or similar conduct in the future.[12] An important secondary effect is to encourage the investment of more resources in research and development, which might also be expected to redound to the public's benefit.

Developing a Public-Private Law Model of Punitive Damages

In relation to this public goal, scholars traditionally have viewed punitive damages as occupying a gray area between the paradigms of criminal law[13] and civil law.[14] The goals of punitive damages to punish and deter the defendant and others bear a superficial similarity to the same goals in the criminal justice system. Likewise, the mental state required of a civil defendant[15] for a grant of punitive damages exceeds mere negligence, demanding instead intentional misconduct or recklessness, which bears a relationship to levels of culpability usually associated with criminal conduct.[16] In contrast to criminal penalties, however, punitive damages are a form of "extracompensatory"[17] damages awarded directly to the plaintiff, and the conduct meriting punitive damages may or may not be subject to separate criminal sanctions. Some scholars have argued that punitive damages represent an erosion of the distinctly conceived paradigms of criminal and civil law, and have proposed a reimagining of the purposes and procedures of punitive damages as a hybrid remedy[18] between criminal and civil law. In any case, the criminal justice model of punitive damages is an uneasy fit for such a uniquely civil remedy.

A more useful characterization of modern punitive damages recognizes that the doctrine falls more broadly at the intersection of public law and private law. Public law refers generally to governmental regulatory systems that set standards for conduct through public participation in democratic processes. Private law, as referred to here, fundamentally involves common-law rules of conduct developed through judicial rulings in individual cases. This public-private paradigm is a more accurate reflection of the goals and purposes of punitive damages than the older criminal-civil hybrid. This fresh paradigm is particularly important in an era in which litigation implicating the public health is commanding a large portion of judicial resources.

Modern tort cases in particular demonstrate an increasing relationship to the public health. Along with that development, courts have had to address the relationship between public law initiatives and private law goals. In toxic tort actions, for example, the parties typically rely upon public law for a variety of purposes. Often the suits are mass torts, with the defendant's conduct affecting large numbers of persons under diverse circumstances and resulting in assorted injuries. In such actions, the common law interrelates with public law in an intricate variety of ways. Thus, for example, a plaintiff in an environmental pollution case who seeks to demonstrate liability may raise the fact that the defendant has been ordered by the State or Federal Environmental Protection Agency (EPA) to clean up the site in question. Or a defendant in a pharmaceutical product liability action may raise as a defense the argument that it should not be held liable because it complied with all federal Food and Drug Administration (FDA) requirements in seeking approval of the drug in question, and because the FDA granted marketing approval for the drug. Such cases, and others, suggest that the public has an important stake in the outcome of much litigation.

Although the punitive damages doctrine recognizes the public interest in its goal of general deterrence, awards are not directed toward correcting the conduct that gave rise to the public harm. Instead, and consistent with the private law model, punitive damages are awarded, in whole or in part, to the successful plaintiff. This fact has led some to suggest that punitive damages perhaps serve a supercompensatory function, either where the compensatory damages award does not adequately compensate the plaintiff or where the defendant's conduct seems to demand greater damages than mere compensation would allow.[19] But the United States Supreme Court has clearly stated that the goals of punishment and deterrence are the sole recognized goals of punitive damages. Accordingly, awarding punitive damages to the plaintiff who, presumably, has already been compensated is not a particularly effective use of the award.

Because a plaintiff rarely has any control over the defendant's conduct, placing punitive damages in the plaintiff's hands only serves a secondary deterrent effect. If the defendant – and others engaging in similar conduct – wants to avoid future monetary losses, they may alter their conduct to enhance safety to both the plaintiff and the community in general. But some defendants are able to shift or spread the costs of liability to other parties or the general public without altering their conduct. Absent direct regulation, they might continue in the same course of conduct that gave rise to the damages, incorporating them into the costs of doing business.[20] Still others may simply not care; these parties would continue engaging in the risky conduct until forced out of business by regulation or priced out of business by the high costs of damages awards. Thus, punitive damages awards are windfalls to plaintiffs, with deterrence an aspirational goal. Plaintiffs are not in a position to direct the conduct of a defendant, let alone an entire industry.

A better approach would be to change the model of distribution of punitive damages awards from the private law model to the public law model, in which the welfare of the general public is directly enhanced by the money paid by defendants as punitive damages. Accordingly, to serve the public health agenda, states should consider the role that punitive damages could play in advancing the health and welfare of their citizens. In particular, states should examine the ways in which punitive damages awards might be diverted to public purposes related to the underlying actions. Such a goal raises numerous legal issues, not the least of which is fashioning a mechanism by which this diversion of funds can be achieved. Such obstacles are substantial, but where financial resources for public health initiatives are dwindling, finding a means to achieve this public goal is worth exploring.

Redistribution of punitive damages is not as difficult as it may sound. Many states have already recognized the fact that punitive damages serve as a windfall to the plaintiff. These states, however, have packaged their reforms as part of all-over tort reform efforts, with little coherent thought to how to redirect the awards to appropriate and effective uses. Any discussion of the redistribution of punitive damages, however, must begin with an examination of the United States Supreme Court decisions grounding the doctrine in due process principles. These decisions establish the legal backdrop against which any reform efforts would need to be conducted. The Supreme Court's decisions on the constitutionality of punitive damages provide a framework for determining when an award is reasonable. Although the Court has articulated limitations on punitive damages awards, its current punitive damages jurisprudence presents no real obstacles to redistributing awards to the general public.

CURRENT SUPREME COURT PUNITIVE DAMAGES JURISPRUDENCE

The basic prerequisites for punitive damages have remained constant. Thus, punitive damages are available only where the plaintiff has proved that the defendant acted in a manner that went beyond mere negligence.[21] Within that standard, there is much variation in the mental state required of the defendant, with standards characterized variously as willful, wanton, malicious, reckless, or intentional.[22] Another consistent feature of punitive damages has been the need to apply some measure of fundamental fairness in awarding them. In general, this has required the application of constitutional due process principles to punitive damages awards, both substantively and procedurally. It has not, however, demanded the level of due process scrutiny that applies in the criminal justice system.[23]

In recent years, the United States Supreme Court has explored the due process parameters of punitive damages, but the test the Court has developed is often difficult to apply in individual circumstances. Most of the Supreme Court cases defining the due process standards for punitive damages have focused on the factors to be applied in measuring the amount of punitive damages, to ensure that they do not exceed an amount that reasonably could be expected to punish and deter. In other words, the award must not be arbitrary and must bear some relationship to the case and to the conduct sought to be deterred. In *Pacific Mutual Life Insurance Company v. Haslip*,[24] a health insurance fraud case, the Court upheld an award of punitive damages, but stated that there is no bright line between an award that is constitutionally acceptable and one that violates due process for excessiveness. The Court emphasized that the key factor in assessing the amount of a punitive damages award is whether a reasonable relationship existed between the amount of the punitive damages award and the harm to the plaintiff. In *Haslip*, the punitive award was four times the compensatory damages. The Court there stated that the ratio of four to one "may be close to the line" of due process, but found that it "did not lack objective criteria."[25] Among the factors recognized by the Court in *Haslip* as appropriate in evaluating the fairness of the award were the reprehensibility of the defendant's conduct, the degree to which the defendant profited from its wrongful actions, and the amount of other sanctions – both criminal and civil – that may be available for the same conduct.[26]

Haslip established a theme for subsequent Supreme Court cases. Since then, the Court has continued to reject a bright-line ratio, but its guidance has not always been consistent. Thus, while one might reasonably read *Haslip* as implying that an award that exceeds a four-to-one ratio might be deemed excessive in violation of due process, in *TXO Production Corp. v. Alliance Resources Corp.*, the Court approved a punitive award that was 526 times the amount of the compensatory damages awarded in the case.[27] *TXO* involved an alleged conspiracy over oil and gas rights, and the Court stated that it was "appropriate to consider the magnitude of the potential harm that the defendant's conduct would have caused to its intended victim if the wrongful plan had succeeded, as well as the possible harm to other victims that might have resulted if similar future behavior were not deterred."[28]

In *BMW of North America, Inc. v. Gore*, however, the Court struck down an award of punitive damages that was 500 times the compensatory damages awarded and offered more explicit general guidelines for other cases.[29] The plaintiff in *Gore* claimed that the defendant had fraudulently withheld material information in selling him a car because the new car he purchased had been repainted prior to the sale.[30] The Court set down several guiding principles on the amount of punitive damages. First, the court stated that the excessiveness of the award should be judged by the defendant's conduct that occurred solely in the state of the alleged misconduct to the plaintiff.[31] Second, the Court stated that a smaller award was more appropriate in a case in which the harm alleged was only economic, where no third parties were threatened, and where the defendant's conduct was not directed at health and safety.[32] Third, the Court continued to reject a bright-line test for the ratio between a punitive award and compensatory damages.[33]

Finally, the Court articulated three principles essential to due process that have been dubbed the "Gore Guideposts." In considering whether a particular award meets this constitutional requirement, courts are to consider: (1) the reprehensibility of the defendant's conduct; (2) the reasonableness of the ratio between the amount of punitive damages and the amount of compensatory damages; and (3) a comparison of other sanctions available for the same conduct under relevant criminal or civil statutes.[34] In applying these guideposts to the *Gore* case, the Court held that (1) the conduct was less reprehensible because of the lack of harm to the person of the defendant; (2) that the ratio therefore raised "a suspicious judicial eyebrow"; and (3) that available sanctions under the relevant consumer protection statutes were only $10,000.[35] Accordingly, the Court held that the punitive award of $2 million was excessive.

Subsequently, in *State Farm Mutual Automobile Insurance Co. v. Campbell*, a bad-faith insurance case on an underlying motor vehicle accident, the Court appeared to follow a more rigid ratio while simultaneously continuing to insist that a bright-line test is inappropriate. The Court, which ruled that the punitive award of 145 times the compensatory damages violated due process, stated that "in practice, few awards exceeding a single-digit ratio … will satisfy due process."[36] The Court stated that in a case in which the compensatory damages award is substantial, due process would require that a lesser award of punitive damages would suffice to effect the necessary punishment and deterrence.[37]

Campbell was then applied to a case with a more direct public health implication. In *Boerner v. Brown & Williamson Tobacco Co.*, a federal appeals court reduced a punitive damages award made to the estate of a smoker from $15 million to $5 million because the compensatory damages were approximately $4 million.[38] The court stated that a ratio of slightly more than one to one was within the allowable due process parameters, per *Campbell*.

The Supreme Court's latest word on the subject was issued in an action brought by a smoker. In *Philip Morris USA v. Williams*, the Court expressed concern that the punitive damages award may have been based in part on harm to persons outside the litigation, namely other smokers using the defendant's product.[39] The claim involved was a deceit claim. The jury had awarded the plaintiff a punitive award that was almost 100 times the compensatory damages award based upon the following jury instruction: '[Y]ou may consider the extent of harm suffered by others in determining what [the] reasonable relationship is [but] you are not to punish the defendant for the impact of its alleged misconduct on other persons, who may bring lawsuits of their own in which other juries can resolve the claims.'[40] The Court held that this instruction lacked clarity on the manner in which the jury could consider harm to persons outside the litigation, and therefore raised the risk of jury confusion and misapplication. The Court stated: "In our view, the Constitution's Due Process Clause forbids a State to use a punitive damages award to punish a defendant for injury that it inflicts upon … those who are, essentially, strangers to the litigation."[41] The Court was concerned that defendants would be prevented from mounting a meaningful defense when such other persons are not before the court and allowing consideration of harm to persons outside the immediate case "would add a near standardless dimension to the punitive damages equation."[42]

Ironically, the rule that emerges from *Williams* is itself nearly standardless and confusing. The Court failed to clearly articulate the precise relationship between punitive damages in a particular case and the public harm the defendant's conduct caused. Although the *Williams* Court held that harm to persons outside the litigation remains an appropriate consideration on the matter of reprehensibility, which reaffirms the first Gore Guidepost, the Court stated that special care must be taken in instructing the jury:

> [G]iven the risks of arbitrariness, the concern for adequate notice, and the risk that punitive damages awards can, in practice, impose one State's (or jury's) policies (e.g., banning cigarettes) upon other states … it is particularly important that States avoid procedure that unnecessarily deprives juries of proper legal guidance. We therefore conclude that the Due Process Clause requires States to provide assurance that juries are not asking the wrong question, i.e., seeking, not simply to determine reprehensibility, but also to punish for harm caused strangers.[43]

The question remains whether courts can ever be certain that juries do not misuse evidence of reprehensible conduct toward strangers to the litigation in setting the amount of punitive damages in the case under consideration.

Reflecting on this line of Supreme Court decisions, a paradoxical mix of confusion and clarity emerges. The Court has consistently applied the Gore Guideposts – even before the *Gore* decision established them as a test – to determine whether an award of punitive damages contravenes the Due Process Clause. But the results sometimes have been confusing and contradictory. The ratio of punitive damages to compensatory damages in the individual cases had seemed subjectively fair, but do not always seem justified under the test developed by the Court. Furthermore, the Court's edict in the multiple-harm situation – that harm caused by the defendant's conduct to other persons not before the court may not be considered in determining the amount of punitive damages, but may be allowed for determining the degree of reprehensibility – is difficult to apply in practice.

These issues play a role in assessing how punitive damages may impact the public health. To put this into context, the due process rulings of the Supreme Court demonstrate that punitive damages and the public health intersect in several important ways:

- Juries deciding whether to award punitive damages, and the amount of those damages, may take into account the impact on the public health and welfare.
- Constraints on the amount of punitive damages apply when the defendant's conduct harmed persons outside the litigation.
- Punitive damages may reflect the impact on the public health and welfare in determining the reprehensibility of the defendant's conduct.
- In cases that are either directly health-related (e.g., tobacco, pharmaceutical cases) or indirectly health-related (e.g., insurance bad-faith cases), punitive damages awards have the potential for resulting in deterrence of undesirable conduct and improvement of the public health and welfare.

In *Gore*, the Supreme Court indicated that it considered pure economic injury to be less reprehensible than personal injuries for determining the amount of a punitive damages award. By logical extension, matters that harm the personal health and welfare of members of the public could be appropriate for consideration in awarding punitive damages. These cases need not be personal injury lawsuits. *Haslip*, for example, was a health insurance fraud case that injured the targeted consumers financially, but which seemed even more reprehensible because the consumers' health care was placed in jeopardy by the defendants' conduct. Furthermore, the reprehensibility of the defendant's conduct may be measured by, among other things, "the magnitude of the potential harm that the defendant's conduct would have caused to its intended victim if the wrongful plan had succeeded, as well as the possible harm to other victims that might have resulted if similar future behavior were not deterred."[44] Thus, it is allowable, and in fact prudent, to consider the scope of the defendant's scheme and its likely full impact in determining a punitive damages award. Damage – actual and potential – to the public health and welfare fits this rule exactly.

Although the Supreme Court's due process parameters seem well suited to using punitive damages to advance the public health and welfare, this goal is hindered by the fact that punitive damages awards typically go directly to the plaintiffs with no assurances that the public health will, in fact, benefit. The Court, while placing some due process limits on the amount of the award when persons outside the litigation have been harmed,[45] has largely left to the states the decisions on the distribution of the awards. If punitive damages were to go to the government, or public service groups, instead of the plaintiff, punitive damages could be put to direct public use to enhance public health and safety. Shifting the award from the plaintiff to where it will do the maximum good may be a way to ensure that deterrence in the interest of the public is more likely to occur. Some states have begun to move in this direction, as discussed below.

STATE LIMITATIONS ON PUNITIVE DAMAGES

The United States Supreme Court has always recognized the interests of the individual states in setting their own limits and rules for awards of punitive damages, within due process limits. In *Gore*, the Court stated: "In our federal system, States necessarily have considerable flexibility in determining the level of punitive damages that they will allow in different classes of cases and in any particular case."[46] While the Court has addressed the outer parameters of due process with regard to the amount of punitive damages a state may allow, it has not entered the discussion of how the award may be distributed.

Much debate has ensued over the relative merits of giving the plaintiff what amounts to a punitive damages windfall. Professor Dobbs has stated that "[t]he windfall to the plaintiff is tolerated as a means of securing public good through a kind of quasi-criminal punishment."[47] The private plaintiff often assumes the role of a private attorney general, vindicating public rights through his or her private lawsuit.[48] However, much of punitive damages doctrine has focused on the defendant's conduct, and only recently has scholarly debate turned to assessing whether the windfall meets the goals of the doctrine.[49] This attention to whether punitive damages amount to an unwarranted overcompensation of the plaintiff arose during the emergence of the tort reform movement several decades ago and has remained a focus of debate. The plaintiff's right to recover punitive damages has been cited by reform-minded groups as an example of tort damages run amok.[50] As a consequence, over the past two decades, there has been a trend toward limiting punitive damages. This trend has primarily advanced a specific social and political agenda and has occurred on both the legislative and judicial fronts. The states have enacted a variety of broad tort reform measures, all of which have been directed at limiting the liability primarily of business enterprises,[51] and many of which have limited punitive damages awards.[52]

Commentators have noted that punitive damages may serve a restitutionary value to society in addition to their primary purposes of punishment and deterrence. Professor David G. Owen has identified several distinct restitutionary purposes, including "restoration of the losses to society,"[53] and other scholars have concurred.[54] As a matter of moral theory, one could reasonably argue that the acts of the defendant that warranted punitive damages also adversely impacted society as a whole. Citing Kantian theory, Professor Owen has reasoned:

> In comparison with the [wrongdoer], the law-abiding members of society are impoverished in proportion to the gain appropriated

> by the law-breaker. In this respect, the [wrongdoer] has stolen value from society by breaking the reciprocal security pact based on equal rights. In the process of restoring the victim's worth and freedom, therefore, punishment serves to restore the community's value of equal rights as well. Punitive damages thus serve to repay the offender's "debts" to both the victim and society, and so to restore the proper moral balance.[55]

It seems counterintuitive to allow the full amount of punitive damages to be placed in the hands of the plaintiff who will likely not spread it within the community that was injured. It is not a stretch to propose, then, that society receive a portion of a punitive damages award that would otherwise constitute a windfall to the plaintiff.

Furthermore, the broader utilitarian goals of society are advanced by punitive damages.[56] Both the specific and general deterrence functions of punitive damages focus on the broader public welfare, not merely the well-being of the plaintiff. Moreover, the amount of an award must tread a fine line between the undesirable results of overdeterrence and underdeterrence. Both overdeterrence and underdeterrence may result from an excessive punitive damages awarded. Overdeterrence results when an award is so excessive that it prices the defendant out of the market. Rather than adjust its activity to be safer and thereby avoid future liability, the defendant who is overdeterred decides not to engage in the activity at all. This may be of crucial importance to society generally when the activity is necessary to the public good, such as the development and manufacture of pharmaceuticals. The overdeterrent effect extends beyond the defendant in the lawsuit to other parties engaged in similar activities.

Underdeterrence, on the other hand, may also result from an excessive award. An award of punitive damages should reasonably be related to the harm the defendant caused or was likely to cause. If not, the defendant may reason that any amount of safety adjustments to its activities would still result in damages awards, and possibly also punitive damages. As a result, a defendant may refuse to adjust its activities appropriately yet continue to conduct the same unsafe activities that gave rise to the award to begin with.

Given the need to assure a balance among complex policy goals, measuring punitive damages is a tricky enterprise.[57] The future conduct of the defendant is unpredictable at best. Conceiving of a public purpose[58] for punitive damages may make it more likely that an appropriate level of deterrence will result by directing the money to a particular use without needing to rely on the defendant's actions. Thus, diverting some or all of the punitive damages award from the plaintiff to a public purpose would have the dual effect of eliminating an undesirable windfall to plaintiffs and assuring that utilitarian goals are met. Some state legislatures and courts have begun to incorporate this concept into their punitive damages rules.

STATUTORY LIMITATIONS ON PUNITIVE DAMAGES AWARDS

Within the due process parameters set by the United States Supreme Court, the states are free to limit punitive damages awards as they wish. Accordingly, many states have placed some limitations on punitive damages. Some states have banned punitive damages absolutely[59] or have allowed punitive damages only as authorized by statute.[60] Some states have also barred or limited punitive damages in certain kinds of cases. In Arizona, for example, in pharmaceutical cases in which the defendant has complied with applicable (FDA) regulations, punitive damages are not available.[61]

States have also limited the amounts of awards by imposing dollar limits,[62] setting maximum ratios between punitive damages and compensatory damages,[63] or keying the award into the defendant's annual gross income[64] or net worth.[65] States also combine the above types of limitations, sometime in complex ways. For example, Kansas caps a punitive damages award at the defendant's annual gross income or five million dollars, whichever is less, but provides alternatively that "if the court finds that the profitability of the defendant's misconduct exceeds or is expected to exceed the [above] limitation ...," the limitation instead will be "an amount equal to one-and-a-half times the amount of profit which the defendant gained or is expected to gain as a result of the defendant's misconduct."[66] Profitability from misconduct – or, in the Supreme Court's terms in *Gore*, reprehensibility – is thereby directly reflected in the award.

Beyond placing limitations on the amount of punitive damages, some states have legislatively mandated that a portion of each punitive damages award should go directly to the state. Such statutes clearly recognize the public goals that punitive damages serve, but little attention has been given to how punitive damages should be used, either by the plaintiff or the state. As a private award in the hands of the plaintiff, the plaintiff is entitled to do with the money as he or she wishes. States that have taken a portion of the plaintiff's punitive damages award have generally designated the general fund of the state as the repository of the money. These states give no assurance – indeed, they do not appear to so much as contemplate – that the money will be directed to remediate the injuries suffered by the state as a result of the defendant's conduct that necessitated the award.

These statutes, generally referred to as split-recovery statutes, vary considerably. Alaska has enacted a statute that requires that 50 percent of any punitive damages award go to "the general fund of the state."[67] Iowa provides that 75 percent of each punitive damages award be deposited in a civil reparations trust fund, which sums "shall be disbursed only for purposes of indigent civil litigation programs or insurance assistance programs."[68] The state of Missouri has created a Tort Victims Compensation Fund, into which 50 percent of each punitive damages award must be deposited.[69] The fund was enacted to provide compensation to tort victims who were unable to collect the full amount of compensatory damages awarded in their actions.[70] In Indiana, 75 percent of each punitive damages award must be deposited in the state fund to compensate victims of violent crimes.[71]

In Georgia, the punitive damages statute has been used to effect legislative product liability and tort reform. The statute provides that when a defendant in a product liability action has paid a punitive damages award based upon a particular product, no further punitive awards based upon that product are permissible.[72] Seventy-five percent of that single punitive damages award, after attorney fees and costs, must be deposited in the state treasury.[73] No similar restriction applies in other kinds of cases, but various other restrictions, including a monetary cap on punitive damages, apply for other kinds of tort actions.[74] The Georgia Supreme Court has upheld these provisions against a constitutional challenge.[75] The court held that although product liability defendants are treated differently from other defendants under the statute, the distinction was not arbitrary. With respect to the constitutional challenge of the split-recovery portion of the statute, the court stated that "[a] plaintiff has no vested property right in the amount of punitive damages which can be awarded in any case, and the legislature may lawfully regulate the amount of punitive damages which can be awarded."[76]

Such split-recovery statutes have generated much criticism. The statutes have been criticized for turning punitive damages into a form of compensatory damages, compensating the state for injury suffered by the citizens generally as a result of the defendant's conduct.[77] This argument has some validity where the state simply accepts its share of the award and uses it as it pleases. But if the state were required to use the money in a manner that would bring about some measure of deterrence of the defendant's conduct, or its after-effects, then deterrence would be the goal, not compensation.

Another criticism leveled at split-recovery statutes is that, far from solving the problem of a windfall to the plaintiff, the statutes would lead to much higher punitive damages awards. This theory suggests that jurors would enhance punitive damages awards if they knew that a portion of the damages would be redirected to the state.[78] This theory is very speculative, based upon some likely erroneous assumptions. It assumes that where a portion of the punitive damages will go to the state, the jury, not fearing a windfall to the plaintiff, would inflate the award. The due process mandates that the United State Supreme Court has placed on the excessiveness of punitive damages should mitigate this concern, even if it has some validity.

This criticism also assumes that jurors will be informed of the split-recovery statute prior to deliberations.[79] Some courts have dealt with the propriety of disclosing to the jury that a punitive damages award would be divided between the plaintiff and the state. Courts holding that such disclosure was reversible error typically have done so because disclosure was deemed to be prejudicial[80] or simply irrelevant to the proper process the jury must follow in determining whether to award punitive damages.[81] To avoid these problems, states could prohibit any such disclosure to the jury, much as states may prohibit mention of the availability of insurance to pay a judgment.

A third argument against split-recovery statutes is that they encourage states to rely on the revenue that the awards produce, which in turn could lead the states to take steps either to make punitive damages more readily available or to advocate in individual cases for plaintiffs seeking punitive awards.[82] This state-agenda argument has some rational basis, and there is some precedent for the suggestion that the states quickly become "addicted" to money that lands in their coffers. An important example is the money paid to the states by the tobacco industry under the terms of the 1998 Master Settlement Agreement (MSA) with the states. Several states had brought suit against the tobacco industry, seeking reimbursement for health-related public expenditures necessitated by the industry's products. The MSA, joined by all states that had not previously settled actions with the industry, set forth a schedule of payments to the states of $206 billion over a period of twenty-five years.[83] Although many assumed that the states would use the MSA money for smoking reduction programs and other health- and tobacco-related initiatives, the MSA lacked the teeth to enforce that use, and the states have largely spent the money on programs unrelated to public health. By 2005, only 4 percent of the money distributed pursuant to the MSA had been used to promote anti-smoking efforts.[84] In an economically challenged climate, this percentage is likely to drop. Moreover, because the MSA distributions are scheduled to occur over a period of twenty-five years, the states have an interest in the continued vitality of the tobacco industry, so that the companies can continue to make the scheduled payments.

Thus, the argument that the states may view split recovery of punitive damages as a revenue producer for any and all public programs has some merit. But the problem associated with the $206 billion MSA is less likely to occur when punitive damages are involved. For one thing, punitive damages lack the certainty of the MSA. Most punitive damages are awarded in individual cases, and although they can be in millions of dollars, there are no assurances that awards will be granted, or in what amounts. Moreover, the state has limited control over the question and none at all in cases where it is not a party. Further, most punitive damages awards are not as high as media reports would have the public think.[85] Finally, if the punitive damages awards were designated to be used in programs related to the underlying matters in the cases, these undesirable incentives would be minimized.

Another criticism of split-recovery statutes has argued that plaintiffs' attorneys, particularly in personal injury cases, would have greater incentive to settle cases in states with such statutes. The argument suggests that because any amount by which the settlement is enhanced by the threat of punitive damages if the case were to go to trial would go to the plaintiff by virtue of the settlement agreement, the plaintiff's attorney would favor settlement in the interest of collecting his or her contingency fee.[86] Of course, this argument is spurious if the state takes steps to assure that costs and attorney fees are paid first, before any portion of punitive damages awarded by verdict is distributed to the state.

CHANNELING PUNITIVE DAMAGES TO SERVE THE PUBLIC HEALTH AGENDA

The first issue raised when considering redirecting punitive damages to serve specific public health purposes is whether it is constitutionally permissible to deny the plaintiff some or all of a punitive damages award. The second issue is whether, assuming the authority of the legislature to redirect punitive damages, the legislature may designate a particular purpose for the portion of the award to which the plaintiff is not entitled. The third issue is whether, in the absence of a legislative designation, the court may exercise its discretion to redirect the award to a particular program or function.

Does a plaintiff have a property right in a punitive damages award that prevents a portion of the award from going to the state? In *Cheatham v. Pohle*, the Indiana Supreme Court likened punitive damages to criminal sanctions and noted that states have wide discretion in allowing and restricting awards of punitive damages.[87] Just as crime victims have no right to recover criminal sanctions imposed in their cases, so too, civil litigants have no direct interest in punitive damages, giving state legislatures broad discretion over the distribution of a punitive damages award.[88] The court stated: "For our purposes, the essential point is that because punitive damages do not compensate the plaintiff, the plaintiff has no right or entitlement to an award of punitive damages in any amount."[89]

The Indiana Supreme Court went on to consider whether the split-recovery statute violated the Fifth and Fourteenth Amendments to the United States Constitution and the state constitution for taking property without just compensation. Reading the provisions consistently, the court stated that any interest a plaintiff may have in a punitive damages award is only that which is defined by the state. In Indiana, the state legislature has defined that interest as 25 percent of the award.[90] The remaining 75 percent "is not the property of the plaintiff .... Rather, the claim she had before satisfaction was, pursuant to statute, a claim to only one fourth of any award of punitive damages."[91] Thus, the court concluded that no taking existed.

Most state courts that have addressed the taking issue have reached the same conclusion as the Indiana Supreme Court. Not all courts have agreed, however. The Colorado Supreme Court held to the contrary and ruled that the Colorado split-recovery statute – which required deposit of a one-third of a punitive damages award into the state general fund – was an unconstitutional taking because the judgment, once rendered, was deemed to be the plaintiff's property.[92] The court reasoned, in part:

> In our view, forcing a judgment creditor to pay to the state general fund one-third of a judgment for exemplary damages in order to fund services which have already been funded by other revenue-raising measures, and without conferring on the judgment creditor any benefit or service not furnished to other civil litigants not required to make the same contribution, amounts to an unconstitutional taking of the judgment creditor's property in violation of the Taking Clause of the United States and the Colorado Constitutions.[93]

The court found it irrelevant that the state had to power to limit the amount of punitive damages awards or even to eliminate them altogether.[94]

Another constitutional issue that has been raised is whether split-recovery statutes violate the Excessive Fines and Penalties Clause of the Eighth Amendment to the United States Constitution. The threshold issue is whether the Excessive Fines Clause applies at all to state split-recovery statutes. In *Browning-Ferris Industries, Inc. v. Kelco Disposal, Inc.*, the Supreme Court held that it did not apply to verdicts awarded by juries in civil cases.[95] Upon analyzing the original purpose underlying the amendment, the Court concluded that the Excessive Fines Clause was intended to address the government's prosecutorial role.[96] The petitioner argued that because courts, as an arm of the state, awarded punitive damages, and because punitive damages share similar goals to the criminal justice system, the state's role in awarding punitive damages in civil cases is analogous to its prosecutorial position in criminal cases. The Court disagreed:

> The fact that punitive damages are imposed through the aegis of courts and serve to advance governmental interests is insufficient to support the step petitioners ask us to take. While we agree with petitioners that punitive damages advance the interests of punishment and deterrence, which are also among the interests advanced by the criminal law, we fail to see how this overlap requires us to apply the Excessive Fines Clause in a case between private parties.[97]

Language elsewhere in the opinion, however, left room for argument that when the state receives a portion of the punitive damages award, the Excessive Fines Clause might apply.[98] The Supreme Court revisited this issue in 1993 in *Austin v. United States*,[99] which raised the question whether the clause applied to a civil forfeiture because the state took possession of the defendant's property. Focusing on the federal forfeiture statute invoked in the case, the Court stated that whether the Excessive Fines Clause applied was directly related to whether the penalty could be deemed, in whole or in part, a punishment. The Court held that although the statute set forth a civil action, the forfeiture could still be considered punishment and that whether a sanction was punishment did not depend solely on whether it was criminal or civil.[100]

Reading *Browning-Ferris* and *Austin* together, it is unlikely that the Court would decide that the Eighth Amendment bars split-recovery punitive damages statutes. In *Austin*, the United States government brought the forfeiture action. As a party, the government exercised control over the litigation as a governmental entity, a sovereign pursuing its right to exact a penalty related to criminal acts. Thus, the forfeiture action invoked "the potential for governmental abuse of its 'prosecutorial' power, not concern with the extent or purposes of civil damages," and therefore ran afoul of the Eighth Amendment.[101] In contrast, split-recovery statutes provide only that the government be a beneficiary of a portion of the damages awarded in the case. Even civil suits in which the government is a party lack the potential for abuse of prosecutorial power that is associated with the Eighth Amendment; the government generally has the same rights and obligations as any private party in the action.

Consistent with this argument, the Ninth Circuit Court of Appeals ruled in 2007 that the Oregon split-recovery statute did not exact a fine for the purpose of the Eighth Amendment because the statute was not a form of punishment. In *Engquist v. Oregon Department of Agriculture*, the court, noting that the United States Supreme Court had previously held the Excessive Fines Clause applicable only for "punishment for some offense,"[102] held that the Clause was not applicable to the split-recovery statute because "operation of the statute is unrelated to Engquist's culpability."[103] While it is still early to predict a trend in the federal courts, the Ninth Circuit's succinct reasoning supports the notion that the Excessive Fines Clause simply does not apply in civil litigation in which the government is not acting in its prosecutorial role.

The next issue of relevance to using split-recovery statutes to advance the public health agenda involves the use to which the money may be put. As previously discussed, although deterrence is a major goal of punitive damages awards, not all defendants who must pay punitive damages will take measures to reduce the dangers of the activity that harmed the plaintiff. The results of the tobacco MSA have demonstrated that states are unlikely to use such funds for programs related to the underlying wrongful conduct if left to their own designs. And while some states have directed a portion of punitive damages awards to go to a specific program, rather than to the general state treasury, those programs are likely to be unrelated to the specific case. For example, Indiana's split-recovery statute designates 75 percent of each punitive damages award for the state's compensation fund for victims of violent crime. While some crime victims will likely also bring civil actions against the perpetrators of their crimes, most punitive damages will be awarded in cases unrelated to a specific violent criminal activity or to any violent crime at all. Although designating the state's portion of the award to such a social program is perhaps preferable over giving the money unrestricted to the state treasury, it may not enhance deterrence of the specific wrongful conduct in which the defendant engaged. Thus, from a public health standpoint, optimal deterrence will be achieved only when legislatures designate a more focused use of the portion of punitive damages awards directed for state use.

Some commentators have suggested that state legislatures should enact statutes that require a designated percentage of each punitive damages award to go to charitable non-profit organizations, with the plaintiff selecting the beneficiary organization.[104] This idea, while commendable, must be viewed as largely academic. Legislatures, given a choice between providing the state with a portion of punitive damages or designating it for a charitable organization that may do most of its work outside the state, will opt for the former. But state programs should fare better in the legislative mindset, as the money goes to the state for programs that the citizens of the state would have to pay for in any event.

In states lacking a split-recovery statute, is it permissible and advisable to allow the trial court to designate a program, either state or private, to which a portion of any punitive damages award in the case must be given? The Ohio Supreme Court took it upon itself to allocate a portion of a punitive damages award to a specific research fund in *Dardinger v. Anthem Blue Cross & Blue Shield*.[105] The plaintiff sued the decedent's health insurer for mishandling the decedent's requests for a certain kind of chemotherapy, resulting in premature death. In reinstating the trial court verdict on breach-of-contract and bad-faith claims, the Ohio Supreme Court reduced the punitive damages award from $49 million to $30 million in light of the Gore Guideposts and conditioned the punitive damages award on its total allocation to a cancer research fund in the name of the decedent at a hospital of the state university.[106] The court stated: "At the punitive-damages level, it is the societal element that is most important. The plaintiff remains a party, but the de facto party is our society ...."[107] The court held that in the absence of a split-recovery statute in Ohio, redirection of punitive damages awards could be made by the court on a case-by-case basis, "with those awards making the most significant societal statements being the most likely candidates for alternative distribution."[108] The court found just such a societal interest in this case and allocated the full amount of the reduced punitive damages award to the state research fund.

A similar effort ultimately fell flat in Alabama. In 1996, the Alabama Supreme Court approved of an allocation of 50 percent of any punitive damages award to the state general fund. In *Life Insurance Company of Georgia v. Johnson*, the court stated its belief that the primary purpose of punitive damages is "vindication of the public interest and deterrence," and that therefore, a portion of punitive damages awards should be used for "the general welfare of all citizens" of the state.[109] The United States Supreme Court vacated the judgment and remanded the case for consideration in light of *BMW v. Gore*, a case that had also originated in the Alabama state courts. On remand, the Alabama Supreme Court stated that its previous holding that a portion of the punitive damages award should go to the state treasury was to prevent unwarranted windfalls to plaintiffs. The court then reasoned that allocations of a portion of punitive damages awards to the state thenceforth would be unnecessary in the light of the Gore Guideposts, which were designed to prevent such windfalls.[110] As discussed earlier in this chapter, the Gore Guideposts do not directly address the allocation of punitive damages awards to persons other than plaintiffs. Furthermore, the Alabama Supreme Court took an undesirably narrow approach in basing its ruling simply on the policy of avoiding windfalls to plaintiffs.

Recognizing, as the Ohio Supreme Court did, judicial discretion to allocate some or all of a punitive damages award to a third party – the state or otherwise – would advance the agenda of the public health community. It would also ensure that the portion of the punitive damages that does not go to the plaintiff would be used in a remedial and deterrent way directly related to the defendant's conduct. Notwithstanding these advantages, the approach taken by the Ohio Supreme Court is fraught with problems.

First, the redirection of a portion of the punitive damages award to a third party is left solely to the discretion of the court, thus lacking consistency and predictability. In *Dardinger*, the allocation to the state research fund was made by the Ohio Supreme Court in the last instance. As one of the other justices pointed out, the issue had not been raised on the appeal, and there was no opportunity for the plaintiff to object.[111] Even where the allocation is made by the trial judge, plaintiffs have no way of knowing, in advance of judgment, whether the court will let them keep any portion of punitive damages that may be awarded. Thus, plaintiffs have a diminished incentive to seek punitive damages. In contrast, plaintiff's attorneys might have incentive, if they are working pursuant to a contingency fee agreement, but under those circumstances the attorney's interest might conflict with representation of the client, as the attorney may seek to maximize the award – and the ultimate legal fee – regardless of the allocation.

More troubling is the possibility that this exercise of judicial discretion violates the constitutional guarantee of equal protection under the law. In *Mack Trucks v. Conkle*, the Georgia Supreme Court held that the state's split-recovery statute, which provided that 75 percent of a punitive damages award in a product liability action should go to the state treasury, did not violate equal protection because all plaintiffs similarly situated – that is, plaintiffs bringing product liability actions who have recovered punitive damages – were subject to the same reduction in their punitive awards.[112] In contrast, allowing the court to exercise its discretion to decide in a particular case whether any or all of the punitive damages award should go to a third party treats similarly situated plaintiffs unequally, because inevitably some plaintiffs will be allowed to keep the full award, or a portion thereof, whereas others would not.

These problems, however, may be overcome by devising a method that provides a compromise between traditional split-recovery statutes and judicial discretion, one that meets the social goals of the punitive damages doctrine and provides a means to advance the public health agenda of the state. The state legislature should enact a split-recovery statute that sets a fixed percentage of the punitive damages award to be redirected from the plaintiff to a third party for the specific benefit of the public in the area of society impacted by the defendant's wrongful conduct that gave rise to the punitive award. The statute would then leave it to the trial court, in its discretion, to decide the recipient, with full opportunity for input from the parties. This mechanism would provide for uniformity and grant plaintiffs predictability and the incentive to seek punitive damages. But it would also advance the deterrent goal of punitive damages, as well as satisfy the needs of the community that have been compromised, delayed, or harmed by the conduct of the defendant.

The flexibility of such a mechanism would allow resources to be directed to where they are most needed in matters relevant to the conduct underlying the punitive award. For example, in an insurance bad-faith case in which the claims involved health care, the court would have wide leeway to designate a medical research or health care fund for the statutory percentage of the punitive award. In contrast, if the bad faith involved mishandling of an automobile case, it may be more appropriate to direct the statutory percentage of the punitive damages award to the state's uninsured motorist fund. In cases not involving health care or personal injuries, the trial court would have other options available related to the case at hand. Non-tort cases involve the public welfare in other ways, and the court would be in the best position, after hearing all the evidence in the case, to designate the recipient of the portion of the punitive damages that the plaintiff does not receive. Thus, for example, in a breach of contract case, the court could direct the statutory percentage to go to a program that promotes consumer rights or corporate ethics, depending on the nature of the case. The selection of the program would be open, but the amount would be limited by the statutory percentage.

CONCLUSION

Given the goal of deterrence underlying the punitive damages doctrine in civil litigation, it is beneficial to fashion a means to spread the deterrence throughout the community, particularly in cases involving personal injuries and health care. Although punitive damages traditionally provide what some have characterized as a windfall to the plaintiff, the states have the authority to establish their own rules for punitive damages, within constitutional parameters. Some states have enacted split-recovery statutes to direct a percentage of each punitive damages award to the state general treasury or a specific state fund. But from a public health standpoint, it would be sensible to require that the portion of the punitive award that the plaintiff does not receive be allocated to a state or private program that will enhance deterrence of the conduct that gave rise to the award in the particular case. States should explore an alternative to the plaintiff's windfall by enacting a split-recovery statute with a fixed percentage allocated to the plaintiff and authorizing the trial court to select a program related to the litigation and to the misconduct for which punitive damages are warranted to which the remaining percentage should go.

Notes

1. See, for example, Huckle v. Money, 2 Wils. 205, 95 Eng. Rep. 768 (K. B. 1763) (upholding a verdict that included "exemplary damages").
2. Fay v. Parker, 53 N.H. 342, 382 (1873). Predictably, New Hampshire has banned punitive damages altogether. N.H. REV. STAT. ANN. § 507:16 (2009).
3. Theodore B. Olson, *The Parasitic Destruction of American's Civil Justice System*, 47 SMU L. REV. 359, 359 (1994).
4. James B. Sales & Kenneth B. Cole, *Punitive Damages: A Relic That Has Outlived Its Origins*, 37 VAND. L. REV. 1117, 1154 (1984). There is nothing to support such blanket statements about the escalation of damages awards. See Michael J. Saks, *Do We Really Know Anything About the Behavior of the Tort Litigation System – And Why Not?* 140 U PA. L. REV. 1147, 1156 (1992) ("Much discussion of the tort litigation system consists of conclusory assertions, unsupported by evidence."). Although widely advanced in popular culture, "the impression that damage awards have soared out of control is almost certainly incorrect." *Id.* at 1242.
5. BMW of N. Am., Inc. v. Gore, 517 U.S. 559, 568 (1996) ("Punitive damages may properly be imposed to further a State's legitimate interests in punishing unlawful conduct and deterring its repetition.").
6. See Dan B. Dobbs, LAW OF REMEDIES § 3.11(2), at 318 (2d ed. 1993) [hereinafter DOBBS, LAW OF REMEDIES] (stating that under the goal of punishment, "the defendant is made to suffer in a way that appropriately corresponds to his wrong").
7. Dan B. Dobbs, *Ending Punishment in "Punitive" Damages: Deterrence-Measured Remedies*, 40 ALA. L. REV. 832, 846–49 (1989).

8. See Philip Morris USA v. Williams, 549 U.S. 346 (2007); State Farm Mut. Auto. Ins. Co. v. Campbell, 538 U.S. 408 (2003); Cooper Indus., Inc. v. Leatherman Tool Group, Inc., 532 U.S. 424 (2001); BMW of N. Am., Inc. v. Gore, 517 U.S. 559 (1996); Honda Motor Co. v. Oberg, 512 U.S. 415 (1994); TXO Prod. Corp. v. Alliance Res. Corp., 509 U.S. 443 (1993); Pac. Mut. Life Ins. Co. v. Haslip, 499 U.S. 1 (1991).
9. See Dan B. Dobbs, THE LAW OF TORTS, § 11, at 19 (2000) [hereinafter Dobbs, LAW OF TORTS]; Richard C. Ausness, *Retribution and Deterrence: The Role of Punitive Damages in Products Liability Litigation*, 74 KY. L.J. 1, 70 (1985).
10. For a survey of product liability cases in which punitive damages have been an issue, see generally Richard C. Ausness, *supra* note 9, at 10–38.
11. Borel v. Fibreboard Paper Prods. Corp., 493 F.2d 1076, 1084–85 (5th Cir. 1973).
12. Pac. Mut. Life Ins. Co. v. Haslip, 499 U.S. 1, 19 (1991).
13. Dobbs, LAW OF TORTS, *supra* note 9, § 2, at 4 ("The purpose of criminal punishment is primarily to vindicate the state's interests in deterring crime and imposing justice.").
14. See, for example, Dorsey D. Ellis, Jr., *Fairness and Efficiency in the Law of Punitive Damages*, 56 S. CAL. L. REV. 1, 2 (1982) ("The concept of punitive damages lies in the borderland that both bridges and separates criminal law and torts.").
15. Courts disagree as to whether employer vicarious liability may support an award of punitive damages without the employer possessing the requisite mental state. *Id.* § 381, at 1063.
16. The states employ a variety of terminology in describing conduct that qualifies for punitive damages, including malicious, reckless, willful, wanton, and grossly negligent. See DOBBS, LAW OF REMEDIES, *supra* note 6, § 3.11(2), at 319. These standards may differ from specific requirements of *mens rea* for criminal acts.
17. Professor Dan B. Dobbs prefers the term "extracompensatory" damages, arguing in one article that the punitive justification of these awards should be eliminated in favor of their deterrence goal. See Dobbs, *supra* note 7, at 842; see also DOBBS, LAW OF REMEDIES, *supra* note 6, § 3.11(1), at 457.
18. For example, Professor Kenneth Mann has argued that the blending of the civil and criminal paradigms in punitive damages favors the recognition of a "middleground" jurisprudential category with its own set of procedural rules. See Kenneth Mann, *Punitive Civil Sanctions: The Middleground Between Criminal and Civil Law*, 101 YALE L.J. 1795, 1870 (1992) (focusing on state-invoked punitive sanctions). Professor Catherine M. Sharkey has proposed a new category of "societal damages" to replace punitive damages in most circumstances. See Catherine M. Sharkey, *Punitive Damages as Societal Damages*, 113 YALE L.J. 347, 352 (2003).

19. See David G. Owen, PRODUCTS LIABILITY LAW, § 18.2, at 1139–40 (2005).
20. See Ausness, *supra* note 9, at 82–83 (stating that "punitive damages will have little deterrent effect if the product manufacturer is able to pass on the cost of such awards").
21. Dan B. Dobbs, LAW OF REMEDIES, § 3.11(2), at 468 (2d ed. 1993) [hereinafter 1 DOBBS].
22. *Id.* § 3.11(2), at 468–69. Courts and commentators have debated the relative weight to be given to the defendant's mental state and his or her conduct. *Id.*
23. This, too, has been a matter of some debate. See Ann Gillespie Pietrick, Note, *Punitive Damages in Mass Tort Litigation – Froud v. Celotex Corp.*, 32 DEPAUL L. REV. 457, 468 (1983).
24. 499 U.S. 1 (1991).
25. *Id.* at 23.
26. The factors listed by the *Haslip* Court were:(a) whether there is a reasonable relationship between the punitive damages award and the harm likely to result from the defendant's conduct as well as the harm that actually has occurred; (b) the degree of reprehensibility of the defendant's conduct, the duration of that conduct, the defendant's awareness, any concealment, and the existence and frequency of similar past conduct; (c) the profitability to the defendant of the wrongful conduct and the desirability of removing that profit and of having the defendant also sustain a loss; (d) the "financial position" of the defendant; (e) all the costs of litigation; (f) the imposition of criminal sanctions on the defendant for its conduct, these to be taken in mitigation; and (g) the existence of other civil awards against the defendant for the same conduct, these also to be taken in mitigation. *Id.* at 21–22. These factors reflect the traditional policies of punishment and deterrence.
27. TXO Prod. Corp. v. Alliance Res. Corp., 509 U.S. 443, 459 (1993).
28. *Id.* at 460.
29. BMW of N. Am., Inc. v. Gore, 517 U.S. 559, 574–75 (1996).
30. *Id.* at 563.
31. *Id.* at 573–74.
32. *Id.* at 576.
33. *Id.* at 582.
34. *Id.* at 575.
35. See *id.* 576–85.
36. State Farm Mut. Auto. Ins. Co. v. Campbell, 538 U.S. 408, 425 (2003).
37. *Id.*
38. Boerner v. Brown & Williamson Tobacco Co., 394 F.3d 594, 603 (8th Cir. 2005).
39. Philip Morris USA v. Williams, 549 U.S. 346, 353 (2007).
40. *Id.* at 356.

41. *Id.* at 353.
42. Upon remand, the Oregon Supreme Court upheld the punitive damages award without reaching the due process issue, and the U.S. Supreme Court once again granted certiorari. Williams v. Philip Morris Inc., 176 P.3d 1255, 1263–64 (Or. 2008), *cert. granted*, 128 S. Ct. 2804 (2008). In 2009, the U.S. Supreme Court unceremoniously dismissed certiorari as "improvidently granted," Philip Morris USA Inc. v. Williams, 129 S. Ct. 1436 (2009), thus leaving further explanation of the due process parameters of punitive damages awards for another day.
43. *Williams*, 549 U.S. at 355.
44. TXO Prod. Corp. v. Alliance Res. Corp., 509 U.S. 443, 460 (1993).
45. The Supreme Court has placed constraints on punitive damages awards when the damage has impacted persons outside the litigation. In both *State Farm* and *Gore*, the Court took aim at awards that punished defendants for conduct directed at persons outside the state having jurisdiction over the litigation. Further, in *Williams*, the Court disapproved of punitive awards encompassing damage done to persons generally outside the litigation. This restriction serves two purposes. First, it assures that punitive damages are not awarded in one state for conduct that may have been legal, or at least less reprehensible, under the law of another state. Second, it minimizes the possibility that a defendant would be subject to multiple punitive damages awards for the same course of conduct where individuals complaining of the same conduct sued in multiple lawsuits.
46. BMW of N. Am, Inc. v. Gore, 517 U.S. 559, 568 (1996).
47. 1 Dobbs, *supra* note 19, § 3.11(1), at 457 (citing Loughry v. Lincoln First Bank, N.A., 502 N.Y.S.2d 965 (1986)).
48. See Dobbs, *supra* note 7, at 847 & n.49. Of course, in appropriate cases, public entities may be plaintiffs, thus more directly involving the public good.
49. Sharkey, *supra* note 16, at 370–71.
50. See, for example, American Tort Reform Foundation, Judicial Hellholes 2008/2009 2 (2008) (report of tort reform advocacy organization), online at http://www.atra.org/reports/hellholes/report.pdf
51. See 1 Dobbs, *supra* note 19, § 3.11(12), at 525.
52. Congress has considered product liability reform bills, most of which have sought to eliminate punitive damages in product actions. For example, Product Liability Reform Act of 1997, S. 648, 105th Cong. (1997).
53. David G. Owen, *The Moral Foundations of Punitive Damages*, 40 Ala. L. Rev. 705, 732 (1989).
54. See Michael Rustad & Thomas Koenig, *The Historical Continuity of Punitive Damages Awards: Reforming the Tort Reformers*, 42 Am. U. L. Rev. 1269, 1322, 1993 (stating that punitive damages encourage plaintiffs to act as private attorneys general and "sue in instances where conduct has

caused widespread harm"); Sharkey, *supra* note 16, at 351–52 (stating that "punitive damages have been used to pursue not only the goals of retribution and deterrence, but also to accomplish, however crudely, a societal compensation goal").

55. Owen, *supra* note 51, at 712.
56. *Id.* at 714 ("Liability rules in general may be assumed at least roughly to promote utility.").
57. Dobbs, *supra* note 7, at 850. In arguing for a deterrence-based measure of punitive damages, Professor Dobbs has stated:

    One result of this inconsistency is that no single extracompensatory award really can serve all the purposes identified because those purposes call for different proof and different measures of liability. Part, but only part, of the chaos in punitive damages law lies in our common propensity for trying to achieve a number of only partly consistent goals.

    Id. at 851–52. That chaos, he has said, is manifested in such a manner that "we invoke the 'punitive' award on one ground, justify it on another, and measure it willy-nilly." *Id.* at 852.
58. By "public purpose" I refer to a purpose that is expressly for the benefit of the general citizenry's health, safety, or welfare.
59. For example, N.H. Rev. Stat. Ann. § 507:16 (2009).
60. See, for example, Santana v. Registrar of Voters, 502 N.E.2d 132, 135 (Mass. 1986).
61. Ariz. Rev. Stat. Ann. § 12–701(A) (2009).
62. See, for example, Va. Code. Ann. § 8.01–38.1 (2009) (capping punitive damages at $350,000).
63. See, for example, Colo. Rev. Stat. Ann. § 13–21-102(1)(a) (2008) (limiting punitive damages to the equivalent of the amount of compensatory damages awarded).
64. See Kan. Stat. Ann. § 60–3701(e) (2009).
65. See Miss. Code Ann. § 11–1-65(3)(a) (2009) (providing sliding scale of limitations on punitive damages based upon net worth of defendant).
66. See Kan. Stat. Ann. § 60–3701(e)-(f) (2009).
67. Alaska Stat. § 09.17.020(j) (2009).
68. Iowa Code Ann. § 668A.1(2)(b) (2009).
69. Mo. Ann. Stat. § 537.675(3) (2009).
70. *Id.* § 537.675(1)(6).
71. Ind. Code Ann. § 34–51-3–6(c) (2009).
72. Ga. Code Ann. § 51–12-5.1(e)(1) (2008) ("Only one award of punitive damages may be recovered in a court in this state from a defendant for any act or omission if the cause of action arises from product liability, regardless of the number of causes of action which may arise from such act or omission.").
73. *Id.* § 51–12-5.1(e)(2).
74. *Id.* § 51–12-5.1(f)-(g).

75. Mack Trucks, Inc. v. Conkle, 436 S.E.2d 635, 639 (Ga. 1993).
76. *Id.*
77. Patrick White, *The Practical Effects of Split-Recovery Statutes and Their Validity as a Tool of Modern Day "Tort Reform,"* 50 DRAKE L. REV. 593, 605 (2002).
78. Victor E. Schwartz, Mark A. Behrens, & Cary Silverman, *I'll Take That: Legal and Public Policy Problems Raised by Statutes That Require Punitive Damages Awards to be Shared with the State*, 68 MO. L. REV. 525, 538 (2003) [hereinafter Schwartz et al.].
79. See *id.* at 545–46.
80. See Burke v. Deere & Co., 6 F.3d 497, 513 (8th Cir. 1993).
81. See Honeywell v. Sterling Furniture Co., 797 P.2d 1019, 1021 (Or. 1990).
82. Schwartz et al., *supra* note 82, at 539.
83. Master Settlement Agreement (MSA), *available at* http://ag.ca.gov/tobacco/msa.php.
84. Allan M. Brandt, THE CIGARETTE CENTURY: THE RISE, FALL, AND DEADLY PERSISTENCE OF THE PRODUCT THAT DEFINED AMERICA 432–35 (2007). See, generally, Jean Macchiaroli Eggen, *The Synergy of Toxic Tort Law and Public Health: Lessons From a Century of Cigarettes*, 41 CONN. L. REV. 561 (2008) (discussing Brandt's book in the broader context of developments in toxic substances litigation).
85. See Jennifer K. Robbennolt, *Determining Punitive Damages: Empirical Insights and Implications for Reform*, 50 BUFF. L. REV. 103, 104–07 (2002).
86. Schwartz et al., *supra* note 76, at 545.
87. Cheatham v. Pohle, 789 N.E.2d 467, 471 (Ind. 2003).
88. *Id.* at 471–72.
89. *Id.* at 472.
90. *Id.* at 473.
91. *Id.*
92. Kirk v. Denver Pub. Co., 818 P.2d 262, 267–69 (Colo. 1991); accord Smith v. Price Dev. Co., 125 P.3d 945, 950 (Utah 2005). The Colorado split-recovery provision was subsequently repealed. The Utah statute now reads: "(3)(a) In any case where punitive damages are awarded, the court shall enter judgment as follows: (i) for the first $50,000, judgment shall be in favor of the injured party; and (ii) any amount in excess of $50,000 shall be divided equally between the state and the injured party...." UTAH CODE ANN. § 78B-8–201(3)(a) (2009) (effective Feb., 2008).
93. *Kirk*, 818 P.2d at 272.
94. *Id.*
95. Browning-Ferris Indus., Inc. v. Kelco Disposal, Inc., 492 U.S. 257, 273–74 (1989).
96. *Id.* at 275.
97. *Id.*

98. The Court stated that the petitioner's "concerns are clearly inapposite in a case where a private party receives exemplary damages from another party, and the government has no share in the recovery," appearing to suggest that a different result might occur when the state shares in the award. *Id.* at 272.
99. 509 U.S. 602 (1993).
100. *Id.* at 609.
101. *Browning-Ferris*, 492 U.S. at 266.
102. United States v. Bajakajian, 524 U.S. 321, 328 (1998).
103. Engquist v. Oregon Dep't of Ag., 478 F.3d 985, 1007 (9th Cir. 2007).
104. See Dede W. Welles, *Charitable Punishment: A Proposal to Award Punitive Damages to Nonprofit Organizations*, 9 STAN. L. & POL'Y REV. 203 (1998); Nicholas M. Miller, Note, *'Tis Better to Give Than to Receive: Charitable Donations of Medical Malpractice Punitive Damages*, 12 J.L. & HEALTH 141 (1998); see also Leah R. Mervine, Comment, *Bridging the "Philosophical Void" in Punitive Damages: Empowering Plaintiffs and Society Through Curative Damages*, 54 BUFF. L. REV. 1587 (2007) (proposing that plaintiffs be allowed to voluntarily direct punitive damages for curative purposes and be required to execute binding stipulations).
105. 781 N.E.2d 121 (Ohio 2002).
106. *Id.* at 146.
107. *Id.* at 145.
108. *Id.*
109. Life Ins. Co. v. Johnson, 684 So. 2d 685, 698 (Ala. 1996).
110. Life Ins. Co. v. Johnson, 701 So. 2d 524, 532 (Ala. 1997) (on remand).
111. *Dardinger*, 781 N.E.2d at 148 (Moyer, C.J., concurring in part & dissenting in part).
112. Mack Trucks v. Conkle, 436 S.E.2d 635, 639 (Ga. 1993).

INDEX

ABC link. *See* abortion breast cancer link
abortion. *See also* abortion breast cancer link, postabortion syndrome; reproductive rights
  dangers of back-alley abortions, 16, 17
  mother's health exception, 20, 25
  opposition to, 21–22, 23
  partial birth abortion, 20, 24–26
  public health arguments, 15–16, 21–24, 29, 31
  South Dakota task force study, 23
  Supreme Court role in regulation, 17–20, 28
abortion breast cancer link, 22–23, 29, 31
advance directives, 52
  decision making rights of patients and families, 41
  failure to execute or comply, 47, 48, 51, 52, 57
  legal challenges, 56
  Medicare and, 51, 55, 58
  state role in requiring, 58
  Texas Advance Directives Act, 53
Alexander v. Choate, 84
American Law Institute, 113, 114–16
American Psychiatric Association Task force on Mental Health and Abortion, 23
Austin v. United States, 241–42

Baker v. State, 93
ballistics. *See* criminal law
Batterer Intervention Programs (BIPs), 126, 129, 132
Beauchamp, Dan E., 27
Bell, Carrie, 30
birth control. *See* contraception
BMW of North America, Inc. v. Gore, 228–29, 231, 232, 235, 244
Boerner v. Brown & Williamson Tobacco Co., 229
Bowman, Cynthia Grant, 102
Brady Law, 159
Brind, Joel, 22
Brown v. Board of Education, 78
Browning-Ferris Industries v. Kelco Disposal, Inc., 240, 241
Buchanan, Pat, 73

Case of the Thorns, 198
Center for Disease Control and Prevention, 23
Cheatham v. Pohle, 239
child access prevention laws (CAP), 169–70
child custody. *See* custody of children
City of Akron v. Akron Center for Reproductive Rights, 18–19
civil rights
  access and quality of health care and, 80–83
  American racial lawmaking, 77
  judicial review of Title VI, 84
  public health in communities of color, 10
  racism, effect on health of Black Americans, 74
Civil Rights Act of 1964 (Title VI), 10, 74, 84
civil union laws. *See* same-sex marriage
compensation. *See* tort law
Congressional Black Caucus, 77

contraception
Plan B, 16
public health arguments, 15–16
Cook, Philip, 162
criminal law
abortions and contraception, effects of denial of access, 16–17
battered woman's defense, 130
failure to control domestic abuse, 6, 131–32
gun trafficking, 165–66
historical treatment of domestic violence, 128–29
homicide by domestic partner, 127
illegal trafficking by licensed gun dealers, 163–65
microstamping of bullet casings, 173–75
profile of domestic abusers, 130
Roe v. Wade and reproductive rights, 17
violent-incident model of domestic abuse, 140–41
criminal punishment, punitive damages as, 233
culturally competent health care, 82
custody of children
domestic abuse, effect of, 126, 132, 141
Fathers' Rights and, 132
foster care for abused children, 132

death, definition of, 53, 57–58
Dardinger v. Anthem Blue Cross & Blue Shield, 243, 245
Defense of Marriage Act (federal), 89, 92–93
deterrence
punitive damages and, 225, 237
tort law and, 223–24
developing countries
end of life care, 42, 59–63
palliative care, 59–63
reproductive rights, 32
women's health in, 32
discrimination, definition of, 74–75
Dobbs, Dan B., 233
domestic abuse
children, effect on, 130
chronic nature, 145–46
coercive control and nature of abuse, 6, 127, 135–41, 142, 146–47, 148–49
definition of problem, 133–35
historical treatment of domestic violence, 128–29, 144
homicide by partner, 127
protective orders, 126, 131, 133, 142
state reforms, 129–30
treatment by state, 126–27
Due Process Clause, 222, 227–28, 229–30, 231
right to medical treatment, 56

end of life care. *See also* advance directives
definition of problem, 42–43
developing countries and, 42, 59–63
doctor-patient relationship and, 50
education and access to, 51, 53, 58
extension or termination of care, 43, 48
historical perspective, 40–41
judicial role and individual rights, 41, 44
New Jersey, 48
Oregon, 48
role of private groups, 58–59
usefulness of public health policy, 58
Engquist v. Oregon Department of Agriculture, 242
EPEC (Education of Physicians for End of Life Care), 58
epidemiological evidence
abortion arguments and, 28–29
abortion breast cancer link, 22–23, 32
comparison of Black and White American health, 69–71
comparison of Black and White American life expectancy, 70
domestic abuse identification, 134–35, 144, 146
domestic abusers and firearms, 167–68
end of life care analysis lacking, 47
gun crime, 161, 162
gun ownership and violence in the U.S., 153–54
gun shows and firearm fatalities, 166
palliative care, use of, 47
use in proving ill effects of smoking, 4–5
Epstein, Richard, 54, 58
Equal Protection Clause
historical treatment of domestic violence, 128–29
persistent vegetative state and right to life, 57

equality before the law, state sanctioned marriage rights and, 1
eugenics, 30
 early arguments for birth control and, 15
excessive end of life care, 43, 44, 48, 49, 53
Excessive Fines Clause, 240–42

family court. *See* custody of children
Family Medical Leave Act (FMLA), 111
Feagin, Joe, 74
Ferguson v. Ferguson, 112
Firearm Owners Protection Act of 1986, 156
firearms. *See* gun control
Freeman's Bureau Act, 78

gay marriage. *See* same-sex marriage
Gonzales v. Carhart, 24, 25–26, 28–29
Goodridge v. Department of Public Health, 94, 95, 96–97, 101–02, 106
Good Samaritan laws, 195
Gore Guideposts, 229, 230, 231, 243
government, role of
 battered women, emergency protection, 126
 coordinated response to public health demands, 189–92
 diversion of punitive damages for public health, 226–27
 elimination of discrimination in health care, 85
 end of life care and, 8, 44, 52–54
 gun control, limits on, 156
 individual rights versus community good, 55, 57
 marriage, status of, 104
 marriage, state-sponsored, 92, 101–02
 protection of community of identification, 77
 use of government insurance to impact public health, 58
gun control
 children and access to firearms, 169–70
 domestic abusers and, 167–69
 high risk persons, 154–55, 162–63
 high risk persons, carrying, 171–72
 high risk persons, purchases by, 160
 illegal trafficking by licensed dealers, 7, 163–65
 juvenile access and ownership, 170–222
 Second Amendment debate and, 7
 technology and control, 172–73
Gun Control Act of 1968, 157
Gun Control Act of 1968, Lautenberg Amendment, 168
gun control laws
 background checks, 156, 157–58, 159, 166
 dealers and private sellers, 155, 156, 159, 164–65
 licensing and registration laws, 160–61
 New Jersey, 161
 one-gun-per-month limits, 167
 preemption of local laws, 157
 purchasers, 155–56, 157
 purchasers, limitations on, 161
 state regulation, 157, 166
gun shows
 background checks at, 156
 dealers and private sellers, 165–66
 firearm fatalities and, 166
Guttmacher Institute, 17

Hand formula. *See* tort law
Hand, Judge Learned, 202
handguns. *See* gun control
Hardin, Garrett, 190
Harlan, Justice John, 26, 31
health care costs
 effect on end of life care, 50
 managed care in minority communities, 83
 public health policy and, 45
 role in end of life care, 43
health insurance
 punitive damages in cases, 231
 racial minorities and, 80
 relationships of affinity and, 109
health research, exclusion of women and minorities, 83
Helling v. Carey, 203–04
hierarchy of community needs, 75–77, 79
Hill, B. Jessie, 26
Holmes, Justice Oliver Wendell, 30
hospice. *See* palliative care
hospitals, treatment of minorities, 81
Human Rights Watch, 61, 62

India, Narcotic Drugs and Psychotropic Substances Act, 61
In Re Marriage Cases, 93
Institute of Medicine, 2, 48, 189

Jacobson v. Massachusetts, 25, 26, 30, 31, 191, 199

Kaye, Judge Judith S., 99
Kelly, Alicia, 112
Kennedy, Justice Anthony, 26
Koop, Surgeon General C. Everett, 21, 143

Lager, Lawrence, 16
Last Acts, 48, 59
Lawrence v. Texas, 98
Levy v. Louisiana, 110
Life Insurance Company of Georgia v. Johnson, 244
Lopez, Ian F. Haney, 73
Losee v. Buchanan, 199–200
Ludwig and Cook, 158–59

Mack Trucks v. Conkle, 245
mandatory sterilization. *See* eugenics
Mann, Jonathan, 32
marriage. *See also* same-sex marriage
  consequences of unhappy, 1
  dissolution of, 114–16
  economic benefits, 101–02, 112–13
  family stability in, 102
  gender subordination in, 102–03
  immigration of spouses, role in, 108
  legal benefits to children, 109–12
  New Jersey divorce law, 113
  procreation and, 98–99
  public health questions and, 2
  role in society, 104–06
  same-sex marriage, effect on heterosexual marriage, 91
  Social Security benefits, role in, 107
  state sanctioned marriage rights, 1, 7, 96–97, 100–01, 106–14
Marvell, Thomas, 170
Maslow, Abraham, 75
Master Settlement Agreement, 238–39
Marvin v. Marvin, 114
Medicare. *See* advance directives
morbidity and mortality statistics
  abortion, contraception and maternal rates, 16, 23, 32
  death rate for Black Americans, 69
  infant mortality of Black Americans, 71
  maternal mortality of Black Americans, 71

Nader, Ralph, 188
National Cancer Institute, 23
National Crime Victimization Survey (NCVS), 134
National Family Violence Surveys (NFVS), 137
national instant check system (NICS), 158
National Rifle Association, 157
National Violence Against Women Survey (NVAWS), 134, 144
Nicholson v Williams, 132

O'Connor, Justice Sandra Day, 19
Owen, David G., 233–34

Pacific Mutual Life Insurance Company v. Haslip, 227–28, 231
palliative care
  access to, 47
  developing countries and, 59–63
  public health policy and, 45
  role in end of life care, 43
  role of government, 53
parents and children
  benefits of public health arguments, 105
  interdependence of parents, 98
  legal benefits to children, 109–12
  same-sex parents and children, 98, 99
partial birth abortion. *See* abortion
Partial-Birth Abortion Ban Act, 24–26
PAS (postabortion syndrome). *See* women's health
personalized guns. *See* gun control
Philip Morris USA v. Williams, 229–30
physicians in the minority community, 81
Planned Parenthood of Southeastern Pennsylvania v. Casey, 19–20
police power
  marriage, regulation of, 94–96
  regulation of public health through, 24, 26, 27, 29–30, 51, 55, 56
  role of government in end of life care, 8, 44, 52–54, 58
  same-sex marriage, exclusion, 97
  sanitation laws and, 3
  tobacco, legal restrictions on use, 5
  vaccinations, right of state to mandate, 25, 26
Polikoff, Nancy, 109
population perspective
  anti-gay policies, mental health consequences, 104
  causality of lung cancer in smokers, 4–5
  children, harm from exposure to domestic violence, 130

definition of, 27
domestic abuse in different groups, 6
end of life care analysis, 45
gun control and, 7
hierarchy of community needs, 75–77, 79
marriage, regulation of, 95
minority community treatment, 80–83
racism, effect on health of Black Americans, 73–74
reproductive rights and, 7, 28–29, 33–35
resistance to public health initiatives, 5
same-sex marriage, effect on public health, 91
scientific uncertainty and role of government, 25, 35
use in public health policy, 6, 29–30, 31–32
women of childbearing age and, 15
women, abused, 125

postabortion syndrome, 23, 24, 31

Principles of Family Law Dissolution, 114

products liability. *See* tort law

Proposition 8, 89, 90

protective orders in domestic abuse. *See* domestic abuse

public and private law
public health policy and, 225
punitive damages and, 224, 233

public health
benefits to groups, 2, 50
Black Americans, historical treatment, 73–74
coercive control and, 146–47
coercive policies, 30–31, 51, 52, 54
definition of, 2, 46–47, 48–50, 54, 187, 189
disease reduction, goal of, 3
domestic violence, incidence and prevalence, 144–45
firearms, effect of, 153–54
individual autonomy and, 195
inequality and incidence of domestic abuse, 147
legal rules, relationship to, 3
population perspective, 2
tort litigation used for, 225
violence as an issue, 143–44

public health arguments
abortion breast cancer link, 22–23
denial of access to abortions and contraception, effects of, 16–17
economic and mental health effects of marriage rules, 2
epidemiology, use in proving cause of disease, 4–5
opposition to, 4, 5
partial birth abortion, 7
postabortion syndrome and, 24
reproductive rights and, 16, 20–22
resistance to vaccination, 5
tobacco, epidemiological evidence of damage, 4–5
tobacco, legal restrictions on use, 5

public health policy
affirmative duty to act within tort law, 195
analysis of end of life care and, 44, 45
anti-abortion arguments and, 22, 23
antidiscrimination laws, impact of, 80
benefits or harm, 58
communities of color and, 10, 80, 85
end of life care and, 8, 41–42, 43, 47, 51
extension or termination of care, 48, 49
gun control and, 7, 154
gun shows and firearm fatalities, 166
individual rights versus community good, 8, 31, 34, 189–92
infectious diseases, treatment of, 3, 31
judicial review of, 26, 55
marriage, benefits to all, 97–98, 105
punitive damages, use for public health, 9, 221–23
role of government in end of life care, 52, 56
same-sex marriage, effect on public health, 91–92
sanitation laws and, 3
scarce resources, prioritization of, 200–03
social contract theory and, 191
state intervention benefits, 45, 51
tort damages as incentive for better behavior, 197
tort law and, 8
tort law role in, 206
tort litigation used for, 188, 223
torts, reasonable-care standard and, 200
use in reducing number of smokers, 4–5

punitive damages
  and public health, 231–32
  awards to plaintiff, 225–26
  benefits for society, 233–34
  communicative purpose to society, 197
  deterrence goal of, 225, 232, 237
  diversion to charitable purposes, 243
  diversion to public health purposes, 9, 226–27, 242
  due process scrutiny and, 227–31, 232
  excessiveness of, 222, 227–29, 233, 234–35, 237
  hybrid between civil and criminal law, 224
  judicial discretion to redirect awards, 243, 246
  property rights of plaintiff in, 239–40, 241
  split recovery statutes, 236–39, 240–41, 245–47
  state tort reforms and, 234, 236
  use for public health goals, 197, 221, 223

Quinlan, Karen Ann, 41

racial policy and treatment of Black Americans, 78–79
racism
  access and quality of health care and, 80–83, 85
  effect on health of Black Americans, 69, 73–74, 86
  elimination in health care, 84, 86
  racial superiority need, 79
Rauch, Jonathan, 104
Reardon, David, 22
reproductive rights
  developing countries and, 32
  government interest in, 17–18
  judicial review of, 15, 18–20, 33
  opposition to, 15
  population approach, 7, 33–34
  population of childbearing aged women, and, 15
  public health arguments, 7, 15–16, 18, 28–29
  respect for individual to enhance community good, 32
Robert Wood Johnson Foundation, 59
Roe v. Wade, 17, 18, 23
Rothstein, Mark, 54
Rue, Vincent, 21
Rylands v. Fletcher, 198, 205

same-sex marriage
  California, 89, 93
  civil union law first in Vermont, 93
  civil union, lesser status, 104
  Connecticut, 93
  District of Columbia, 90
  economic and mental health effects of marriage rules, 2
  effect on children, 98
  emotional health in institution of marriage, 102–03
  Hawaii, 90, 92–93
  historical perspective, 92–93
  Iowa, 89, 93
  Maine, 90
  Maryland, 93
  Massachusetts, 89, 93, 94
  New Hampshire, 90
  New Jersey, 90
  New Mexico, 90
  New York, 90, 93
  religious opposition, 100
  social costs of opposite-sex only marriage rule, 1
  Vermont, 90, 93
  Washington, 93
Sanger, Margaret, 15
Scalia, Justice Antonin, 98
scofflaw gun dealers. *See* gun control
separation of powers, public health and, 26
sexual orientation discrimination, 93
Siegel, Reva B., 21
Sierra Leone, 61
Sorenson, Susan, 163
South Dakota Task Force to Study Abortion, 23
split recovery statutes. *See* punitive damages
State Farm Mutual Automobile Insurance Co. v. Campbell, 229
state limitations on punitive damages, 232–33, 235
  dollar limits, 235
  legislative mandates to state treasury, 236
Steinbock, Bonnie, 27

Sternberg v. Carhart, 20, 25
straw purchase. *See* gun control
SUPPORT study, 45

Taking Clause, 240
Texas Advance Directives Act, 53
tobacco. *See* public health arguments
tort damage awards
  dangerous behavior, effect on future, 196–98, 223
  dangerous behavior, strict liability for, 205
  Hand formula, 202–04
  liability and compensation for injuries, 193–94
tort law
  definition of, 187, 193
  failure to act and "no duty rule", 195
  Hand formula of cost-benefit analysis, 202–04
  historical context, 198–99
  individual, protection of, 193–95, 200, 201
  scarce resources, allocation of, 202–04
  strict liability or negligence, 198–99, 200
tort law and public health
  balance with, 200, 202
  class actions and, 188
  conflict with, 194
  deterrence goal of, 223–24, 225
  objectives of, 223
  products liability and, 204, 205
TXO Production Corp. v. Alliance Resources Corp., 228

U.S. Commission on Civil Rights, 80, 83, 85

Varnum v. Brien, 100
Violence Against Women Act, 128, 168
Vittes, Katherine, 163

Wal-Mart, 164
Williams, David, 85
Wintemute, Garen, 162
women's health. *See also* abortion; reproductive rights
  assault, level of in domestic violence, 137–38
  battered women's profile, 139, 141–43
  developing country experience, 32
  domestic violence impact on, 126–28, 131–32, 133, 134
  emotional health in institution of marriage, 102–03
  individual rights versus community good, 25–26, 31
  minority women's treatment, 82
  rape prosecution, 126
  right of privacy and, 27
World Health Organization (WHO), 17, 29, 32, 60, 62, 70, 72